Big Sister

I0893587

WOMEN, GENDER, AND SEXUALITY
IN AMERICAN HISTORY

Editorial Advisors:
Susan K. Cahn
Wanda A. Hendricks
Deborah Gray White
Anne Firor Scott, Founding Editor Emerita

A list of books in the series appears at the end of this book.

Big Sister

Feminism, Conservatism, and Conspiracy in the Heartland

ERIN M. KEMPKER

UNIVERSITY OF ILLINOIS PRESS
Urbana, Chicago, and Springfield

© 2018 by the Board of Trustees
of the University of Illinois
All rights reserved
1 2 3 4 5 C P 5 4 3 2 1
∞ This book is printed on acid-free paper.

Library of Congress Cataloging-in-Publication Data
Names: Kempker, Erin M., 1978– author.
Title: Big sister: feminism, conservatism, and conspiracy in the heartland / Erin M. Kempker.
Description: Urbana: University of Illinois Press, 2018. | Includes bibliographical references and index.
Identifiers: LCCN 2018011128| ISBN 9780252041976 (cloth : alk. paper) | ISBN 9780252083662 (pbk. : alk. paper)
Subjects: LCSH: Feminism—Indiana—History—20th century. | Feminism—United States—History—20th century. | Women's rights—Indiana—History—20th century. | Conservatism—Indiana—History—20th century.
Classification: LCC HQ1438.I6 K46 2018 | DDC 305.4209772/0904—dc23
LC record available at https://lccn.loc.gov/2018011128

Ebook ISBN: 978-0-252-05070-1

For

Martha Swain and Mildred "Mickie" Brandt Mebruer

Contents

Acknowledgments

THIS BOOK HAS TAKEN SUCH a long road to completion, and I have met so many wonderful, supportive people on the way. Like many other books, this one started out to tell a very different story. Initially my interest was strictly midwestern feminism and then strictly female conservatism, but I found that I simply could not understand either feminists or conservatives as they developed in Indiana without studying both and the "nested" nature of each side's political identity and consciousness. Only by researching both sides could I explain what happened when the two sides confronted one another over the meaning of feminism.

The book has undergone many transformations. Throughout its different iterations, I found women willing to share their time and memories with me. On the feminist side, thank you Betty Nelson, Barbara Cook, and Dorothy Mennen, along with members of the Indiana Women's History Association, including Beth Van Vorst Gray, Marianne S. Wokeck, Jill Chambers, and Mary Anne Butters, who graciously invited me to their meetings and volunteered helpful ideas and suggestions for my dissertation. My heartfelt thanks to the many conservative women who talked to me about their work in anti-ERA and anti-IWY politics, including Phyllis Schlafly, Joan Gubbins, Joanne Reynolds, Beulah Coughenour, Jan Conner Wahls, Pat Schneider, and Kathryn Nikou. You let me into your homes and trusted me to listen to you and speak to your experiences. I hope you are pleased with the book and find truth in its argument about conspiracism within the movement, even if conspiracy was not part of your personal experience of the movement. You will not agree with everything I say in the book, but I hope you still see me as fair and respectful of your experience. In attempting to cover both sides, no doubt I will prove the adage "please all, and you will please none."[1] It is worth the risk, but more than anything I would hate to disappoint you.

Teaching a heavy load did not make completing this book easy, but I had many wonderful colleagues and students who spurred me on and an editor who was always patient. At different times Brian Anderson, Bridget Pieschel, Tom Richardson, Amber Handy, Beverly Joyce, Kristi DiClemente, and Nora Corrigan provided support and encouragement that helped me refocus my attention and return, again, to research and writing. My sincere thanks to the entire Mississippi University of Women community, especially the students in my Women in American History classes, who shared openly their thoughts and perspectives on women's politics throughout the twentieth century, and the Faculty Research Committee for grants that provided financial support for the project. My editor, Dawn Durante, offered me patient support and guidance at every crossroad. In connecting to a community of scholars while maintaining a busy teaching schedule, I prioritized reading and journal publication over conferences, and this often left me feeling isolated from the larger field of women's historians. Without the ongoing support of Martha Swain, Melissa Estes Blair, and Janet Allured, who reached out to me and pulled me into whatever they were doing, I would have been even more isolated.

My deep thanks to Donald Critchlow. When I was at my wits' end sorting through potential directions for the project, he helped me find my footing and gave my work a truly insightful and critical read—one that made all the difference. I also thank him for the introduction to Phyllis Schlafly and his substantial help at the Eagle Forum Archives.

Historians are dependent on the archival and library faculty and staff who make their research possible. I am so thankful for the assistance of archivists and librarians at the Indiana Historical Society (IHS), the Kenneth Spencer Research Library at the University of Kansas, and the John Hay Library at Brown University. Their professionalism and warm, friendly manner were always appreciated. I extend heartfelt thanks particularly to Amy Belcher for help with the Women's Manuscript Collection at the IHS. Perhaps there never was a historian more lucky than me in that two of my dearest friends, Sara Morris and Amanda Clay Powers, are remarkably dedicated and brilliant academic librarians. Whatever I asked for, even if the university was closed or if I lost all citation information, they found for me, even sending me sources I did not know to ask for.

Significant portions of chapters 3, 4, and 5 of this book were first published as articles in *Frontiers: A Journal of Women Studies* and the *Journal of Women's History*.[2] I am very grateful to both journals for allowing me to share the material here.

My sincere thanks to my friends and family in central Missouri, West Lafayette, Indiana, and Columbus, Mississippi, who supported me and this project, never asking why it was taking so long. Sara Morris, Megan Birk, Christina Abreu, and Eric Hall stuck with me through all the hardships of finding the first job and surviving the first few years. Calls on Saturday morning provided a link between our supportive world as graduate students together and my new world as an assistant professor. When I moved to Mississippi, Amanda Clay Powers and Kris Lee helped me adjust to my new home and over the years have continued to help me connect to a community of supportive people, including Shalyn Clagget and Alicia Hall. My sincere thanks to Susan and Alan Smith and Susan Hester for welcoming me into their families and helping whenever a research trip necessitated time away from home. Special thanks, too, to Jan DeBlieu and Jeff Smith DeBlieu, whose personal interest in me and this project was deeply appreciated.

Through it all and without question or hesitation, my family has supported me. To my parents, Deborah Mebruer Kempker and Leonard Franklin Kempker, words cannot express my gratitude for your support throughout the years, but especially for showing me by your example how daily work can be an anchor in life and how work, regardless of whether it is pleasant, can provide the foothold that allows you to help push others forward. As this book comes to a close, I frequently think of my maternal grandmother, Mickie Mebruer, who was not allowed to attend high school because of her family's strange notion of fairness. She was the youngest of nine, and although circumstances had changed, since her parents had not been able to send her siblings to high school, she could not go either. From her life to mine in two generations speaks volumes about the wide difference in twentieth-century women's experiences and opportunities. She would be so pleased with this book, as will my grandfather Clarence Mebruer, who shares with me a love of history. More than I can say, I am grateful for my sisters, Emily Short, Tracy Wunderlich, and Megan Boehmer, and their families. What a drab space my office would be without the cat drawings, colorings, and hand-made portraits of my nieces and nephews. Everywhere I work, love is all around.

To my mentor, Nancy Gabin, who has had a profound influence on this project since its inception, I offer sincere thanks. If ever you doubt the impact of good teaching or your work, look to the seemingly endless number of graduate students, myself included, who left Purdue so much the better and wiser for your influence. Years after leaving, you are still the model of the kind of caring, dedicated person and scholar that I hope to be.

Finally, to my partner, Spencer Smith, I can only say thank you for years of encouragement and support. No matter what was going on in our lives, you believed in my ability to write this book. Between you and me, that was only true of you, but you believed it so keenly that you left me no choice but to work to make it true. My reward for a day spent writing was a night off with you—and I would work for that every time. Whatever happens next will be our adventure. I am delighted to be on this journey with you.

Big Sister

Introduction

IN FEBRUARY 1978 conservative Hoosier women opened an exhibit in the rotunda of the statehouse to explain the true purpose and meaning of feminism, as they saw it, to the public. The exhibit displayed materials—posters, brochures, and pamphlets—the women had gathered a few months before in Houston at the National Women's Conference (only the second such conference in the nation's history), part of the International Women's Year (IWY) celebration. The IWY conference developed out of a United Nations initiative to recognize and promote women's public involvement globally and women's well-being around the world. All states and territories held regional and state conferences, elected delegates, and wrote resolutions for the Houston national conference, and most of the delegates and participants were feminists.[1] But Indiana, along with eleven other states, elected a majority conservative delegation, and it was these women who set about creating the rotunda display to demonstrate what they had learned about feminism in the previous years as they struggled against the Equal Rights Amendment (ERA) and the feminist initiatives of the IWY. The exhibit focused on exposing feminism as a treacherous conspiracy of collectivists and sexual libertines; manuals demonstrated techniques of lesbian lovemaking and masturbation, earning the exhibit an X-rated listing from the *Indianapolis News*.[2] Two large signs announced "No Minors Allowed" in case any schoolchildren on field trips wandered into the vicinity. Joan Gubbins, state senator and leader of the conservative IWY delegates, assured the press that although the exhibit materials "disgust and frighten us," the display was necessary "because many of the materials advocated Marxist doctrines, socialism or lesbian relationships," which "generally demonstrate the alien ideology of feminists who are demanding positions of power and influence in our government." The exhibit, according to her, showcased "the complete facts about the composition of the feminist movement": it stripped the movement of its pretensions and revealed the "filthy" reality.[3] Ruth Cartwright, columnist for the *Marion News Herald*, agreed, saying the Houston conference amounted to a "$5 million Lesbian Bash," and she warned her readers not to be fooled into believing that feminism bore no connection to communism, collectivism, or homosexuality. "Start looking under the rug," she told readers, "where ERA's Lesbian and Communist promoters have swept their dirt." Cartwright even hinted that the display was punishment for "naïve Legislators" who voted for the ERA and thereby supported feminists whose "lesbian and communist material" the exhibit showcased.[4]

For feminists in the state, the display was one more in a string of recent travesties. Jane Fribley, chairwoman of Indiana Church Women United, explained in a letter to state lawmakers that while the brochures might have come from the Houston conference, she did not think them representative of the conference.[5] Unwilling to defend the "offensive" display that "desecrated" the statehouse but equally unable to deny that feminism included lesbians and Marxists, Hoosier feminists tried to explain to lawmakers and the public the diversity of individuals, groups, causes, and ideas within feminism—all of whom had access to exhibit space at the Houston conference, including Planned Parenthood, the Religious Coalition for Abortion Rights, Pro ERA, the Girl Scouts, the League of Women Voters, the National Organization for Women, Business and Professional Women, and the National Education Association. Acknowledging the diversity of the movement was not easy, however, since for years Hoosier feminists had worked to explain feminism as a matter of "simple justice," disconnected from radical politics or a critique of the family. After a five-year battle with conservatives, Hoosier feminists had ensured the passage of the ERA, making Indiana the last state in the nation to pass the amendment and leaving it only three states shy of the three-fourths needed to enshrine gender equality before the law in the Constitution. The achievement at the state level had taken its toll, however, and Hoosier feminists were exhausted and exasperated. To them, the claims of conservatives—that feminists were communists, traitors, atheists, and conspirators in league with a world government, just to name a few—were bizarre to say the least. After years of struggle with right-wing women, feminists still could not understand their arguments, much less accept them. But understanding conservative women's arguments was easier than it might at first appear, because these conservative women were not hyperbolic. They meant every word they said.

Over the course of several years, amid conversations prompted in large part by the ERA, some conservative women had come to understand feminism as the most recent addition in a long line of collectivist schemes. This explanation drew on anticommunist arguments developed throughout the postwar era by groups like the Minute Women of the U.S.A., Pro America, and the John Birch Society. Such organizations provided a forum for conservative women to discuss related forces pushing for a "one-world," totalitarian supragovernment—forces these women described as treasonous. While communists often were lumped under the "one-worlder" category, the two were not synonymous. In their literature, right-wing women described a spectrum of subversion that included the fifth column but also those advocating domestic cooperation through federal regionalism and internationalists advocating stronger authority for the United Nations (UN). Because they saw world planners as using "rights" rhetoric to promote and achieve a homogenized total government, right-wing women opposed civil rights, human rights, gay and lesbian rights, and feminist initiatives, especially those supported by the UN. The categories of domestic and foreign policy blended as these women strove to combat a global threat that manifested at all levels of government and sought above all else centralized power and homogenization.

The advent of the second-wave feminist movement in the 1970s proved in the minds of right-wing women that world planners were gaining ground. Feminist calls for equality and "unisex" treatment under the ERA, with provision for federal enforcement power, represented the latest threat in the creation of an overpowering federal government that could (and would) cede control to a world government. Feminists wanted to paint the ERA and related legislation as a matter of "simple justice," but conservative women did not agree. In their eyes, feminists were the most recent in a long line of one-worlders intent on homogenizing gender difference and paving the way for world government through the UN. The conservative Hoosier women who attended the IWY as Indiana's official delegates and who created the rotunda exhibit clearly expressed their fear regarding the final objective of feminism when they wrote state legislators about their experiences. Ultimately, feminism would lead to a form of totalitarianism that would supersede individual difference and individual rights. "We have all worried about 'Big Brother,'" the letter concluded. "'Big Sister' would be much, much worse!"[6]

The reality of conservative women, under the banner of traditionalism and "pro-family" values, operating a pornographic exhibit at the Indiana statehouse helps explain why Beth Bailey and Dave Farber describe the 1970s as "maybe our strangest decade."[7] But in order to understand the rotunda exhibit or how conservative women came to associate feminists with one-worlders, we must understand the context of their politics, the "nested boxes" (as Benita Roth describes them) of ideas and assumptions from which they made sense of the world.[8] When conservative and feminist Hoosier women clashed in the 1970s over the meaning of feminism, they came to the issues of female equality, gender difference, and citizenship from very different political worldviews. Conservative women's activism grew out of anticommunism, conspiracism, and their awareness of an increasingly globalized world. Far from marginalizing their activism, *Big Sister* portrays right-wing women as the inheritors of very old American traditions: fear of concentrated power and millennial prophecy believers. Not unlike anti-Federalists of the revolutionary era, in the face of increased centralization of power, these women demanded local autonomy and control. And as inheritors of nineteenth-century millennialism, they took to heart the belief that America constituted the New Israel, God's Chosen Land. When they looked at feminism, many conservative women saw the advent of a totalitarian world government that carried religious connotations, which only further fueled their activism.

Feminists saw no such world with no such connections. Indiana's Senator Birch Bayh ushered the ERA through the US Senate in 1972, and many hoped Indiana's state legislature would follow his lead by adding Indiana to the quickly lengthening list of legislatures to ratify the amendment. Since the ERA only promised that "equality of rights under the law shall not be denied or abridged by the United States or by any State on account of sex," it appealed to all kinds of feminists.[9] Indiana feminists agreed to "low key" their feminism so that the wider public and male state legislators might ratify the ERA quickly. They created a feminist coalition, Hoosiers for the Equal Rights Amendment (HERA), to ensure that Indiana was on the right side of history by approving the ERA. Over time, however, the strategy of low-key feminism led to tension and frustration. The HERA coalition fell apart as Democrats began to see the state's Republican leaders and Republicans themselves as the enemy in the ratification battle.

In the least, the rotunda exhibit makes clear that Hoosier women did not agree on the meaning of women's rights, feminism, or women's responsibility as citizens, and each side developed very different strategies for how to deal with radicals within their ranks. Understanding that difference and how conspiracism affected the second-wave feminist movement in the Midwest is at the heart of this book. *Big Sister* argues that conservative women's response to feminism was part of a longer history of right-wing countersubversion and conspiracy that extended at least to the Cold War. The Indiana ERA and IWY experience demonstrates that conservative women developed a grassroots movement during the 1970s that grew ascendant within the Republican Party by the 1980s and that their political consciousness developed together with and in opposition to the politics of women's liberation and international cooperation (a tendency or political impulse they called "collectivism"). Just as right-wing activists pitched a "big tent" and welcomed conservatives and conspiracists of many stripes, feminist women on the left attempted to adapt feminism to the goal of ERA ratification and the political climate of their midwestern state by silencing radicals and denying the place of liberationists and radicals in the movement. In so doing, they accomplished the goal of state ratification but challenged the inclusivity of feminism. Two very different strategies emerged on the right and left regarding how to deal with radical flanks; each strategy had its own benefits and costs, which continue to be felt in the politics of the Republican and Democratic Parties today.

The conservative and feminist women discussed in this book agreed on very little, but both thought they acted in the interests of women, and both claimed to speak for the category of "women."[10] Who gets to decide what "women" think? As Ronnee Schreiber explains in *Righting Feminism: Conservative Women and American Politics,* that depends a lot on who starts the conversation.[11] When conservatives make claims as women, they challenge the universality of "women's interests" and "force feminists to concede that identity politics has significant limits."[12] While scholars sometimes consider conservative women to be acting outside the category of women, that they have "false consciousness" or are betrayers of their sex and gender, these arguments fail to recognize that there exists "deep ideological differences *among* women."[13] This tendency to see feminism and women's history as linked is part of what some scholars see as the "exclusionary nature of identity politics."[14] In order to understand women's interests, we must be willing to study women's interactions and the contested terrain of what proper womanhood and citizenship meant to different women at different times. It is important that women's historians continue to explore the diverse meanings of women's politics and women's interests. Lest we give the false impression that women's history coincides with that of progressive politics, suffrage, and feminism, we should not avoid "troubling the waters."[15]

The last quarter century has brought to light much good work about the origins, ideology, and history of right-wing women.[16] Michelle Nickerson's *Mothers of Conservatism* and Kirsten Marie Delegard's *Battling Miss Bolsheviki* contribute to our understanding of American antifeminist, conservative, and anticommunist women.[17] Increasingly, studies of the Right look at the interplay between conservative and left-wing women, such as Susan Goodier's *No Votes for Women,* and across geopolitical boundaries, as does the collection of essays in *Women of the Right.*[18] This book is part of that burgeoning attempt to put feminist and conservative women on the same page and address how an increasingly globalized world affected how women perceived themselves and their community. *Big Sister* is a study of the ideas that informed the conservatism of antifeminists and the activities of feminists in the late twentieth century. The book stays squarely situated in the American Midwest, allowing us to see how consistent threads like anti-internationalism and antistatism adapted to new threats. Continuity seems to undergird much right-wing thought in the twentieth century, but this study allows us to see exactly how and when old fears pivoted to new targets.[19] *Big Sister* represents my best attempt to understand the differences that separated feminists and conservatives, explain the one to the other, and ultimately answer the question of what happened to feminism in a midwestern state like Indiana.[20]

Throughout this book, I utilize the term "liberationist" to denote the small collectives of women in Indiana active before the ERA push and "radical" to describe those who challenged the political powers that be by pursuing public protest. While the two were often closely related—Indiana liberationists adopted radical New Left tactics—they were not synonymous, as not all those in favor of public protest identified as liberationists.[21] "Liberal" feminists are those interested in panstate organization and a reformist political agenda. One of the threads we follow in *Big Sister* is the formation of feminist politics and organizations and how strategy and place affected that formation. I include in the category "feminist" any group or person that supported the ERA and actively worked to eliminate sex discrimination and patriarchy.[22] I group all pro-ERA women's activism as feminist not to obscure the diversity of their "feminisms" but to better understand the intersection of their interests and the fault lines.[23]

I use the terms "conservative" and "right-wing" interchangeably to describe anticommunist women. What it means to be "right-wing" and "left-wing" changes over time, as does what it means to be "centrist." While right-wing women attacked female pacifists in the International League for Peace and Freedom in the 1930s for trying to employ the rhetoric of "motherhood" in arguing against war, right-wing women during World War II employed motherhood themselves to argue against American involvement.[24] Conservative women were not monolithic, and according to George Nash, it is a "misdirected" endeavor to attempt an all-encompassing definition of a conservative.[25] What constitutes right-wing in a global context is an ongoing discussion, but it probably includes at least three features: (1) a focus on the creation of the "Other" and the use of anti-Other rhetoric, (2) the valorization of motherhood, and (3) an emphasis on the importance of the heteronormative family.[26] Ultimately, relative positions on a political spectrum must be tied to a specific time and place. Rooting feminism and conservatism to an ongoing conversation about the meaning of gender, equality, and citizenship allows us to see the diversity within the conservative movement and understand how that diversity of thought developed.

A conspiracy theory is an idea of how a person or people act, often criminally and clandestinely, to gain and abuse power. As Kathryn Olmsted describes in *Real Enemies: Conspiracy Theories and American Democracy, World War I to 9/11*, conspiracism refers to "the tendency to see conspiracies *everywhere*," meaning that a person may look to conspiracy theories, either interlocking or even contradictory conspiracies, to explain much of what he or she sees happening in the world.[27] Belief in a conspiracy correlates to conspiracism. Once an individual finds the utility of conspiracy in explaining an issue or event, he or she seems likely to use it repeatedly. In a summary of the field in 2012, Michael J. Wood, Karen M. Douglas, and Robbie M. Sutton reported that "the most consistent finding in the work on the psychology of conspiracy theories is that belief in a particular theory is strongly predicated by belief in others—even ostensibly unrelated ones."[28] Conversely, someone who has adopted a conspiracist worldview is more likely to adopt individual conspiracies.[29]

Conspiracy belief is so common and has such deep historical roots within the United States that Robert Alan Goldberg titles it "an American tradition," but that has not translated into considerable scholarly attention.[30] Nationally representative surveys suggest that most Americans have heard of a range of conspiracy theories, and half of those people believe at least one.[31] It is possible that in the near future most Americans will report belief in conspiracy theories.[32] While conspiracy theory may be commonly associated with those who favor authoritarian approaches and ideas, including those who support human rights violations and restricted civil liberties, historians find conspiracy belief alive in all strata of American society.[33] Conspiracism knows no gender, race, class, or political ideology—and it is certainly not limited to the political Right. Political affiliation may determine the kind of conspiracy belief a person holds but not whether or not that person believes in conspiracy.[34] From belief in 9/11 being a government plot to belief that President Barack Obama is an alien Muslim, and from left-wing ideologues like Michael Moore to right-wing extremists like Alex Jones, conspiracy belief is everywhere but acknowledged by few. As Olmsted wryly observes, "No one admits to being a conspiracy theorist."[35] Given its prevalence as a shaper of mass opinion, we know very little about how conspiracy belief functions as a political narrative or who is more likely to employ conspiracy theories to explain the world. Political scientists J. Eric Oliver and Thomas J. Wood concluded that the paucity of work in the field amounts to "a significant oversight."[36]

Conspiracy theories predate the founding of the country, but Michael Barkun argues that since 1963 and the assassination of Kennedy, conspiracists have built "a veritable cottage industry of conspiracy."[37] In part, conspiracism grew in the twentieth century because government officials promulgated "a certain conspiracist style—a deep, pervasive fear of hidden plotters" in order to solidify power and squash enemies.[38] Consider that some government conspiracies are real (think of the Tuskegee syphilis experiment run by the US Public Health Service, CIA attempts to kill Castro, or President Nixon's "hit list" of enemies targeted with government surveillance or worse), and sometimes the government perpetrates its own conspiracy theories (as when President Woodrow Wilson blamed World War I on the "military masters" of Germany, or, more recently, President George W. Bush implying that Osama bin Laden plotted 9/11 with Saddam Hussein).[39] Over the course of the twentieth century, this trend of increasing use of conspiracy by the government, along with increasing government surveillance and changes in media and news culture, led many Americans to a startling reversal. Olmsted argues that instead of fearing conspiratorial attacks *on* the federal government, increasingly, ordinary American focused on the federal government *as the perpetrator* of conspiracy.[40] The growth of the federal government in the twentieth century has had significant impact on the development of conspiracy theories in America and the development of the political Right.

Not all, and perhaps not even most, right-wing and conservative women engaged in conspiracy theories to explain their world, but ignoring the degree to which belief in conspiracy motivated the activism of some and the conservative movement as a whole, especially regarding the federal government, obscures an important part of their politics. The history of right-wing women and conspiracy is emerging, and these are active fields, but the two do not converge. While histories of twentieth-century conspiracy theory tell us much about the changing focus of conspiracy theories and theorists, often the focus is on national organizations and male actors.[41] Scholars in these fields have not yet adequately addressed how conspiracy theories shaped politics in a specific place and time or how conspiracy affected right-wing women's perspective in the late twentieth century. The central theme of this book is that right-wing women's understanding of one-worldism—a conspiracy theory refined by grassroots anticommunists during the height of the Cold War—shaped conservative women's response to the second-wave feminist movement and circumscribed feminist activism. This book places the experience of Indiana women in battles over the ERA and IWY in the larger context of countersubversive history and the history of conspiracy belief to reveal the important part right-wing women played in helping the Old Right and the anticommunist grassroots transition to a focus on globalism and social issues like feminism and homosexuality.

One way of exploring conspiracism more fully is to explore conservative women who came from the heart of America, in this case Indiana, as a means of detailing the political and social vision that motivated their political activism. As a unit of analysis, the state study provides an important "missing link" between the activities of national leaders like Phyllis Schlafly and Gloria Steinem and the political activism of grassroots women.[42] While feminist histories have begun to examine how identity formation is shaped by local events, this book adds to a growing body of literature, such as Stephanie Gilmore's *Feminist Coalitions,* that seeks to understand how feminist organizing was achieved and undone locally and how conservative and feminist women politicized one another.[43] Only by understanding the political context of this midwestern state can we understand how and why feminism and conservatism manifested as they did there or how radical movements of the Right or Left fared in a place so firmly committed to the status quo.

Defining what it means to be midwestern is like being asked to catch smoke. Historian of the region Andrew R. L. Cayton noted that unlike other areas of the country (the South, the West, and the East), there is no contested meaning of the term "midwestern"; there is a total absence of a "regional discourse itself."[44] Farming and family farms of the nineteenth century are the "dominant image" of the Middle West thanks to L. Frank Baum's *The Wizard of Oz,* Mark Twain, Willa Cather, and other writers, but what the Midwest meant in the twentieth century is less clear.[45] With an industrializing economy and a collection of mid-sized cities, Indiana, like the rest of the Midwest, no longer seemed to conjure a shared pastoral story or image. It became a "mushy place" without much of a conversation about itself.[46] Geographies of the Midwest vary (Does it include Missouri? Does it include the Great Lakes region?), and I will offer no exact co-ordinates for its location on the map. The Midwest is a big place (larger in size than the East or the South) and very diverse. Any single midwestern identity would be a gross oversimplification, and I do not wish to essentialize that complexity. One avenue by which we can approach the question of what it means to be midwestern is in a shared concept of identity for those who live or lived there. Region is something more than location or statistics. It is emotional and exists in our concept of ourselves, our community, and our environment.[47]

Self-identity is at the heart of the question of midwestern studies, and I argue that one important aspect of midwestern identity is an appreciation of (or at least an understanding of the perceived importance of) conformity and the personal quality of "nice." A common theme that emerges in this work is that midwesterners value conformity and are intensely uncomfortable with difference.[48] Midwesterners were and are a people concerned with public civility and appearing friendly, even if that civility reflects an ideal more than a reality.[49] This is not a trait that exists only in the Midwest, and in making this claim I do not intend to say that it is true in all times and places. However, the tendency is noted repeatedly by scholars of the region. Cayton explains: "The premium in the Midwest is on politeness, on the vague and unthreatening universal rather than on the unfamiliar and dangerous particular. Midwesterners, while privately proud of their private idiosyncrasies, take public refuge in the clichés of bourgeois patriotism. They appeal to a national set of values emphasizing freedoms that protect their local interests and autonomy. They are all Americans; they are not unique Midwesterners. More than anything else, they want to be thought of as normal and respectable."[50] It was not easy to be different or to push for change in such an environment, which is why William J. Spurlin argues in *Reclaiming the Heartland* that being queer in the Midwest is different and more contested than elsewhere in the country, since the heteronormative culture requires "assimilation into larger heterosexual worlds," while the individual still holds the desire to resist "invisibility through asserting difference," leaving lesbian and gay men in a "continuing struggle" to understand and define their sexuality and identity.[51] In such a political environment, the advantage falls heavily on the side of traditionalists and supporters of the status quo—notions of change become highly suspect, and those arguing in its favor would be aware that they were challenging not just a specific issue but a way of life, a way of being in a community. A question that not all political activists ask themselves but one that behooves the midwesterner to consider more than "Is this good?" is "Is this nice?"

In this sense, Indiana is a thoroughly midwestern place. While housing a vibrant two-party tradition, it is a place committed to "evolutionary, not revolutionary change," and still Hoosiers believe that they set themselves apart by their intense politicking.[52] In the nineteenth and early twentieth centuries, "politics, Indiana style" meant highly competitive two-party elections that often acted to swing national campaigns.[53] On the right, the state has given rise to some important conservative institutions: the American Legion's national headquarters have been in Indianapolis since 1925; the Youth for Christ (1943) and the John Birch Society (1958) got their start in the state.[54] Kathleen Blee's groundbreaking work *Women of the Klan* makes clear that Hoosier women actively and eagerly took part in the creation of a political culture infused with notions of white supremacy and countersubversion. Hoosier legislators voted to support women suffrage in 1920, but only after a lengthy fight that included counterarguments about women not desiring the vote, women's place in the home being ordained by God, and fear that the "vulgar rowdyism" of political culture would unsex women.[55] Even James Madison holds in *Hoosiers: A New History of Indiana* that "campaigns for women's suffrage and for prohibition were largely middle-class reform movements and generally not radical in their goals or methods."[56]

From the Ku Klux Klan of the early twentieth century to antitax campaigns throughout the century, Indiana has proven a hotbed of right-wing thought and organization.[57] Its antigovernment flair seems to have been manifest continuously from the frontier era through the twenty-first century. Madison writes: "For many Hoosiers, there were twin evils in government. One was high taxes; the other was federal power. For pioneers the federal government had removed Indians, surveyed and sold public lands, and boosted economic development. Hoosiers were strongly patriotic but seldom grateful. From the outset they tended to distrust government, particularly at a distance in Washington."[58] As the federal government expanded with the New Deal and two world wars, Hoosiers adapted to its growth begrudgingly and in ways neither rapid nor radical. Madison notes that in the early twentieth century the two major parties remained strong despite Populism's draw in other midwestern and southern states, as Populists were "too far from the center of Indiana's traditions."[59] While Indiana saw Progressive reforms like the Indiana Railroad Commission (1905), a revised child labor law (1911), and the Indiana Public Service Commission (1913), "moderation" and "conservative restraint" characterized the era.[60] Cayton is quick to point out that exceptions abound throughout the twentieth century in the life and work of Robert M. Lafollette, Jesse Ventura, even Phyllis Schlafly and Betty Friedan. Still, he argues, "such figures tended to be seen as anomalies who had little discernable impact on the region's popular reputation" for "middle-of-the-road" politics.[61]

In a place devoted to conformity, nicety, and the politics of moderation, female activists faced particular scrutiny. Midwestern women found the commitment to "niceness" especially challenging, since the gendered expectation is that women should not make men uncomfortable. On the contrary, women were to smile and please, be the perennial hostesses, and work tirelessly but effortlessly to achieve the comfort of everyone around them, especially the men in their families and communities. In their battle over the meaning of feminism, conservative and feminist women each argued that they spoke for the majority of Hoosiers; as such, they "read" the political scene and crafted strategies to work in such an environment. Feminists in Indiana demonstrate what can happen when activists pushing for political change, even radical change, meet a political culture that prioritizes politeness and tradition.[62] Since it was feminists who demanded change, their behavior and activism become suspect. They made decisions based on how they thought their cause and their organizations would be perceived by the general public, thus attempting to silence radicals in their midst and denying a radical flank. Conservative women, arguing in favor of gender difference and "traditional family values" as they described them, had no such obligation to nicety. Since they were acting in defense of God and country and attacking the purveyors of radical change, they were freed from the constraints of conformity and nicety to let loose apocalyptic rhetoric and devastating criticism of women who threatened the systems conservative women loved. Overall, both sides show us how the perceived conservatism of a state and its political culture acted on even radical activists and how women from very different ideological backgrounds crafted gender identities to suit a specific place.

Chapter Overview

Chapter 1 surveys Cold War America and looks at the experience of American women coming out of World War II. This chapter explains the history of world federalism and the desire for increased global cooperation after two world wars in the twentieth century. It also introduces important anticommunist organizations that challenged world government, like Pro America, the Minute Women, and the John Birch Society, and activism in Indiana. Finally, it discusses right-wing women's politics during the postwar era. Like their left-wing counterparts active in Women Strike for Peace, the labor movement, and the civil rights movement, right-wing women were intensely active during the 1950s and 1960s. In that way, they too defy the notion of apolitical housewives and offer more proof that American women were "not June Cleaver." Unlike their leftist counterparts, however, conservative women rooted their political activism in maternalism and essentialized the nature of women to include antisubversive political activity.[63]

Chapter 2 uncovers the rhetoric of national anticommunist organizations, especially the Minute Women and the John Birch Society, with regard to fears of a totalitarian world government during the 1950s, 1960s, and early 1970s and explores the related history of one-worldism and millennialism. Activities of the Minute Women in Indianapolis prove they acted as guardians of their local communities and sought to block the formation of local groups they believed were connected to the communist conspiracy. Also discussed is the appeal of conspiracy theory to right-wing women and connections between anticommunist fears of one-worldism and the burgeoning feminist movement in the early 1960s.

In chapter 3 we zero in on Indiana to investigate how conservativism infused with one-world conspiracism developed there and affected feminist goals like the Equal Rights Amendment. Feminism was alive and well in the state, and existing liberal groups formed a coalition that called itself the ERA Coordinating Committee (later renamed Hoosiers for the Equal Rights Amendment) in the early seventies in order to achieve state ratification of the ERA. Feminists adopted a "low-key" approach—a strategy to make feminism palatable to the general public in the state. On the right, conservative women effectively transitioned old anticommunist fears to a new target and in editorials described the ERA as communist directed. State ERA ratification riled and rallied the Right and made conservatives all the more determined to stop "the planners" in their next showdown, the International Women's Year.

Chapter 4 focuses on how Hoosier feminists adapted feminism to the particular political environment of Indiana. Specifically, the chapter examines feminists' decision to forward their low-key image to achieve greater respectability and support for the ERA in a conservative political milieu. This decision ultimately proved successful in ratification of the ERA but also led to dissent and hard feelings within feminist coalitions as many started to see the low-key strategy as a muzzle. This chapter explores the strategy decisions and contours of the Hoosier feminist movement, rooted as it was to place.

In the final chapter we see conservative women's fears come full circle as they faced down a feminist initiative directed by the United Nations. The International Women's Year called for a series of events, including regional and state conferences, leading up to the national conference in Houston in 1977. Because UN initiatives were being voted on in Indianapolis, the IWY represented the growing reach of the world government conspiracy, and feminism was the latest vehicle used by internationalists to achieve control. While feminists saw the conference as a chance to capture the national spotlight and bring attention to women's issue like the ERA, conservatives saw it as the ultimate showdown with satanic forces pushing for a totalitarian government they decried as "Big Sister."

CHAPTER 1

Women's Experience in Cold War America

The great majority of Americans understand very well that this war is not a war only, but an end and a beginning—an end to things known and a beginning of things unknown. . . . We know that whatever the world will be when the war ends, the world will be different.

—Poet and author Archibald MacLeish, 1943[1]

THE COLD WAR, with its rhetoric of good and evil and grassroots focus on subversion and domestic saboteurs, is a critically important time in the creation of a divided worldview within the United States and the formation of right-wing thought around the world.[2] Kim Nielson and, more recently, Kirsten Delegard have uncovered the roots of female conservatism in turn-of-the-century antifeminism and antiradicalism, which manifested most stridently during and after World War I, but even the divisions that existed among Americans and their political worldviews before World War II were disrupted and altered by the war itself. Conservative and liberal Americans were affected by the war, but differently. They derived different meaning from recent events and felt differently about the enormous changes of the previous decades, especially the advent of totalitarian and communist governments in the Western world, the growth of the federal government (during World War I, the New Deal era, and World War II), and the creation and use of nuclear weapons. Alan Brinkley in *Liberalism and Its Discontents* notes the growing separation:

> Americans greeted the prospects for change in many different ways. MacLeish—liberal, a New Dealer, and an administrator in the wartime government—wel-

> comed change and believed it could be harnessed (through the efforts of an enlightened government) to the goal of creating a better and more just society. Others viewed the future with trepidation, many of them hoping to preserve the patterns of power and wealth that had shaped the world they had known before the war. The social and cultural legacy of World War II was the product of broad social forces that no individuals or institutions could control. But it was also the result of many visions of the postwar world among many groups of Americans—almost all of them certain that the war validated their often sharply different, and even conflicting, expectations.[3]

Perhaps nothing better demonstrates the optimism of the immediate postwar era—the desire for change and the belief that problems of the past could not and should not be repeated—than the movement for world government. Some liberals responded to the problem of global war by calling for greater international cooperation, even if that meant sacrificing some measure of national sovereignty to a world government. Since at least the League of Nations, Americans had considered the possibility of joining a world government, but not until the late thirties, as the Second World War loomed on the horizon, did American support for the idea really grow.[4] The Campaign for World Government, led by Rosika Schwimmer and Lola Maverick Lloyd, began in 1937, and in 1939 California congressional representative Jerry Voorhis called for the president to plan for a convention to discuss writing a constitution for a world government.[5] Journalist Clarence Streit's manuscript "Union Now" (1939) laid out the basics for how a world government might be created and maintained. His book received little attention from publishers until World War II, when it became "the possible answer of the democracies to Adolf Hitler's *Mein Kampf*."[6] In 1943 Streit created the Federal Union, Inc., to promote the "federal union of 'the democracies'" around the world. His version was not as expansive as other world government propositions because, as Lawrence S. Wittner notes, "for one thing, it did not foresee a world government but only a union of a minority of nations, not very persuasively defined as 'democracies' yet which included countries like the Union of South Africa."[7] Perhaps because Streit's plan was so supportive of the political status quo, it received praise and support from *Fortune* magazine, corporate executives, and one former president of the US Chamber of Commerce.[8]

The creation and use of atomic weaponry had a dramatic effect on the world government movement, prompting some to see the creation of a world government as a dire necessity. Atomic scientists joined both the peace movement and the world government movement, which often stemmed from related impulses. After the war, according to Wittner, an "avalanche of books and articles advocating various forms of world government" hit the market, most notably, Wendell Willkie's *One World*, which sold over three million copies.[9] World government supporter Robert M. Hutchins explained their cause in dire terms: "The task is overwhelming, and the chance of success is slight. We must take the chance or die."[10] Many ordinary Americans seemed to agree. World federation resolutions came from such unlikely places as North Carolina and New Jersey state legislatures, and by the end of 1945, that number had grown to fourteen state legislatures that petitioned Congress to create a world government.[11] By the end of 1946, seven US senators (13 percent) "openly advocated" for a world government, while another dozen "admitted privately that they supported it."[12] In the House the numbers were even more impressive. Wittner estimates that between fifty and one hundred representatives supported "some form of world government."[13]

In his survey of the history of the global world government movement, Joseph Preston Baratta finds the peak just before the Korean War in 1950, with a little over 150,000 members in the various movement groups, the largest of those in the United States being the United World Federalists, Inc. (UWF), led by Norman Cousins and Grenville Clark.[14] The World Movement for World Federal Government also formed in 1947 (it changed its name to the World Association of World Federalists in 1956 and to the World Federalist Movement in 1994).[15] World government advocates and European federalists amended the constitutions of many nations, including France, Italy, Denmark, West Germany, and the Netherlands, after the war to limit national sovereignty. In its new constitution under the direction of Gen. Douglas MacArthur, Japan renounced war and belligerency. In the United States, Voorhis and his resolution calling for the United States to join a world government became known as the California Plan and was supported by six states before the Cold War—specifically, the Korean War and the Bricker Amendment—stopped its progress.[16] Wittner and others argue that despite surveys suggesting grassroots support, the bedrock of world government support came not from the bottom but from elite opinion makers such as writers Thomas Mann and Upton Sinclair, socialist Norman Thomas, and influential lawyers Grenville Clark and Thomas H. Mahoney.[17] Norman Cousins summarized the popularity of the idea: "It is today the hall-mark of intellectual and moral respectability to say that one believes in 'world cooperation' or 'world government' after the war."[18]

During the war, World Federalists split with Streit's Federal Union over whether "democracies" should be favored over a world government body that included more countries.[19] These advocates of world government feared that the United Nations, which was created as a result of the Dumbarton Oaks agreements, was too weak, incapable of preventing war, and undemocratic in its structure.[20] They largely supported ratification of the UN charter, even though they had had little influence over its creation, so that the larger idea of world organization and world government might proceed in the postwar era and not meet the same fate suffered by the League of Nations a little more than two decades before.[21]

When Truman called on Congress and the nation "to support free peoples who are resisting attempted subjugation" by communists around the world, particularly in Greece and Turkey, he used the language of a divided world facing irreconcilable choices.[22] The world would need to choose between good and evil, between "free peoples" and "totalitarian regimes" under communism, and in such an environment the idea of world government became dangerous and further from reality than perhaps ever before. There could be no shared mission or experiment in cooperative government between mortal enemies. World government advocates around the world and within the United States persisted, but with limited success. Along with the founding of the UWF, 1947 also witnessed the formation of the University of Chicago's Committee to Frame a World Constitution and the work of Robert Hutchins and G. A. Borgues to publish *Common Cause*, a scholarly journal devoted to world governance.[23] By 1989, twenty nations around the world had amended their constitutions along lines similar to those of the California Plan and had limited national sovereignty, thus paving the way for European union and, perhaps at some point in the future, even Latin American and African federation. These regional unions, the thinking goes, might lay the groundwork ultimately for world federalism.[24] The Cold War severely dampened world government prospects and enthusiasm, but the intellectual movement survived and continued its work throughout the late twentieth century. The existence of the movement and the shared impulse of so many Americans toward global cooperation and collective security planted the seed of what would become innumerable conspiracy theories. What seemed common sense regarding the fate of humanity to some seemed the road to destruction to others.

For many liberals, the conclusion of World War II seemed to indicate that colonialism, imperialism, systems of racial superiority and segregation, even sexual inequality might be in their last days. The work of black Americans to fight the "Double V" campaign, which called for victory over fascism abroad and over racism at home, forced liberals, especially New Dealers, to reconsider race as an issue and the inequality African Americans faced in accessing even the basic necessities of life. Membership and activism in existing civil rights organizations like the Urban League and the NAACP grew, and new organizations like the Congress of Racial Equality began. Gunnar Myrdal's *An American Dilemma* examined the "race problem" as both economic and moral in nature and forced liberals to recognize the deep and lasting inequalities that limited black access to the "American Dream" of democracy and material comfort.[25] The war against Nazism had a connection to the system of racial hierarchy at home, and propaganda films like *The Negro Soldier* forced liberals in the Roosevelt administration to acknowledge that the participation of African Americans in the war effort called for increasing respect and opportunity (if not an end to Jim Crow).[26] While white supremacists and segregationists rallied to fight the rising tide of black activism, World War II held the potential to be "Jim Crow's Last Stand," as Langston Hughes envisioned.

Women, too, found the war to be "an experience of unprecedented freedom."[27] Almost six million American women joined the workforce during World War II, and in a complete reversal of opinion since the Great Depression, the public supported working women as patriotic and necessary.[28] Artists created icons of the female war worker in Rosie the Riveter and Winnie the Welder that portrayed women workers as powerful and beautiful—Norman Rockwell's Rosie was even haloed by her welding mask. Real-life Rosies and Winnies could boast that they were "making history working for victory."[29] They could earn a living and in the process challenge ideas about "women's place" in the home, ideas that had been popular in the United States throughout the nineteenth and twentieth centuries, and prove that women's place might be wherever women made good. Women's wartime work was understood by manufacturers, unions, and government officials as temporary—a wartime necessity that was not intended to alter women's view of themselves or their place in the world, but it did. As historian Alice Kessler-Harris argues in *Out to Work: A History of Wage-Earning Women in the United States*, women's work during World War II was "a natural response" to the war effort, the opportunity to make money in employment while husbands were absent.[30] However, it also marked "the dawning recognition within families" that women's work outside the home could provide the important leg up families needed in ways that frugality within the household could not.[31] While women returned to domestic pursuits in droves after the war, the number of unemployed women did not drop to prewar numbers, and the percentage of working women increased throughout the 1950s. Women's overall percentage of the workforce grew at an astonishing rate in the decades after World War II: from 29 percent in 1950, to 35 percent in 1965, to 40 percent in 1975. This, Kessler-Harris notes, matched the percentage increase of the previous sixty years combined.[32] For many women, the question increasingly shifted from whether they would work to what kinds of employment opportunities were available to them.

For all this, the new notions of racial and gender equality forged in World War II were often ambiguous and incomplete. For women, work did not immediately challenge gender difference, since after the war the workforce was again sex segregated by job title and category. Women and men did not compete for the same kinds of employment often, nor were they paid equally if they did work the same jobs. But Kessler-Harris notes that women's experience with work prompted questions: "If wage work spread to most women, could job-related restrictions continue? For how long would women continue wage work without attempting to shed some of the responsibilities of home? And for how long would they earn wages without taking some of the freedom that their new economic status offered: the freedom not to marry, not to play submissive roles, the freedom to express their own sexuality?"[33] These questions did not seem ascendant immediately; still, they fed postwar politics. It was these questions, which took shape in the 1950s, that would have an "explosive impact" in the 1970s and help create the second-wave feminist movement.[34]

World War II affected conservatives differently. For some, the war's end gave witness to terrifying new technologies, especially the advent of the nuclear bomb and its use against the Japanese, the creation of the United Nations, the creation of the political state of Israel, and the global growth in power and status of atheistic communism. These all suggested that the postwar era might signal the approach of the biblically prophesied end-time. Many saw the operation of vast conspiracies of power in the global reach of the United States and the United Nations. The federal government expanded enormously during the New Deal, but that growth paled in comparison to its growth during World War II. In the postwar era, the role of the president and the executive office expanded at the expense of the states.[35] The growth of the federal government created enormous unease among conservatives, which was only made worse by government abuses in the postwar era, including lies about the extent of American involvement in Vietnam and Watergate. Perhaps not surprisingly, in 1964 75 percent of Americans believed that their government would "do what is right always or most of the time," but by 1995 75 percent believed the opposite, that their government could not be trusted to do the right thing.[36] Robert Alan Goldberg notes that by 1996 one survey found that 63 percent of Americans had "little to no faith that government officials tell the truth."[37] This distrust of the intentions and trustworthiness of public officials both encouraged and reflected the prevalence of conspiracism among the American public.

While the end of the war raised the specter of nuclear holocaust and subversive infiltration, it also created a new focus on domesticity for many families. Material comforts were more readily available than ever before. The middle class expanded enormously, suburbia became the site and symbol of that growth, and American families prepared for a postwar era that was built around larger families headed by a breadwinning father and a stay-at-home mom.[38] All those trends were real, but they might also represent "the way we never were."[39] One quarter of Americans were poor, suburbs were racially segregated, and not everyone who lived the life of Ozzie and Harriet was happy with it.[40] We are left with a contradiction in postwar America. Brinkley concludes: "On one side was the new reality of women moving in unprecedented numbers into the paid workforce. On the other side was the growing power of a more traditional image of women as wives, mothers, and homemakers. But the postwar paradox is simply a continuation of the contrary experiences of women and men during the war itself: for many women, the exhilarating discovery of new freedoms and opportunities; for many men, a fear of independent women and a strengthened expectation of traditional family."[41] However, even that paradox was not so simple or neat, because women too were on the side of those who feared the rise of female independence and what it might mean to family cohesion and structure (just as there were men who supported feminism and women's liberation).

By the late 1940s, nothing mattered more to conservatives than the effort to stop the spread of communism globally and root out communist influence and subversion at home. The Soviet apparatus was far-reaching and intent on fomenting worldwide communist revolution, and in 1949 the Soviet Union detonated a nuclear bomb. Any conflict between the United States and the USSR could potentially ignite a nuclear war that would lead to "mutually assured destruction." Even some advocates of world governance began to question whether they were spending their energies on the right front. In his memoir *Facing Reality: From World Federalism to the CIA,* Cord Meyer, president of the United World Federalists between 1947 and 1949, explains that he went to work for the CIA and later headed the International Organizations Division of the CIA because of the threat the Soviet Union posed to the United States and the world.[42] Cold War ideology motivated American military involvement in the conflicts in Korea in the 1950s, Vietnam in the 1960s and 1970s, and Afghanistan in the 1980s—it is a critically important aspect of American life and international relations in the last half of the twentieth century.

Assessing the reality of the threat communism posed to the United States is at the heart of assessing the American response, and historians are deeply divided over the issue. Ellen Schrecker speaks for many scholars who see anticommunism as an overreaction to the threat postwar communism posed to America. In *Many Are the Crimes: McCarthyism in America,* she unfolds how through varied means a broad anticommunist coalition turned "dissent into disloyalty and, in the process, drastically narrowed the spectrum of acceptable political debate."[43] The wave of anticommunism that swept the United States in the late 1940s and 1950s was "the longest lasting wave of political repression in American history," as she describes.[44] The ongoing release of previously unseen archival documents from the former Soviet Union in the last ten years has shed new light on the issue, though debates about interpretation continue. Few deny any longer that Alger Hiss was a communist spy, as was Julius Rosenberg (aided by Ethel Rosenberg), but there is no convincing evidence that Robert Oppenheimer, Henry Wallace, and Harry Hopkins were.[45] Schrecker argued in 1999 that new documents did not change her conclusions that the communist espionage that existed in the United States before 1945 was squashed by the efforts of the FBI after the war, effectively forcing the KGB to go underground and resort to paid informants. She maintained that "fear of Communist espionage that provided the main rationale for the political repression of the McCarthy era was largely unfounded."[46]

Others interpret the new evidence differently. John Earl Haynes and Harvey Klehr challenge the idea that American communism was harmless or that communists were victims. Comparing scholars who whitewash communism or Stalinism to Holocaust deniers, Haynes and Klehr argue that "many American historians hold America to a moral standard from which they exempt the Soviet Union and practice a crude form of moral equivalence."[47] For all the "ugly motives" of some anticommunists and the resulting injustice to their victims, Haynes and Klehr argue that "the anticommunism of the postwar era was a rational and understandable response to a real danger to American democracy."[48] Careful not to support the argument of right-wing ideologues by mounting a defense of Senator Joseph McCarthy, Haynes and Klehr nevertheless argue that it was anticommunists in the general public and in the US government who effectively circumscribed the action of American communists and stopped them from using the Communist Party USA (CPUSA) for purposes of espionage: "American communism declined *because* of the determined campaign by anticommunists of every political hue."[49]

Big Sister explores grassroots anticommunism and right-wing conspiracy theory, but not actual communists. As a result, it does not add to our understanding of communist infiltration or espionage. The focus of this book is right-wing anticommunists who saw no distinctions of allegiance when it came to the Left, grouping all manner of left-leaning ideas into the categories of communist and subversive. Haynes and Klehr's criticism of academia's treatment of anticommunists does not go far enough for many on the contemporary Far Right. Haynes and Klehr demonstrate how the CPUSA acted as a spy network in the United States, but Haynes argues that this spy apparatus did not attempt to subvert American policy; it solely sought information.[50] Here, too, is a distinction not made by the right-wing women in this study who believed that communists were actively subverting American domestic and international policies. My purpose is not to argue that communist espionage within the United States was not real or that communism was not a threat but to demonstrate how the work of anticommunists extended beyond countering the subversive threat of communists. Anticommunism is a much larger field of study than communist espionage or the work of the CPUSA.

Domestic Red hunters often focused less on the Soviet spy apparatus and more on subversion at home and in local communities. They saw danger in the sometimes mundane institutional operation of their local library, and for this reason they were considered by some to be extremists, even called a "lunatic fringe."[51] Many point to Senator William Ezra Jenner as the symbol of both anticommunist vigor and conservatism in the heartland state of Indiana. Elected to a US Senate seat for two terms from 1947 to 1959, Jenner served as chairman of the Senate's Internal Security Subcommittee and proved a dedicated friend and supporter of his colleague Joseph McCarthy. In speeches, letters, and editorials, Jenner revealed to Hoosiers the true nature of the communist conspiracy in Washington, DC. A secret and sophisticated "invisible super-state" controlled the federal government and ensured that the Truman and Eisenhower administrations would not take serious action against the Soviet threat.[52] He told Hoosiers that "Communists and fellow travelers" were already in charge of the Democratic Party, and he warned that seventy thousand communists were on the federal payroll.[53] By the late 1950s, Jenner counted the Democratic Party, the Supreme Court, and most Republicans as part of a fifth column. The foreign policy of Secretary of State John Foster Dulles amounted to a "planned retreat before the communist advance." President Eisenhower's policies were no more than a "global giveaway." Even his Indiana colleague and fellow Republican, US Senator Homer Capehart, was a "New Deal sonofabitch."[54] According to national reports, Jenner was a "blowhard" and a "hack," "completely irresponsible and intellectually vacant," and in 1950 *Time* magazine counted him among the "Senate's Most Expendable," but many in Indiana agreed with Jenner's assessment of the national and international scenes.[55] Irving Leibowitz, longtime political reporter for the *Indianapolis Times*, attempted to reconcile how Indiana could produce sons as different as Eugene Debs, Wendell Willkie, and William Jenner and tried to determine who among them best embodied Indiana's political legacy. In the end, the answer was simple: "No one ever represented the thinking and feeling and heart of Hoosierland with more fidelity than Bill Jenner."[56]

Jenner was an important voice in the state anticommunist milieu, but he was one of many operating under similar assumptions about the nature of the communist conspiracy and working toward similar goals of eradicating the world of communism, starting with cleaning up local communities. Anticommunism included politicians, policy makers, bureaucrats, and grassroots activists who worked tirelessly at the local, state, and national levels to track individuals and organizations and make public their perceived covert activities. Women's anticommunist organizations proliferated in the 1950s, and women made anticommunism the work of ordinary housewives. And this appeal to housewives was more than just common language. Mary Brennan argues in *Wives, Mothers, and the Red Menace: Conservative Women and the Crusade against Communism* that by gendering anticommunism and claiming it as the work of stay-at-home wives and mothers, conservative women created a "special mission" that empowered them to be politically active, especially on the local level, and helped them build community with other women.[57] It also disarmed critics, since conservative women's ambition, ironically, supported women's connection to home and hearth.[58] The Minute Women motto, "Guarding the Land We Love," suggests that they saw themselves as watchdogs over their families and by extension the whole nation. Michelle Nickerson finds that conservative women created a niche for themselves within the anticommunist movement by "asserting that housewives and mothers were better suited than men to the work of anticommunist vigilance."[59] Housewives had the time to thoroughly research the problems of the day and the responsibility of keeping the home and raising the children, which made all manner of political concerns relevant to them, from UN genocide treaties to domestic education policy. In the mold of Progressive maternalists, they essentialized women's nature as morally superior and extended housewifery to include cleaning up society and the government.[60]

Postwar conservative women engaged in politics outside the home in order to defend the home—another paradox of the era—and for this reason their understanding of politics and conservatism may be different from that of men. Rebecca Klatch argues in *Women of the New Right* that while postwar conservatives interpreted their world differently, they shared a "common hostility" toward communism and big government; still, gender divided how men and women interpreted and reacted to that threat.[61] Feminism particularly divided conservatives along gender lines, since it was more relevant and personal to women than to men and because advocates of feminism were typically female.[62] Kirsten Delegard notes that since the first wave of anticommunist, countersubversive activism after World War I, the motto of conservative women seemed to be "It takes women to fight women."[63] Conservative women believed themselves to be especially needed in the fight against female Progressives, and when they conceived of the dangers of centralized power and communism, they did so in ways most relevant to their lives as stay-at-home wives and mothers in largely middle-class white communities. However, anticommunism did not challenge inherently the ideal of woman as submissive, patriarchy, or the authority of men.[64] Women's political activism did not radically alter the power structure within the home or their daily lives of housework and mothering; nonetheless, Brennan sees these women as "warriors" seeking "the complete destruction of their communist opponents": "They were not nice little old ladies telling everyone to calm down before someone got hurt or suggesting some kind of peaceful dialogue. No, anticommunist women disparaged compromise as a weakness and spoke of the need for their enemies to be annihilated. They might have looked like 'girls,' but they talked like men. Distracted by the fact that these activists looked like respectable women [middle class and white], most Americans missed their adoption of masculine behavior. By the time anyone noticed, it was too late to rebuild the old mold of femininity."[65] The ferocious way in which these happy housewives attacked perceived communist subversion would be mirrored by antifeminists during the 1970s. Across the last half of the twentieth century, conservative women forged an identity that blended their commitment to gender difference, gender-distinct social and familial roles, and countersubversion.

Like the fear of communism, the fear of world government was common on the right in the postwar years; Minute Women, Pro America, and the John Birch Society were part of a cacophony of voices describing the threat. Typically, men like Robert Welch are credited as important one-world conspiracists; less well understood are women-specific organizations like Pro America and Minute Women and their part in creating and transmitting anticommunist and antigovernment conspiracy theories. By 1954 right-wing publisher Ida Darden of the *Southern Conservative* credited Minute Women and Pro America for providing the model of "a new and responsible type of womanhood" who, "with a firm determination," would "retrieve feminine leadership from their bumbling, fumbling, and addle-brained sisters and . . . exert their organized influence in restoring orderly government in the United States."[66]

In Connecticut in 1949 Suzanne Silvercruys Stevenson, a sculptor and wealthy Belgian refugee of World War II, founded the Minute Women of the U.S.A. as a national organization to mobilize women to defend the "Traditional American Way of Life."[67] Stevenson was a devout Catholic and described herself as the "Paul Revere of the Fair Sex," warning Americans of the dangers of communism.[68] She encouraged conservatives across the nation to launch a "Women's Crusade" to save their country from communist control and subversion.[69] All Minute Women members pledged to uphold twelve principles when they joined the group and made a personal commitment to vote in every election (along with providing the two-dollar membership fee).[70] The twelve principles included "Belief in God and Country," "Principles Embodied in the Constitution," "States' Rights," "Clean Politics," "Economy and Efficiency in Government," "Fairer Taxes," "A Sound Dollar," "Free Enterprise," "Right to Work," "Courageous and Enlightened Foreign Policy," "Free Press and the Truth," and "Patriotic Teaching in Schools and Colleges."[71] As historian Don Carleton notes, Minute Women often interpreted states' rights as the preservation of racial discrimination, fairer taxes as the elimination of the graduated income tax, and right to work as the elimination of labor unions.[72] Minute Women opposed liberalism, socialism, communism, the New Deal, and nearly every reform of the Progressive Era.[73]

The Minute Women grew nationally, but exact numbers are difficult to ascertain. Stevenson claimed in 1952 that the organization included five hundred thousand members in 104 chapters and forty-six states, but she revised those figures months later to fifty thousand members in several states.[74] In his 1953 series for the *Houston Post,* reporter Ralph O'Leary stated that of the five hundred local members, most were wealthy residents of the exclusive River Oaks subdivision. In fact, wives of physicians or oil and personnel executives accounted for one quarter of the chapter, while relatively few members came from less affluent circumstances.[75] Carleton argues that conservative upper-middle-class, mostly Republican-affiliated, stay-at-home wives and mothers in their late thirties to fifties made up the bulk of the membership in Houston.[76] No survey of Hoosier Minute Women exists to document their background and circumstances, but the general perception of the group conformed to the more publicized Houston set. Indianapolis Minute Women appeared to be middle-class white women who did not work outside the home.[77]

The origins of Pro America are found in the New Deal, although the group saw its high-water mark during the Cold War. The women of the Lake Washington Garden Club of Seattle, Washington, were troubled by Franklin Delano Roosevelt's election in 1932 and the growth of the Unemployed Citizens' League of Seattle that same year.[78] The elite clubwomen formed the National Association of Pro America, National Organization of Republican Women, Inc., known as Pro America, as an anti–New Deal, anti-Roosevelt women's organization loosely associated with the Republican Party.[79] Pro America women were disturbed about changes in American life after World War I, especially changing sexual mores among youth, challenges to traditional religious authority by modernists and intellectuals, and the changing demographic of the country brought on by new immigrants.[80] Lake Washington clubwomen sought to return to a simpler time "when there was less government bureaucracy and more power in the hands of families and communities."[81] Ostensibly, the group was nonpartisan, and they did attempt to appeal to Democrats disgruntled with Roosevelt's politics, but they were largely Republican in makeup, acting as an unofficial Republican women's club in many western states.[82] Nickerson documents Pro America's work in the Los Angeles area and agrees with Catherine Rymph that the primary focus of the group was to push the Republican Party further right.[83] Women who joined the organization consistently saw themselves as "more anti-Roosevelt than Republican, and more anti-Communist than partisan."[84] Pro America had a large following in the West and began calling itself a national organization in 1935, although it did not have chapters in all states.[85] It is unclear when or how the organization came to Indiana, but it was still active in the state in the 1970s and led by Jean Harvey of Monticello. It was this group—local chapters of Pro America—that led the charge in explaining feminism as part of a conspiracy theory in the state. During the Equal Rights Amendment and International Women's Year battles, Pro America's pamphlets and newsletters most explicitly connected feminist initiatives to the older threat of one-worldism.

The activities of these anticommunist women were myriad. Minute Women disrupted leftist speakers at their podiums and succeeded in keeping "controversial" speakers off public and private event agendas, but since the local manifestation of the communist and liberal menace differed, so too did local projects. Mary D. Crain, leader of the Memphis Minute Women chapter, refused to collect Social Security from her newspaper employees, claiming that "Social Security is Communism!"[86] Carleton details the diverse efforts of Houston Minute Women, including banning a United Nations essay contest from the public schools; launching a book-stamping crusade intended to publicize, if not ban, "subversive" public library books; and publicizing, erroneously, that the United Nations had not only seized but ruled several American cities.[87] Members conducted investigations into the political activities of prominent personalities, from Hollywood actresses and Truman appointees to more mundane public school officials.[88] In Indianapolis, Minute Women alerted the American Legion to the formation of the Indiana Civil Liberties Union in 1953 and worked to keep the union from finding space to meet in the city.

Minute Women organized for local, state, and national efforts but did not admit coordinated action. Each woman claimed to act as an individual in phone calls, letters, or any other form of protest. Stevenson perceived that the effect of the organization would be heightened if the public and targets believed protest to be a spontaneous outpouring of concerned citizens.[89] The feigned spontaneity and individual nature of Minute Women work also protected the group from censure, since the organization denied responsibility for protest or any other form of action. In some apparent confusion as to the purpose of the rule, Marguerite Dice, leader of the Indianapolis Minute Women, confirmed the policy to the *Indianapolis Times*, saying that she could speak only for herself, since the Minute Women "never act as a group."[90] Dorothy Frankston of Wheeling, West Virginia, national chairperson for the Minute Women, confirmed that Minute Women always worked as individuals, "never as a group," but also denied any connection between the Minute Women and the War Memorial incident. The media had "smeared" the Minute Women in Houston, and she concluded that by connecting the Minute Women to the Indiana Civil Liberties Union struggle, the Indianapolis press must have "thought we needed another slap."[91]

In order to maintain anonymity and their claim to strictly individual action, Minute Women relied on skillful use of the telephone as a tool for organization and harassment. Stevenson implemented a detailed telephone pyramid through which national leaders passed orders to chapter leaders, who in turn passed the message to five chosen members, who contacted five others, and so on through the membership list. Members had alternate contacts in case the chain broke somewhere along the line. The telephone network constituted a major factor in the coordinated action of the group. The effectiveness of the telephone chain was such that some chapters even dispensed with formal meetings.[92] Members implemented organized telephone networks to inform one another of group plans and used larger phone networks to stay abreast of the work being done by sister chapters in other localities. Using the telephone as a tool for harassment, Minute Women called organizations, businesses, and churches to blacklist the Indiana Civil Liberties Union. Whether for organizational or protest purposes, the telephone was an essential tool of Minute Women and one that conveniently coincided with their preference for secrecy and anonymity and housewives' access to technology, as the Indianapolis War Memorial incident or "Argument in Indianapolis" makes clear.

To understand the War Memorial incident, it is necessary to understand how the American Legion headquarters got to Indianapolis. Historian Richard Clutter explains that at the close of World War I founding members of the Indiana state affiliate of the newly created American Legion entered into a "gentlemen's agreement," whereby veterans agreed to forgo demand for a state bonus for their war service if state authorities provided the American Legion a national headquarters.[93] With the help of the Indianapolis Chamber of Commerce, Legionnaires got their headquarters in 1920 when a special session of the Indiana General Assembly approved funding for construction of the War Memorial complex.[94] The state legislature's authorization determined that the facilities were to be open to state veterans' organizations and "for other public meetings and other public purposes not inconsistent with the purposes of this act."[95] Legionnaires sat on the board of trustees for the complex, and many understood the facilities to be their own.[96] Although paid for with public monies, Legionnaires remembered the memorial as payment in lieu of the cash bonuses other states awarded veterans, and as a result, Legionnaires dominated issues relating to the building and grounds. The War Memorial Building was the site of Legionnaires' power in state politics, and with important help from groups like the Minute Women, Legionnaires patrolled and policed other political organizations in the state.

The American Civil Liberties Union (ACLU) formed in the early 1920s at roughly the same time as the American Legion, dedicated itself to ensuring the individual liberties guaranteed in the Bill of Rights. Throughout the postwar era, the national organization corresponded with dedicated liberals in the state, but Indiana had no chapter affiliate of the ACLU. Given the political climate after World War II, Hoosier liberals reported that the chances of generating much interest in the ACLU were slight; potentially sympathetic people, they explained, were "extremely cautious" for fear of being labeled "pinkos."[97] That changed in 1953, when a group of nearly seventy people, "physicians, lawyers, [and] housewives," met at an Indianapolis hotel and formed the Indiana Civil Liberties Union (ICLU) to be a state affiliate of the national ACLU.[98]

At the initial ICLU meeting, participants created several committees, one of which was to handle logistics, including finding a place to hold subsequent meetings. Within days the group booked the East Room of the War Memorial Building for a November meeting that they anticipated would include several hundred people. In a surprise decision four days before the meeting, the board of trustees for the memorial revoked the ICLU reservation. Felix J. "Star" Brown, executive secretary for the board, explained that he initially approved the request because he believed that the ICLU represented "very reputable people . . . [of] business and learning in Indiana," but protest letters and calls from Minute Women alerted him to the "controversial nature" of the group.[99] He promptly cancelled the meeting.[100] Ralph Fuchs, Indiana University law professor and leader of the ICLU, promised that the meeting would proceed in a different location with scheduled guest Arthur Garfield Hays, national director of the ACLU, as the principal speaker.[101] But because of the late notice (only days prior to the meeting), and especially because of Indiana Legion and Minute Women pressure, another room was not easy to find. The ICLU contacted the Claypool

Hotel, which agreed, only to rescind shortly thereafter; the Continental Hotel, the Riddick Piano Company, the Indianapolis Public Library, and the Indianapolis YMCA all declined to provide space.[102] Initially, the Knights of Columbus on North Delaware Street could see no problem with the ICLU's use of their hall, but "upon further investigation" they found the decision constituted a "controversial issue" and declined to get involved for fear the choice would "lead to internal strife" among the knights.[103] Less than two days before the meeting, Rev. Father Victor L. Goossens, pastor of St. Mary's Catholic Church, stepped forward to provide the ICLU a space at the church's family center, and although no one in his parish criticized his decision, he received hostile phone calls from several Minute Women.[104]

The Indiana Legion's attack on the ICLU did not end with denying them use of the War Memorial Building. Roy Amos, Indiana Legion state commander, challenged the very existence of the organization. Amos argued that Hoosiers ought to know that the ACLU "is under the control of individuals who are either outright Communists or fellows with long records of affiliation with groups cited by the attorney general as subversive." "Well authenticated records," he said, proved that "90 per cent" of its monies and efforts had gone to protect "Communists, fellow travelers, subversive aliens and other enemies of our country." The ICLU would not meet in the War Memorial Building; moreover, the Indiana Legion would oppose the formation of an ACLU affiliate in the state. "We don't want any such sanctuary for Communists in this state," Amos explained. "We don't want an organization in Indiana whose record and reputation provides . . . assurance to every Communist uncovered in this state of free legal defense of his treasonable activities."[105] Minute Women alerted the Indiana Legion to the threat posed by the ICLU and, consistent with their function in other states, likely provided the Legion with some of the ICLU's "well authenticated records." The cooperation of the Minute Women, Indiana Legion, and other conservative organizations demonstrates how the anticommunist consensus was created and maintained and how women were integral to the growth and maintenance of anticommunist networks.[106]

With the Indiana Legion and Minute Women intent on making Indiana "into a dust bowl, arid of divergent thought," the ACLU had to weather a "terror-psychology" to survive in the state, as one ICLU member asserted.[107] Father Goossens agreed with the larger purpose of the ICLU, telling reporters, "There is something much more basic involved here than merely the idea of a meeting place." As a Catholic priest in a state with a strong association with the Klan, Goossens poignantly defended minority rights, reminding Catholics that "we all of us at some time or other are going to find ourselves in a minority group."

"If one organization can prevent another group of people who are not traitors, who are not subversive, from gathering together in peaceful assembly to discuss and speak freely," he asked, "then what guarantee would there be that later on another group might not decide that when I or my people . . . gather together . . . to worship . . . that we should be stopped?"[108]

The War Memorial incident became a national cause célèbre when Edward R. Murrow sent reporters to cover the story as it broke. The "Incident in Indianapolis" episode aired on *See It Now,* a Columbia Broadcasting Station program, on 24 November 1953 to a nationwide audience as part of Murrow's focus on McCarthyism and anticommunism's deleterious effects on human rights.[109] Indianapolis Minute Woman Marguerite Dice (and Midwest regional leader of the Minute Women) told *See It Now* reporters that she objected to the ICLU's use of the War Memorial Building because "it was erected in memory of those men who gave their lives for the protection and preservation of the principles on which this country was founded. The inscriptions, in and outside of it, bear witness to this. What a travesty it would be to open its doors for a meeting to which Communists are welcome when we know the open and avowed purpose of such is to overthrow our government by force and violence as well as by infiltration."[110] This disagreement about the meaning of patriotism, civic obligation, and public discourse would last another twenty years and then only be solved after a ruling by the Indiana Supreme Court to allow the ICLU use of the facility. On 13 October 1973 the ICLU held an official meeting in the War Memorial complex.[111] The struggle demonstrates the stamina of anticommunist crusaders in Indianapolis and the support of ordinary citizens for countersubversive activities.

When Robert Welch, a Massachusetts candy manufacturer, founded the John Birch Society (JBS) in Indianapolis in 1958, Minute Woman Marguerite Dice offered support. It was at Dice's home that Welch laid out the status and nature of the communist world conspiracy and founded the JBS to combat that menace.[112] Dice was a personal acquaintance of Welch and reportedly admired his writing concerning the communist threat.[113] Despite Dice's presence and experience in anticommunist organizing, the initial members of the JBS were all male, and Dice was only credited with providing coffee and refreshments. According to Welch, the many anticommunist organizations and groups operating in the country in the late 1950s did not dampen the need for the JBS, they hastened it. Since the death of Senator Joseph McCarthy in 1957, anticommunism lacked "a dynamic personal leader," "a hardboiled, dictatorial, and dynamic boss."[114] Politicians like Barry Goldwater (Arizona), Senator Jenner, and Senator William F. Knowland (California), though of sound "Americanism," would inevitably seek redress in the political system and fail to take on the "broader overall action" that Welch believed the situation required.[115] "With all my shortcomings," he told the eleven men assembled in Dice's living room, "there wasn't anybody else on the horizon willing to give their whole lives to the job, with the determination and dedication I would put into it."[116] Dice's life and work with the Minute Women belied that claim, but apparently she did not count.

While women were critical to the grassroots success of the organization, they were largely ignored in the official literature of the JBS and as paid field workers. The JBS did not understand anticommunism to be the special prerogative of women. Women, like men, were encouraged to join if they met the moral and patriotic criteria, but Welch did not acknowledge their special contributions within the JBS or acknowledge their work in the larger anticommunist movement. Annual JBS dues were twenty-four dollars for men and twelve dollars for women, which might suggest Welch thought women were less capable of providing financial assistance and therefore less desirable than men as members.[117] But women were active participants and leaders within the JBS. Michelle Nickerson's work concerning conservative women in the Los Angeles area is informative of the way individual women understood their role within the JBS. Nickerson details the involvement of two JBS members who, although active in JBS causes (one even ran an American Opinion bookstore), did not rely on the JBS exclusively to fulfill their political or social impulses. Previous work in the anticommunist movement provided their formative activist experiences, and that initiation had occurred mainly in the company of other women in groups like Pro America, Minute Women, and various other Republican women's clubs.[118]

Minute Women supported men in the American Legion and JBS, but there is some evidence to suggest that, at least at times, right-wing women were frustrated and angered by men abdicating their gender role as protector. Under the title "The Enemy Is Landing," Pro America lamented that "today's Minute Man . . . [are] more apt to be Minute women and their guns are 'papers' and their voices muffled."[119] In criticizing the welfare state, Minute Women criticized male leaders and the "common man" for their predilection for dependency. Social welfare programs endangered masculinity and male prerogatives of dominance. In an article in a Minute Women newsletter, the author begins by saying that Americanism means choosing not to be a common man, associating the common man with a preference for "having the state look after me," the dole, and being content with the "stale calm of Utopia" as opposed to seeking the "thrill of fulfillment." Such a dependent man amounted to a "kept citizen" who had traded "freedom for beneficence" and "dignity for a handout." Perhaps because the essay was so critical, the author assumed a male identity and used masculine pronouns, but the piece likely was written by a woman. She reminded men that it was their duty and "heritage" to "stand erect, proud and unafraid [before would-be masters]: to think and act for myself, enjoy the benefit of my creations and to face the world boldly and say, 'This I have done.'"[120]

Total membership of the John Birch Society at any given time is difficult to calculate since that number was secret, and Welch so often spoke in generalities. In early 1960 Welch claimed to have four thousand members.[121] The society boasted chapters in thirty-four states in the winter of 1961, and the Anti-Defamation League backed up that estimate, noting that most chapters were in the South and Midwest.[122] The society reported thirty-five full-time salaried field managers in 1962 aided by seventy volunteers and a staff of over forty at the Belmont, Massachusetts, headquarters for *American Opinion*, the society's organ and formerly *One Man's Opinion*.[123] Historian Lisa McGirr believes that at the height of the society's popularity, it enjoyed a membership of between eighty and one hundred thousand, roughly matching the support of the CPUSA during the Popular Front.[124] And that number meant millions of dollars in revenue for Welch and the society coffers. Based on annual dues, membership rates alone would have netted the JBS organization $1.2 million in 1961, which is a conservative estimate, considering that some of those members may have donated other amounts or committed to lifetime membership for $1,000.[125] In 1965 operating costs totaled $5 million, with salaries, printing, and postage being the major expenditures.[126]

We will look more thoroughly at the nature of right-wing rhetoric regarding collectivist and one-world conspiracism in the next chapter, but it is important to lay out here how anticommunist organizations communicated with and cross-fertilized one another. Transmission of ideas across the conservative spectrum was important, and many organizations, including the JBS and Minute Women, made it part of their mission to help one another connect with literature and like-minded people. The big tent philosophy of the JBS effectively joined all manner of persons interested in conservatism, right-wing conspiracy, and anticommunism into a powerful movement that captured the attention of Republicans. The JBS did not expound a purist ideology but blended important variations of right-wing thinking and added to the "fusion" of the libertarian antistatist, moral traditionalist, and anticommunist strains an active and energetic core of workers and leaders in communities across the country.[127] Welch employed a secular approach with regard to religion, encouraging all monotheists to join his movement. The different kinds of conservatives within the JBS do not appear to have been a problem for the organization. "Conservatism encompasses a broad range of ideas, impulses, and constituencies," Brinkley explains, "and many conservatives feel no obligation to choose among the conflicting, even incompatible impulses, that fuel their politics."[128] Carleton and Nickerson agree that conservatives worked together through Republican clubs, Pro America, Minute Women, and a host of other organizations in an often informal but highly effective national network that shared ideas, literature, and speakers. "Cross-fertilization among such groups was rampant," Carleton argued, "especially since some persons held memberships in several of these groups at the same time."[129]

A major focus of the JBS was the operation of bookstores so that conservatives could access a wide range of right-wing literature inexpensively. Letter-writing campaigns, support for conservative radio programs and publications, and the organization of speakers' bureaus constituted the straightforward educational mission of the JBS. As his first directive, Welch urged local chapters to create reading rooms in their local areas, like those of Christian Scientists, staffed by volunteers in rented or donated space that would offer "any good American" books telling "the true history of events and developments of the past two decades," as well as magazines such as Welch's *American Opinion*, William F. Buckley's *National Review*, and the *Dan Smoot Report*.[130] While ostensibly all conservatives were welcome to peruse the shelves, Nickerson notes that persons of color likely would have felt uncomfortable.[131] The reading rooms served as hubs of local activity, and by 1967 there were 350 such reading rooms nationally.[132] These reading rooms became local "nerve centers" for grassroots conservatism throughout the 1960s, and, at least in southern California, the bookstores seemed to be largely run by right-wing women.[133]

Similarly, when Minute Women took on the role of guardian, they performed that work largely through research, reading, and writing. Newsletter articles make clear that Minute Women scoured the *Congressional Record*, local and national newspapers, congressional and government reports, other right-wing literature, and a variety of organizational and church literature. More than anything, they encouraged voracious reading, but mostly of literature authored by colleagues on the right. Before the founding of the JBS, Minute Women newsletters recommended Welch's book, *One Man's Opinion*, as required reading and singled him out by encouraging Minute Women across the country to arrange for him to speak in every state. "In one woman's opinion," wrote Florence Post of Welch, "we have no better speaker on the patriotic platform."[134] Like the JBS, Minute Women sought to help its members afford and access conservative literature.[135] Dorothy Frankston recommended that members read books published by the Devin-Adair Publishing Company, including John T. Flynn's *The*

Decline of the American Republic, Orval Watts's *The United Nations—a Planned Tyranny*, and Merrill Root's *Collectivism on the Campus*, and to help them afford new titles she passed along to Minute Women members the 20 percent commission the publisher gave to sellers.[136]

The telephone was another important tool in this "get out the message" work, just as it had been for Minute Women in the 1950s. In the mid-1960s Indiana chapters of the JBS instituted the Let Freedom Ring campaign, which provided a prerecorded message to anyone who dialed a specific unlisted telephone number.[137] Local chapters publicized the number in a variety of ways, including distributing candy with the local number printed on it.[138] While the recorded messages did not mention the JBS, the address given to listeners interested in more information was the local American Opinion bookstore. The first message transcribed by the Anti-Defamation League in November 1965 attacked the civil rights movement as a "rising tide of criminology and Communist inspired racial revolution" and encouraged listeners to support their local police in their defense of America against "communist slavery." The message concluded, "For an article that reveals the Communist designs behind the drive to destroy your local police, and for a support your local police window sticker, send 10 [cents] in coin to Support Your Local Police in care of 1538 N. Meridian Street, Indianapolis, Indiana. Let Freedom Ring."[139]

Let Freedom Ring operated sporadically in the state throughout the mid- and late sixties. Indianapolis and Hammond reported JBS messages in 1965 and through at least the following year; the town of Anderson reported an active Let Freedom Ring campaign throughout 1967.[140] The transcribed messages touched on a range of issues, most of which indicated that communism was the root cause of all left-wing or reform-minded organizations and movements. Themes included communist control of the National Council of Churches, communist direction of the antiwar movement, communist direction of the war in Vietnam and America's involvement there, and the treasonous Panama Canal "give-away" started by Eisenhower.[141] Charles de Gaulle, whose "dictatorship executed 100,000 anti-communist patriots after World War II," was an "anti-American megalomaniac determined to remake Europe in alliance with the Communists."[142] Johnson's Great Society was communist inspired. "While Americans worry about atomic attack," a recording explained, "the Communists prepare to destroy from within by using our own government-financed revolutionists." Antipoverty programs resulted in salaries for "goons and assassins" and supported "burglary, drunkenness, rape and even murder" in youth groups across the country. "The War on Poverty is truly an invitation to mob rule," the recording concluded.[143] In addition to writing the *American Opinion* for more information, outraged listeners could write letters to public officials, corporations, and newspaper editors.

Not limited in its activities to the Let Freedom Ring campaign, the JBS effectively worked to bring conservative speakers to Indiana to further educate the public. Between 1964 and 1967 the American Opinion bookstore of Anderson sponsored such speakers as Maj. Pedro Diaz Lanz, anticommunist Cuban air force officer and former pilot for Castro; Billy James Hargis of the Christian Anti-Communist Crusade; Sheriff Jim Clark of Selma, Alabama; and Phyllis Schlafly.[144] Indianapolis Birchers brought former communist Julia Brown to speak about her experiences within the party and the degree of communist infiltration within the civil rights movement. Brown did not disappoint members when she confirmed their suspicion that the movement was really an attempt by communists to "stir up racial strife."[145] Although Indiana historian Dale Sorenson argues that anticommunism had "lost much of its virility" by the late 1950s, the growth of the John Birch Society challenges that trajectory and documents how anticommunists sustained their activism—and even gained momentum—throughout the 1960s.[146]

When Minute Woman Marguerite Dice invited Robert Welch to found the John Birch Society in her home in 1958, her role as the silent hostess symbolized the way right-wing women provided critical support to like-minded men, but often that help failed to leave much of a footprint in the historical record. In a 2008 article commemorating the fiftieth anniversary of the founding of the JBS, *Indianapolis Monthly* magazine dubbed Dice the "Mother of the Movement," crediting her as a "revolutionary woman," albeit one standing "behind the founding men of the JBS."[147] The reality is that by the late 1950s, Welch and the JBS arrived on the scene after right-wing women had accumulated years of experience researching the communist conspiracy and tracking its progress. Through the JBS, right-wing women found a larger field for their contributions and ideas, as well as new insight into the history and trajectory of the conspiracy toward total government, but the JBS was only an extension of work already under way.

Leaders of the Indiana antifeminist coalition developed their political consciousness and worldview from within this anticommunist milieu. Minute Women were an important organization locally in the 1950s, but they disappeared from the historical record after Dice opened her home to the founding of the JBS. Still, Minute Women ideas lingered long after the group was active, probably because they were so well connected to the larger conservative network they helped create. Little is known of the history of Pro America in Indiana during the middle decades of the twentieth century, but they quickly emerged as a powerhouse in the 1970s in the fight against the IWY and ERA. Jean Harvey effectively mobilized conservative women as the state Pro America leader, and her influence loomed large in the Indiana resolutions related to federal regionalism at the Indiana IWY state conference.[148] Local Pro America literature provides the most consistent and explicit discussion of feminism as part of the one-world conspiracy. A survey of IWY participants to the Indiana conference revealed that while only 2 percent belonged to the Eagle Forum, 12 percent of respondents belonged to Pro America, making it also the most well represented conservative women's organization at the event.[149]

For conservative women, anticommunism gave meaning to the varied problems they perceived in the world as it developed after World War II, problems that related to moral depravity (including sexual promiscuity, pornography, and divorce), growth of the federal government, loss of local autonomy, and, increasingly, women's abdication of their responsibility to home, hearth, and family. Anticommunism also provided conservative women a means of expressing their ambition and political interests outside the home in a way that reaffirmed their position within the home. From within anticommunist grassroots organizations like the Minute Women, Pro America, and the JBS, women learned to think, speak, and organize for political action and successfully forged a connection between their roles as housewives and countersubversives. Feminists of the 1970s struggled to understand the quick response of conservatives to the ERA, and the puzzle piece that eluded them was the part played by still-active anticommunists, their ideas, and the groups they created.

CHAPTER 2

Anticommunists and the World Government Conspiracy

Of course, they want us to go to work so they can take over the indoctrination of our children—making them into one-worlders and zombies.

—Dorothy Frankston on the threat posed by second-wave feminists[1]

THE COLD WAR and the growth of the federal government in the twentieth century had a significant impact on the development of conspiracy theories in America and the development of the political Right. Historian Kathryn Olmsted argues that the major shift in twentieth-century conspiracy theory is the switch from a fear of conspiratorial attacks on the federal government to a belief that the federal government is the perpetrator of conspiracy.[2] She also notes that after 1960 the field of conspiracy became more democratic and open to women's participation and ideas.[3] However, the rhetoric of anticommunist organizations throughout the Cold War era makes clear that the transition was well under way by the 1950s. Throughout the postwar era, Pro America, Minute Women, and the John Birch Society warned of a world government or one-worldist conspiracy, which would become known as the New World Order by the 1980s, and it was through this lens of conspiracy that some conservative Hoosier women understood the second-wave feminist movement and the growing push for women's equality.

Studies of right-wing women in the twentieth century reveal that they "accepted motherhood as the essence of women," as Glen Jeansonne explains, "and male primacy as the essence of national strength," but these women still called for a voice equal to men's in the political sphere.[4] They were not feminists for a number of reasons, including their advocacy of hierarchical relationships of power and their belief in gender difference, as opposed to sameness, even if they believed women ought to have more access to the political process. Even before the New Deal of the 1930s, antifeminists effectively accomplished what Kim Nielsen described as the "gendering of conservatism" by combining opposition to an active interventionist government with the perpetuation of patriarchy in private and public life.[5] Before the Second World War, isolationist women motivated by "maternal love and fanatical prejudice [against Jews]" fought the Roosevelt administration and any attempt to enter the United States into the war.[6] While groups like the Women's National Committee to Keep the U.S. out of War did not appear as players in the postwar era, their causes often did. Leaders of the isolationist mothers' movement hit upon postwar issues that continued to resonate with right-wing women. Agnes Waters, whose activism earned her the title "the loudest mothers' leader," focused on opposition to the United Nations in the postwar era, arguing that it threatened to "overthrow this republic and every nation on the face of the earth."[7]

Conservative women of the postwar era built on the mothers' movement rhetoric, which counterbalanced the "warm individualism and personal character" of mothers with a United Nations that fostered one-worldism and homogeneity.[8] Postwar conservatives were different from members of the prewar or wartime mothers' movement, especially since they avoided and possibly disagreed with the blatant anti-Semitism of Elizabeth Dilling and Waters. While profascist mothers did not rematerialize in the postwar era, right-wing women after the war adopted many of their critiques, especially of anti-internationalism. "Isolationist mothers," Michelle Nickerson argues, "gendered anti-internationalism in ways that became meaningful for Cold Warriors," making combating the United Nations "mothers' most significant legacy."[9] Conservative women's groups after World War II described the United Nations as the ultimate threat to the home. Heartland mothers made a mantra of the idea that "one could not be internationalist and patriotic at the same time"—a message that Nickerson argues became a "guiding principle" for conservative women across the country during the Cold War.[10]

Anticommunism was the name given to a host of connected, though distinct, threads of right-wing thought in the 1950s, and much work remains to be done in unpacking the phrase "anticommunist."[11] Lisa McGirr argues that within the symbols of the UN and communism were a number of interrelated fears, including the growing prominence of Asia and Africa on the world stage and millennial fears of the rule of the Antichrist.[12] While right-wing women often lumped communists under the one-worlder umbrella, the two were not synonymous. A study of Minute Women, Pro America, and the John Birch Society rhetoric reveals how conservatives understood the connections between millennialism, one-worldism, and feminism.

In 1950 the American Legion stated their opposition "to any form of world federation or world government," and the National Americanism Commission of the American Legion released a report denouncing world government as a communist attempt to "destroy our sovereignty," "confiscate our economic wealth," and "strip the United States of military independence and power."[13] Even though "none of the leading organizations actively engaged in promoting world government have been cited as Communist fronts, the presence of individuals [as indicated by a letterhead of the 1949, the United World Federalists, for example] who have been cited as being affiliated with Communist front movements shows the Communists hope to control eventually any world-government administration."[14] By 1953 the National Economic Council newsletter explained that "'world government' is today's phrase, as 'National Socialism' and 'Communism' were yesterday's phrases." The article, entitled "When World Government Moves In," outlined the basics of how a world government would make "the West (the United States and Canada, Britain and the Commonwealth countries, and Western Europe)" "a vassal area of Asia."[15] Far from isolated voices in the wilderness, anticommunist women added to this postwar discourse on the threat of world government.

Minute Women and Pro America contributed their own understanding of the one-worldism threat and argued that it was the job of women as mothers and "guardians" of the home to counter it. Early in the Cold War, right-wing women perceived that the real enemy lurked behind the front of communism. Minute Women described how programs and agencies inside the United Nations and the federal government aimed to end national sovereignty and make US citizens part of a "socialist world government."[16] In June 1953 in a speech delivered to the Connecticut Veterans of Foreign Wars, Susanne Stevenson, founder of the Minute Women of the U.S.A., Inc., argued that the educational mission of the United Nations Educational, Scientific and Cultural Organization (UNESCO) was to teach "world mindedness," which was a threat to America's youth.[17] When Dorothy Frankston took over for Stevenson as national chairman for the Minute Women in 1954—a position she held until 1968—she expanded on Stevenson's vision of the problem. Frankston sensed that postwar Americans felt a growing unease with the world around them and their government; this feeling would finally lead them to the right questions. "Are you being led into Collectivist = Statism? Is your Faith in Divine Providence being supplanted by social goals and the illusion of security?" she asked.[18] By 1959 Frankston explained that communism was no monolith and that communists themselves were often the dupes of a larger movement of collectivism: "True, communism is the enemy of the free world (if there is such) but communism is the forceful imposition of a socialistic rule. Socialism then is the conditioning prerequisite for Communist take over. Metro Government, Urban Renewal, Public Housing, TVA, Aid to Education, Mental Health are all part of the conditioning program."[19] Programs that aimed to coordinate human activity and diminish local autonomy, challenge individualism, or provide assistance to racial minorities or the poor were often categorized as "planning" or "collectivism" and were deemed part of the master conspiracy. Often these ideas overlapped, as when Frankston described the United Nations International Children's Fund (UNICEF) Halloween campaign in 1961. UNICEF was "in fact a powerful propaganda agency for the world-wide Communist conspiracy" whose "most familiar activities in this country are the collection of money by sending children to beg from door-to-door—(Halloween), and the sale of subversive greeting cards, which emphasize racial mixing and U.N. one-world concepts." The point of the UNICEF campaign included the desire to "intrude on the celebration of our great national and religious holidays and thereby obscure the traditional meaning of these occasions."[20] One-worlders desired to create a homogenized country of interracial citizens without loyalty to nation, state, or local community and without a firm grounding in tradition, which, as Frankston understood it, included segregation and nationalism.

The fear of centralization and planning appears repeatedly in Minute Women newsletters of the postwar era. Minute Women worked tirelessly to identify and report to one another the exact programs and agencies inside the United Nations and the federal government that they believed aimed to end national sovereignty and make US citizens part of a world government. Minute Women read UNESCO literature and reported on its contents to one another. Under the title "Another UNESCO Booklet," Frankston detailed the professional affiliations of the author of a pamphlet entitled *The Universal Declaration of Human Rights: A Guide for Teachers*. The author appeared to be working alone, without collaborators, and the pamphlet encouraged use of the declaration in "every subject—English, History, Civics, or what have you" with the intention of making the declaration more universally understood and accepted. Her coverage implicated the International Federation of Teachers Association, the New Education Fellowship, the International Federation of Secondary Teachers, and the World Organization of the Teaching Profession as involved in the effort to spread world-mindedness.[21] Words like "international" and "worldwide" were suspect when said by educational professionals. Throughout the 1970s conservative women were committed to fighting, as Rosemary Thomson, a leader in the anti–International Women's Year campaign, explained, the "NEA's brave new world forecasts," challenging groups like the National Science Foundation, which received federal grant money to ask "open-ended discussions that don't teach values one way or the other," a technique "right out of humanism's bag of no moral absolutes."[22] The "let him alone and let him be happy" thinking of educators did not mesh with conservative women's way of thinking.[23] As Thomson explained, "We are in a battle for our children's minds."[24]

In 1967 Minute Woman Jo Hindman explained that Executive Order 11386, which established the Federal Advisory Council on Regional Economic Development during the Johnson administration, was "another precedent-shattering bureaucratic achievement." Since the New Deal and by using pull-at-your-heartstrings initiatives such as the War on Poverty, "commerce has been the gateway to centralized control." Through the "notorious concept of social engineering" the powers of Congress would be "by-passed in [a] CONVERTED American government." According to Hindman, this plan had been foretold by "J[acob] L[evy] Moreno, a European emigrant" who "graphically explained the plan wherein the surge of human 'wants' would sweep directly from the masses toward a central national head, completely by-passing state legislatures."[25] Under headings like "One-World Activity" and "More One-Worlders," newsletters updated members on new organizations like the Campaign for a World Constitution and listed the Americans affiliated with such efforts, or Americans who participated in suspect conferences like the European-American Assembly in Bürgenstock, Switzerland, which included members of the despised Council on Foreign Relations.[26]

Pro America, too, groped for answers to what lay behind problems plaguing postwar America. Socially conservative women saw moral decay everywhere, in changing sexual mores, pornography, juvenile delinquency, the film industry.[27] Under the title "The Enemy Is Landing," one woman asked: "If we could figure out what is disturbing our way of life so deeply, might we not find a way to correct it before it goes too far? May not all the obvious troubles be actually related parts of a much less obvious but deeper scheme—one which will affect the high and low, the rich and the poor, one which will change law and order, religion and faith, work and play?"[28] Citing the work of Anthony Sutton in *Wall Street and the Bolshevik Revolution,* a Pro America author noted that Leon Trotsky in 1917 "was for world revolution, for world dictatorship; he is in one word, an internationalist. Bankers and Bolsheviks have this significant common ground—internationalism," proving that one-worldism was the ultimate aim of a conspiracy that included communism.[29] In an article titled "World Government, Whether You Want It or Not," Pro America's newsletter warned readers that instigators of one-worldism would not be explicit or honest about their goals: "The ultimate dream of this century's 'planners' would not come to pass through voluntary surrender by governments of their political and economic affairs to a world state because it is unworkable and contrary to human nature. Therefore the world government wishers have adopted a new strategy which is being put into action piecemeal, through rear doors, almost clandestinely."[30] Ultimately, "world government" and totalitarianism were the enemies behind myriad social and political ills, including communism. Conservative women had to be on guard to subvert planners on whatever front they moved. Catherine E. Rymph summarizes the trend: "Conservative women activists of the Cold War era would, in the name of home rule and parental authority, devote much of their energy to fighting the influence of the United Nations in their local schools. Referring to the UN as a 'world government,' they fused antistatist and anti-internationalist discourse into a collective critique of authoritarianism."[31] If early Cold Warriors worried about the global scope of communism, conservative women of the 1960s and beyond associated any scheme with a global perspective to be "communistic" and, more importantly, totalitarian or authoritarian.

Minute Women blended a strong measure of Christian fundamentalism and millennialism into their countersubversive arguments. Millennialism has a long history in the United States, dating to the utopian vision of the Puritans and their understanding of their settlement as the biblical "city on the hill."[32] Minute Women believed, like the Puritans, that America was the New Israel, God's chosen land. Therefore, as goes America, so goes Christianity. Throughout the nineteenth century, millennial religions like the Millerites and the Shakers exhorted Americans to prepare for the Second Coming, which they believed was nearly at hand. Disappointment followed in the wake of lapsed deadlines, but the millennial tradition continued into the twentieth century. Millennials believe that the end-time will include a period of one thousand years in which there will be utopia and peace on Earth. Disagreement exists between pre- and postmillennials about whether the one-thousand-year utopia will begin before or after the Second Coming of Jesus Christ. Among premillennials there is also disagreement about whether "the great tribulation," or a period of war, disaster, and terror, will be experienced by all. Pretribulationists believe that some—true believers—will be "raptured," or saved from Earth and the tribulation, while others believe that all will experience the great tribulation but that true believers will be saved after.[33]

Overall, both millennials and conspiracists believe in a dichotomous world of good and evil, and most believe in the inevitability of an apocalyptic showdown between the two. A recent study suggests that these two factors—a belief in supernatural, unseen, and intentional forces operating in the world and a belief that history is a battle between good and evil—are the best predictors for who will believe in conspiracy theories.[34] While not all American conspiracists were or are millennials, there is a strong "symbiotic" connection between the two.[35] Conspiracy is antithetical to randomness and chaos; believers of conspiracy look for covert purpose in overt action and discourse because they believe that with enough information and insight they can uncover connections between seemingly unrelated events. In this way, conspiracy correlates to a belief in an ordered world and good and evil. If conspiracy is built on anxiety, it might also provide comfort. The existence of a grand conspiracy is unnerving, but understanding how world events fit into old patterns—even believing that there is a pattern to world events—might be comforting, as is believing there is something a single individual can do about global problems and cultural shifts. "Conspiracy theories locate and describe evil, while millennialism explains the mechanism for its ultimate defeat," explains Michael Barkun in *A Culture of Conspiracy: Apocalyptic Visions in Contemporary America*; and the strength and variety of American millennialism throughout the eighteenth, nineteenth, and twentieth centuries were matched by a diversity of conspiracy beliefs.[36]

The manifestation of an all-powerful world government had religious connotation for "prophecy believers," especially premillennial dispensationalists who believed that the tribulation, a period in which the Antichrist would exercise complete rule on Earth, was at hand.[37] Premillennial dispensationalists were evangelicals who "conceptualized history as partitioned into certain ages with a definite end."[38] Watching throughout the postwar era for signs of the end-time, conservative Protestants found abundant evidence—in the global fight with atheistic communism, the advent of the state of Israel, and the creation of the nuclear bomb—to support their belief that they had passed into a new age in which Christ would return to Earth (specifically the United States) and signal the beginning of the end of the world.[39] Cold War historian Angela M. Lahr, in *Millennial Dreams and Apocalyptic Nightmares,* argues that anticommunist rhetoric of good and evil fit easily into "the premillennial worldview" and allowed evangelicals to engage more comfortably in national life and political culture.[40]

By the late twentieth century, conspiracists, especially fundamentalists and millenarians, viewed "the Antichrist" less as an evil person and more as a mechanism or system of control, so much so that world government became a synonym for the Antichrist.[41] In 1964 Florence Post, a Florida Minute Woman, bluntly stated that "the enemy we now fight is the Anti-Christ," and this claim in no way competed with an understanding of the enemy as communism, socialism, totalitarianism, and liberalism.[42] Minute Women had always understood their work as a "crusade" and used the language repeatedly throughout the postwar era. "In these troubled times," wrote a Minute Woman in 1970, "having put on the whole armor of God, we are fortified with hope and are able to stand."[43] While Minute Women conspiracy theory drew heavily from the millennial tradition, over the course of the late twentieth century millennials created an "improvisational millennialism" that was neither strictly secular nor religious.[44] Freed from any mooring in specific religious or secular texts or traditions, this "improvisational style" of millennialism "has a much freer hand," explains Barkun.[45] The result is conspiracy theories with endless adaptability.[46] Minute Women conspiracy theory blended secular and sacred evils with no method to their application beyond utility in explaining current events and situations.

According to Minute Women, the threat posed by psychological experts and mental health programs was part of the world government conspiracy. Gene Birkeland of San Fernando Valley warned Minute Women in 1955 that "'they' are making plans for YOU. You are going to have your brain 'washed' so you can become a well regulated little citizen of the world." "Who are 'THEY'?" she asked. "They" were the National Association of Mental Health, which "was liberally sprinkled with its own set of 'one-worlders, Atlantic Unioners, etc.'" and was intent on discrediting those who fought communists "with bare knuckles and no holds barred" by labeling them "'crackpots' or 'lunatic fringe.'"[47] Birkeland expanded this understanding of the postwar mental health movement by focusing on an Alaskan mental health bill in her 1955 exposé, entitled "Now—Siberia U.S.A.," in which she argued that the seemingly innocuous state bill that sought to create a mental health facility in the state of Alaska was an attempt to create a gulag where anyone deemed mentally ill could be shipped off to.[48] "Don't get the idea that, simply because this was designed for Alaska that you . . . couldn't be sent there," she warned and cited part of the law that allowed for "prompt transfer" of residents of other states to the Alaska facility if the state had a reciprocal agreement with Alaska.[49] Psychologists like Gordon Allport offered explanations of right-wing and racist politics that signaled delusion and mental illness; psychological experts often used nonreligious or even antireligious theories to explain the human condition; the National Institute of Health, created by Congress in 1946, was part of ballooning federal bureaucracy. But the most commonly cited problem with psychology was its connection to one-worldism. Birkeland used this equation to explain the relationship: "Mental Hygiene = Human Relations = U.N.E.S.C.O."[50] Nickerson found that Minute Women often quoted two lines from the founding statement of the World Mental Health Federation: "Principles of mental health cannot be furthered in any society unless there is progressive acceptance of the concept of world citizenship. World citizenship can be widely extended among all peoples through the applications of the principles of mental health."[51] Siberia U.S.A. became a Minute Women campaign to stop the advance of psychology and state- or community-sponsored psychological programs, and through it they gained important allies and supporters.[52] In the mid-1950s, Minute Women led the charge against community mental health initiatives at the local, state, and national levels and effectively created a new front in the fight against world government.

Few issues mattered more to right-wing women in the 1950s than the Bricker Amendment. In the postwar era, conservatives of all stripes worried about the growth of the federal government, especially the expanding welfare state and executive authority at the expense of state authority. As the United States increased its participation in international affairs, conservatives worried that the expansion in power would have domestic effects. Particularly galling was the possibility that UN treaties might be enforceable within the country. If so, the 1948 Universal Declaration of Human Rights might be used to challenge Jim Crow or any number of other state prerogatives. Republican Senator John Bricker of Ohio introduced a constitutional amendment to the US Senate in 1952 that stipulated that any treaty conflicting with the Constitution would be void and that any treaty that included measures pertaining to "internal law" would only be valid if enacted through congressional legislation.[53] While Bricker was no isolationist—he supported the Marshall Plan and NATO—he was worried about the increasing trend of unilateral action on the part of presidents who involved the nation in international affairs without consulting Congress.[54] The amendment was well received among conservative circles, and all but one Republican Senate colleague asked to cosponsor the amendment with Bricker.[55] The conservative leadership of the American Bar Association provided important help in drafting, revising, and lobbying for the amendment.

Minute Women immediately rallied to the cause and made the amendment a top priority. Passage of the amendment was the "number-one issue" for Minute Women in 1954 (followed by rescinding the Status of Forces Treaty), and the

Bricker Amendment appeared again in 1956 and 1957 in Minute Women literature as congressional debate over the amendment continued.[56] Conservative women joined together to form Vigilant Women for the Bricker Amendment, of which the Minute Women claimed to be the largest part. They gathered half a million signatures on a petition in support of the amendment and brought a group of over two hundred women to Washington, DC, to hand deliver the petition to Bricker, lobby senators, and hold a pro-Bricker rally in January 1954.[57] Frank Holman, former president of the American Bar Association (1948–49), wrote to the Minute Women to encourage their efforts and called on them to "carry the fight to the grass roots level."[58] By organizing "a great nationwide campaign," women would galvanize the electorate to vote in primaries and conventions and ultimately pave the way for the defeat of the "internationalists." He characterized the Bricker Amendment as "the greatest issue which faces America today, greater than taxes or inflation or even communist infiltration," and as fundamental as whether "we and our children are to have a government of men or a government of adequate Constitutional safeguards." Implicitly, Minute Women's roles as mothers and wives explained why a "government of men" needed women to spur it to action. "The women of America have the power of winning this fight. You need only organize," Holman encouraged.[59]

Minute Women followed the Bricker Amendment throughout the 1950s, reporting on congressional elections with the potential to impact the progress of the amendment and the status of the amendment in the House and Senate Judiciary Subcommittees.[60] Indianapolis Minute Woman Marguerite Dice, along with fifty-four other citizens of Indianapolis, sent a petition to the US House Committee on the Judiciary in 1956 that advocated a number of Far Right policies, including "early passage without change of Bricker amendment, enforcement of McCarren-Walter Act, adoption of Hoover commission recommendations, end deficit spending, balance budget, cut taxes, withdrawal from International Labor Organization, keep out of the Atlantic Union and World Government, terminate Status of Forces Treaty, advance no Federal aid to education."[61] Despite the Minute Women's best efforts, the amendment failed to achieve support from the Eisenhower administration. Eisenhower and liberal Republicans, as well as most Democrats, saw the amendment as hampering the president's authority to deal with international affairs. While Eisenhower attempted to avoid overtly breaking with the Right over the amendment, ultimately his administration waged a campaign to stop its progress through Congress.[62]

Disappointment over the Bricker Amendment made Minute Women even more disgusted with the Republican Party. Frankston was critical of Eisenhower Republicans from the beginning and warned that their tactics were so nefarious as to include weakening the Republican Party (by alienating supporters of conservative Senator Robert Taft of Ohio, who challenged Eisenhower for the Republican presidential nomination in 1952) in order to encourage Democratic victories.[63] She warned women that "sitting on the sidelines, we Americans have allowed the two major political parties to approximate each other . . . until today 'bi-partisan' policies and candidates are making our votes a matter of fading significance."[64] The solution was to "start thinking" and question the political status quo.[65]

Minute Women did not always understand Democrats as the enemy; however, they criticized politics they saw as liberal regardless of party affiliation. Florence Post filled in for Frankston as editor of the Minute Women newsletter in January 1964, and she wrote that she hoped the new Johnson administration would put on the brakes in the "our rush for a total world government."[66] Democrats could, potentially at least, be allies, even if more often than not they disappointed. Minute Women more commonly focused on the politics of the Republican Party and redeeming Republicanism from internationalists. Right-leaning newspapers like the *Chicago Daily Tribune* noted that the Minute Women, a laudable group, would not be necessary if the Republican Party would "get its [anticommunist] message to the people."[67] The *Daily Tribune* was not surprised that Minute Women were popular, since "the vast majority of Americans, men and women," favored their goals, but the newspaper was surprised that the group operated outside the GOP. Since Republicans were so often "crypto-Democratic" who offered "watered down New Dealism," the editor concluded that "the rapid growth of the Minute Women is just another evidence that the most numerous segment [the middle classes] of the American population has been without a voice in contemporary American politics."[68]

The Minute Women's response to the Bricker Amendment reflected their growing belief that the United Nations represented a powerful challenge to American sovereignty. Cathal J. Nolan argues that opposition to the Bricker Amendment "represented broad, popular, and nationalist support for the whole United Nations system" and was the "last hurrah" of conservative isolationists in the postwar era.[69] The Bricker Amendment uncovered the deep "forests of anger on the political right" concerning America's position as a global power broker willing to intervene in conflicts and enter treaties with nations on wide-ranging issues.[70] The Minute Women were not isolationists—they were often hawks advocating for American involvement in the world, but only in ways that forwarded an expansion of capitalism and that demonstrated national power. For many right-wing women, the failure of the Bricker Amendment proved that "internationalists," as opposed to nationalists, called the shots in Eisenhower's administration, just as they had done in the presidencies of FDR and Truman. Right-wing women's activism concerning the Bricker Amendment further demonstrates how conspiracy could live alongside a more mainstream critique of the expansion of presidential power and international cooperation and motivate women to more actively participate in the political process.

Pro America and the Minute Women thought women particularly suited to the work of fighting one-worldism.[71] Since the threat of internationalism and one-worldism meant an end to the "American way of life" and a bleak world for their children, Minute Women sounded a gendered call to action by specifically challenging their members to educate themselves regarding foreign policy in order to protect their homes and families from totalitarian world government. "If you don't like this drift to world government, just remember one thing," Frankston explained. "You will have to stop it. It will not stop itself. You will have to do something." "The left-wingers, the Communists and the One-Worlders, know who are the party leaders," she argued and asked, "How much time is it worth to you to find out who they are?"[72] Minute Women literature routinely discussed the need for housewives to expand their understanding of care for the family to include countersubversive work. Despite the fact that "correspondence, card files, reading and a smattering of housekeeping" meant that there were "never enough hours in the day to do it all," Frankston argued that it was the job of Minute Women to "make Government their business."[73] She rallied women to action: "Women CAN do it and they WILL. . . . Keep constantly alert. Watch the actions and reactions of your Senators. Continue your messages to them. The job is not done until victory is won."[74]

Although the JBS is known and remembered as an anticommunist organization, Robert Welch followed the path laid out by the Minute Women and transitioned from anticommunism in the mid-1960s, branching out to focus on a much older and more elusive foe. In a pamphlet entitled *The Truth in Time*, published in 1966, Welch alerted members to the possibility that the real enemy was not communism but a much older adversary that he had difficulty pinpointing:

> The communist movement is only a tool of the total conspiracy. As secret as the Communist activities and organizations generally appear, they are part of an open book compared to the secrecy enveloping some higher degree of diabolic force. The extrinsic evidence is strong and convincing that by the beginning of the Twentieth century there had evolved an inner core of conspiratorial power, able to direct and control subversive activities which were worldwide in their reach, incredibly cunning and ruthless in their nature, and brilliantly farsighted

> and patient in their strategy. Whether or not this increasingly all-powerful hidden command was due to an unbroken continuation of [Adam] Weishaupt's Illuminati, or was a distillation from the leadership of this and other groups, we do not know. Some of them may never have been Communists, while others were. To avoid as much dispute as possible, therefore, let's call this ruling clique simply the INSIDERS.[75]

Like the Minute Women, Welch thought communism only part of a conspiracy aimed at world "collectivism," but he provided more historical context for understanding the conspiracy than Frankston. Welch divided people into several camps: the cadre of insiders, who were few and elite; their stooges, including communists, liberals, government officials, bankers, and so on; and the ill-informed and apathetic public. Fighting them all were patriots like Welch.[76] The "Insiders," explained Welch, were a group of amorphous "big shots" in government and international affairs.[77] Men like Dwight Eisenhower, George Marshall, and Charles de Gaulle were not communists but insiders and thus still part of a collectivist conspiracy that aimed to rule the world.[78] In the face of skepticism, Welch asked, "How do you think their actions all eventually mesh together so well, to bring an incredibly brutal one-world tyranny ever nearer, unless there is central conspiratorial planning of the whole show in which they are leading actors?"[79] The fantastic nature of the revelation made Welch cautious about disclosing it to the JBS membership. Revealing it "little by little," he hoped to expose the larger world threat of the insiders without alienating his anticommunist members.[80]

Welch included in his list of potential "insiders" what D. J. Mulloy called "one of the mother lodes" of conspiracy theory in the United States and around the world: the Order of the Illuminati.[81] When Welch linked the "insiders" to the Illuminati, he brought over two hundred years of American conspiracy belief full circle.[82] Fears of the Illuminati run deep in the United States, dating to the late 1790s and the political divisions separating the first political parties in the country, the Federalists and Jeffersonian Republicans. British and American conservatives argued that revolutionary political elements, including the Jeffersonians, encouraged by and in league with French radicals, were subverting tradition, order, and Christianity. The conspiracy goes that the root of the menace was the Order of the Illuminati, a secret fraternal organization founded in 1776 by Adam Weishaupt, a Bavarian professor of natural philosophy at the University of Edinburgh. The Illuminati were responsible for the French Revolution, and, according to John Robinson's *Proofs of a Conspiracy*, published in 1798, they intended to "establish universal Liberty and Equality, the imprescriptible rights of Man. . . . And as necessary preparations for all this, they intended to root out all religion and ordinary morality, and even to break the bonds of domestic life, by destroying the veneration for marriage-vows, and by taking the education of children out of the hands of the parents."[83] Federalist Congregationalist minister Jedidiah Morse, in a sermon delivered on the Day of the National Fast in Massachusetts in 1799, explained that the Illuminati in New York and Virginia (and likely elsewhere in the country) intended to "subvert and overturn our holy religion [Protestant Christianity] and our free and excellent government."[84] While the existence of a group known as the Illuminati is not in doubt, David Brion Davis characterizes it as a "short-lived organization dedicated to the humanitarian and rationalistic principles of the Enlightenment."[85] There is no historical evidence to support the conspiracy theories associated with the Illuminati, but that has not stopped the theory from flourishing in the American imagination for over two hundred years. Most recently, pop star Beyoncé had to defend herself against the charge of active participation in the Illuminati in part because she used a triangle hand gesture as part of a choreography routine.[86]

Welch did not believe that the conspiracy toward "collectivism" began with the Illuminati; the forces of "good and evil" had forever been locked in an "eternal war"—or at least a war that went back to the sixth century B.C.E., presumably in Greece, and the advent of government by the consent of the governed.[87] The good fought "under the banner of individual rights and responsibilities," the evil fought "under the banner of collectivism," he explained.[88] While self-government was a "huge advance over the Asiatic principle of governmental power resting on sheer might," it also meant that demagogues would use the people to forward their agenda of collectivism. (Democracy was a real problem for Welch; the United States began as a republic, and he routinely connected democracy to the growing demand for minority rights both within the United States and in anticolonial movements around the world.) By the 1700s the "Satanic creed and program" of collectivism had combined to form the Illuminati, "the most important one of these [secret collectivist] groups," which took control of collectivist activities after 1776. Sometime in the twentieth century either communists took control of the Illuminati or the Illuminati took control of the communists; that "there have been one or more such organizations, which have now been absorbed into the top echelons of the communist conspiracy—*or vice versa*—is supported by too much evidence of too many kinds to permit much doubt."[89] Through a long line of dedicated operatives, including the Gracchi brothers, Gaius Marius, Mao Zedong, and Eleanor Roosevelt, "the forces of evil had learned well, from massive experience, to use government as the instrumentality through which to achieve their ambitions, and to use the demagogic appeal of bread and circuses for the masses as a means of controlling that instrumentality."[90] The conspiracy toward totalitarian world government was led by collectivist insiders, and the fight had been going on since before the country was founded.

The Illuminati conspiracy brought Welch closer to European and American anti-Semitic thinkers of previous generations, specifically, Nesta Webster and Charles Coughlin. Nesta Webster was a popular British writer and conspiracy theorist in the 1920s and 1930s who wrote prolifically on the Illuminati and connected the order to Bolshevism and state socialism. She argued that Jews, who hoped to topple Christianity and Christian nations, were part of the conspiracy.[91] Father Charles Coughlin advocated the same ideas in the American Midwest in weekly radio broadcasts throughout the 1930s. In the early 1930s Coughlin stated that international financiers or world bankers controlled world markets and governments around the globe, but by the late thirties Coughlin described these international financiers as Jews who were heading a Jewish conspiracy for world domination and intimately connected with the secret Order of the Illuminati. In his description of Jews as masterminds of a secret plot to control the Western world and maybe the globe, Coughlin echoed Nazi propaganda and sometimes copied it verbatim.[92] At the peak of his popularity, Coughlin broadcast to an audience of roughly forty million people, with significant support from heartland states like Indiana and Ohio, and he received more mail than anyone else in America.[93] Revilo Oliver, a professor of classical languages and literature at the University of Illinois, directly connected Welch's "insiders" to the "conspiracy of Jews" that ultimately forced Oliver to resign in 1966 from the JBS executive committee.[94] Welch never openly or explicitly described the conspiracy of international bankers as Jews, but the argument was an old one, and for many, the connection was obvious and well traversed. He built on the anti-Semitic foundation constructed by others but without the explicit references that the Anti-Defamation League (ADL) and others required in order to link him personally to hate speech.

In their 1966 exposé on the Birch society, Benjamin Epstein, national director of the ADL, and Arnold Forster, general counsel and director of the ADL's civil rights division, explained that almost every month in the JBS *Bulletin* "Welch insists . . . that the UN was planned by Communists, that it is controlled by the Communists, and that it was designed specifically to suit Communist purposes."[95] Welch encouraged the creation of catchy slogans like "Get the U.S. out of the U.N. and the U.N. out of the U.S." It was a tactic he picked up from communists whose effective use of "I like Taft, but can he win?" devastated the Republican's chance for the 1954 presidential nomination, according to

Welch.[96] The Birch campaign against the UN sought to expose the communist principle of reversal, whereby communists secretly coveted and controlled organizations they purported to disagree with, such as the UN.[97] Dictatorship and totalitarian one-world government lay behind cooperation in or with the UN, and JBS publications and speakers frequently warned against such machinations. Regardless of whether the United Nations was controlled by communists or insiders, Welch consistently spoke out against it.

The postwar civil rights movement was another manifestation of the communist conspiracy, and the right-wing response to it set a pattern for how conservatives responded to other identity politics, including feminism. Among the diverse messages of the Let Freedom Ring campaign, anti–civil rights messages predominated in Indiana. JBS speakers and publications promoted the civil rights movement as communist inspired. Reacting to the *Brown v. Topeka Board of Education* decision, Welch argued that Supreme Court Justice Earl Warren "voted 92 percent of the time in favor of Communists and subversives." Inevitably, he said, the Warren Court would destroy "all of the safeguards which made this a republic instead of a mobocracy."[98] Black conservatives Julia Brown and George Schuyler supported this message. Schuyler, longtime reporter for the *Pittsburgh Courier* and a JBS member, frequently published essays assuring conservatives that not all African Americans supported Martin Luther King Jr. and his ilk. Schuyler charged that the Southern Christian Leadership Conference and King particularly were "infecting the mentally retarded with the germs of civil disobedience, camouflaged as non-violence and love of white people."[99] In addition to *American Opinion*, Schuyler wrote for *Review of the News*, another Birch publication, and traveled as a speaker for the group, even sharing the stage with Selma, Alabama, sheriff Jim Clark.[100]

Black women's place in right-wing American politics has been largely overlooked by scholars, but Julia Brown, a popular anticommunist and anti–civil rights speaker on the JBS circuit, offers a glimpse into their thinking and influence within the movement.[101] Brown averaged a dozen speeches a year between 1963 and 1971 to large audiences, including in Indiana, and over that time her speeches increasingly became more similar to the argument of other right-wing ideologues regarding race and conspiracy.[102] Julia and her husband, J. Curlee Brown, were in many ways a success story. Julia left high school in the tenth grade and worked hard, along with her husband, to build up a trucking business and achieve middle-class status in their Cleveland community by the late 1940s. Although joining the CPUSA in 1947 in the hopes of helping promote the welfare of and opportunities for black people, she left the party within a year, believing that communists duped common people and were only using civil rights to forward communist goals. She rejoined the CPUSA in 1951 as a spy for the FBI and provided information about the activities of communists in her area for nearly nine years. Her life as an "undercover agent" culminated in 1962, when she testified before the House Committee on Un-American Activities and identified around one hundred people she thought were communists or communist sympathizers.[103] While Brown began political activism firmly committed to civil rights and integration, by 1964 she protested the civil rights movement, especially the activities of King, whom she decried as "the biggest enemy of my people."[104] A major theme in her message was that "civil rights" agitation was a trick communists used to foment trouble: "The Communists use civil rights as the sugar to catch the flies for the poison. Civil rights is the sugar to entice the people. And after they get an audience then they feed them the poison."[105]

Historian Veronica Wilson documents how Brown transitioned from anti-communism and a liberal commitment to civil rights and integration to supporting George Wallace and Richard Nixon and arguing that "police brutality was a myth" created when "rabble-rousers lure well-meaning police into reprisals that radicals capitalize on to condemn government authority."[106] Like Welch, Brown told her audiences that King was communist led and the civil rights movement was communist inspired. She explained his assassination as communist directed, because King stopped being useful to communists or stopped being amenable to their goals (which, as Wilson points out, would seem to challenge the idea that he was their dupe).[107] According to Brown, Robert Kennedy suffered the same fate at the hands of his communist handlers. Even a decade after King's assassination, she fought the creation of a national holiday in his memory, testifying before Congress at the request of Senators Strom Thurmond and Larry McDonald. She had a long career, telling the prosegregationist Right what they wanted to hear, and she made increasing use of conspiracy theory to explain how the world worked.[108] It is not easy to understand Brown's reasoning, but a belief in conspiracies of enormous scope would help explain how she could deny even the existence of ghettos during the riots in Watts and Newark and lay the entire civil rights movement at the feet of communist saboteurs. By connecting civil rights to the communist conspiracy, she implicitly connected civil rights to the collectivist conspiracy, since for most right-wing conspiracists there was no real difference.

If the ideas of right-wing women seem odd or unusual, that is no reason to take them lightly. The Minute Women's and JBS's fear of one-worldism was not new to the Cold War or even the twentieth century. What the history of conspiracy makes clear is the remarkable longevity of theories like the Illuminati conspiracy and that belief in conspiracy is very common in the United States—especially today. Conspiracism is not aberrant in the sense that belief in conspiracy theories is reported by millions of Americans, but it still troubles scholars since it means believers might no longer accurately or realistically perceive the world around them.[109] "Conspiracism straddles a blurred and shifting boundary between pathology and normalcy," Barkun notes, but he encourages scholars to avoid pejorative descriptors such as "paranoid."[110] Olmsted reminds us that belief in antigovernment conspiracy is "an understandable response to conspiratorial government actions" but acknowledges that understanding or explaining conspiracism can be difficult.[111] "Careful hands" are needed in this work, Barkun warns.[112]

Belief in conspiracy may be popular because it promises individuals insight into the working of the world and perhaps, as a result, access to power and control.[113] Countersubversion has never been limited to the Far Right or Left and has made its influence felt on both political parties and mainstream culture, influencing everything from anti-Catholicism and the political debates during the American Revolution, to the ideologies of abolition and proslavery arguments during the antebellum era, to American support for Japanese internment during World War II.[114] Grassroots anticommunists, like those within the Minute Women and JBS, were not "extremists" and were never seriously investigated by federal or state authorities since, as Sara Diamond explains, their politics "reinforced prevailing state and corporate prerogatives during the Cold War era."[115] Belief in conspiracy per se is not psychopathological, antisocial, or "abnormal." People who report little trust in others and people with heightened levels of paranoia or anxiety are more likely to believe in conspiracies, but conspiracy belief is not limited to this segment of the population. Beliefs in the unseen and in history as a story of good and evil are the best predictors of conspiracy belief, and J. Eric Oliver and Thomas Wood argue that these tendencies are not "irregular"—certainly they would not impede "normal functioning in society." They are predispositions that "originate in cognitive tendencies that would appear normal or even appropriate in other circumstances, such as knocking on wood for good luck."[116] Likewise, belief in conspiracy does not correlate to political naïveté or miseducation on political issues. Oliver and Wood conclude, "Even highly engaged or ideological segments of the population can be swayed by the power of these narratives, particularly when they coincide with their other political views."[117]

If conspiracy is and was popular with everyone, it still may have had a specific appeal to right-wing women. Belief in conspiracy coincides with feelings of powerlessness with regard to the political system.[118] Women, especially those who might otherwise feel isolated in their homes and far from positions of authority even in local communities and especially centers of national power, might be particularly drawn to conspiracy as a way to exert control over their lives.[119] Conspiracy theory becomes the great leveler—Fredric Jameson dubbed it the "poor person's cognitive mapping"—because it allows believers a way to explain the complexities of life in a global age. That explanation might be a "degraded version" of understanding, according to some, because it "either misrecognizes totality as totalitarianism or attempts to represent the unpresentable as analogy" and thereby becomes "an illegitimate form of knowledge." But for many women who had time to read but perhaps not the ability or desire to pursue advanced education or training, conspiracy theory offered a way to explain the world that required creativity and research skills but not access to powerful people or groups.[120] It allowed those without power to imagine themselves with power or at least secret information and insight into the operation of the world and history, which is why conspiracy may be particularly appealing to socially disempowered groups.[121] Conspiracy operated as a "rhetorical bullhorn" for women, Nickerson theorizes, "amplifying female voices that might not ordinarily project the same volume as men's into public debates."[122] When an unnamed Pennsylvania Minute Woman explained that a bill introduced to Congress would overtly increase federal aid to state and local police but that covertly the bill authors wanted to "take over as much local government as possible," she demonstrated how with little more than a copy of the *Congressional Record* women could perform important political work and see their ideas discussed in print.[123]

It is also important to consider that women did not have to be convinced of the conspiracy to see the utility of it. Indiana conservative Kathryn Nikou described her father's interest in conspiracy theories, but she reported that she did not adhere to them—sometimes because she personally knew the individuals involved and the theories purported did not resonate with her knowledge of the facts of the case. She explained, "It's like anything. Sometimes they can stumble on something right, but sometimes they can stumble on something wrong."[124] Conservative state senator Joan Gubbins of Indiana reported that she did not believe in the conspiracy of federal regionalism (the idea that the federal government or liberals wanted to obliterate the states and divide the country into larger federal regions ahead of a world government takeover), but the idea had been around a long time, and she indicated that it was a step in the right direction if it got women thinking about the problem of federal domination and usurpation of the states.[125] Nickerson found similar sentiment among the women she interviewed: "The extent to which they believed the actual conspiracy theory behind 'Siberia U.S.A.' mattered less than the power it gave them to attack the social and political forces they sought to annihilate."[126] The existence of a conspiracy against the shared interests of a group fosters unity and solidarity within the group.[127] This benefit may be true even if all members of the group do not believe in the conspiracy.

Many conspiracy theorists, including Welch and Frankston, had difficulty pinpointing the exact culprits involved in the collectivist conspiracy. There was a strategy to this vagueness, but it also was to be expected, since a "true" conspiracy "would be something that is absolutely unpresentable or absent, proving no signs or clues of its existence. . . . [I]t is invisible and undetectable."[128] Yet varying, even competing, theories for understanding the threat big government and one-worldism embodied did not create cacophony or even competition among conspiracists on the Far Right. Michael J. Wood, Karen M. Douglas, and Robbie M. Sutton find that believers of conspiracy "do not tend to settle on a single conspiracist account as the only acceptable explanation; rather, they simultaneously endorse several [even] contradictory accounts."[129] The result is that, "over time, the view of the world as a place ruled by conspiracies can lead to conspiracy becoming the default explanation for any given event—a unitary, closed-off world-view in which beliefs come together in a mutually supportive network known as a *monological belief system*."[130] Ambiguity regarding the identity of conspirators may derive from uncertainty as to who the real conspirators are, but it may also represent "an element of self-preservation and conflict avoidance in the vagueness. . . . If multiple contradictory theories are simultaneously believed by many in a conspiracist community, endorsing one in particular is tantamount to denying the others and may provoke a backlash."[131] Theodore Sasson agrees, arguing that conspiracy theories "tend to be expressed in terms that are vague and in multiple forms," but he theorizes that perhaps that is because the mainstream media often fails to provide detailed information that would allow those seeking alternate explanations to be more specific.[132]

When Robert Welch identified the Illuminati and "insiders" as the perpetrators of the one-world conspiracy it did not create tension between Minute Women and the JBS, just as it had not created tension when US Senator William Jenner argued in 1956 that NATO was the ultimate culprit. Frankston reprinted large sections of Jenner's speeches that identified NATO as the source of one-world agitation and later supported the JBS and Welch's publications by advertising them in her newsletter. Minute Women could appreciate Jenner's ideas about how the "NATO super government" sought to increase its reach into domestic areas like taxation, labor, and immigration, since he was careful to make clear that no "Generals or Admirals . . . assigned to NATO take part in this carefully planned campaign to make us part of one-world government by regional compacts," although he still maintained that they led America to one-worldism. There were some in government—"probably only a few people"—who knew the larger plan; that others did not was to be expected, since the planners "planned it that way." Under the headings "Only Congress Can Stop World Government" and "The People Must Fight for a Nationalist Congress," Jenner explained that "those Americans who stay home on Election Day . . . are the best friends the One Worlders have."[133] His sentiments deeply resonated with the worldview of Minute Women, as did his solution to the problem, and when Welch arrived on the scene, Minute Women supported his ideas, too. Competing theories of the trajectory of one-worldism and its culprits were welcomed by the Minute Women.

Although Minute Women sometimes despaired that the majority of the country was lost to the rot of internationalism and moral decay, mostly they believed this about the youth. Frankston encouraged Minute Women to focus their activism on the most democratic body of the federal government—Congress—because she believed the Minute Woman way of thinking was that of the majority, even if it was not represented in mainstream politics. Minute Women newsletter articles often closed with a suggestion that women write to their congressman and explain their point of view. Implicit in the Minute Women approach was a belief in the power of their research to uncover the truth and the willingness of Americans to act if and when right-wing women could get the message out. While Minute Women were often exasperated with the apathy of other women and the general public, they believed that through their efforts they would redeem the nation and do it through the democratic process.

Unlike Frankston, Welch was no democrat. He counseled that the framers of the Constitution organized the country as a republic, and only the long and tireless efforts of liberals had convinced the American people that the United States was supposed to be a democracy. Republics are a form of representative government, but they do not require that most people, even citizens, have the right to vote. Democracies operate based on the political participation and will of the majority. In *The Blue Book*, which Welch wrote to explain the need for the John Birch Society, he argues that "democracy . . . as the Greeks and Romans both found out . . . is merely a deceptive phrase, a weapon of demagoguery, and a perennial fraud."[134] Since demagogues "take from the haves and give to the have-nots, and since increasing agencies of the government were always necessary to handle and effectuate these transfers, the meshing of demagoguery and collectivism was as inevitable as sunrise."[135] Both Welch and Frankston proved the connection between conspiracism and feelings of powerlessness with regard to the political system, distrust of authority, and "a belief in the essential malevolence of officialdom—or in the specific malevolence of a certain powerful entity," proposed by psychologist Virun Swami and colleagues.[136] However, Frankston firmly believed in the power of democracy to counter the conspiracy. Sara Diamond argues that even Welch and the JBS should be understood as democratic, since they primarily focused on writing letters and creating reading rooms.[137] This confirms what other studies have concluded, that while conspiracists may be "politically cynical individuals," they can also be supportive of democracy, indicating that "conspiracist ideas are predicted by an alienation from mainstream politics and a questioning of received truths," not necessarily belief in more authoritarian forms of government, although some shade in that direction.[138]

When feminism (re)surfaced on the national agenda, some right-wing women understood it as part of a long-standing conspiracy on the part of collectivists to form a one-world government. President Kennedy formed the Presidential Committee on the Status of Women in 1961 to assess the barriers to women's full participation in law, work, and society.[139] Frankston argued that the commission was Kennedy's "latest trick" in an attempt to bring the United States in line with one-worlders' way of thinking. The "Status of Women business," was connected to the United Nations Commission on Human Rights and the UN charter generally—the entire attitude of all three mirrored the Soviet commitment to support mothers and provide childcare; therefore, all were treacherous, if not treasonous. Frankston plainly laid out the real purpose of the commission: "They want to make us equal to the opposite sex. They say so. They want us to have equal pay for equal work, and have equal political and voting rights. They also say 'the Commission will investigate' our many social, political and civil problems. This smells strongly of the UN, and sure enough, it's the UN's baby and JFK isn't raising Congressional Approval of his Status of Women."[140] That the commission was headed by Eleanor Roosevelt only further proved the connection to collectivists. The "planners," "Red-fronters," and "one-worlders" intended to use gender as a tool to infiltrate American society.[141] To the idea that the commission intended to remove barriers to women in public life, Frankston asked, "Had you felt any barriers? We had not and are perfectly contented to be left entirely alone." Since the "UN Declaration of Human Rights is nearly identical to the Soviet Constitution," Frankston had little doubt that the commission and, more generally, the push for equality evidenced the growing threat of one-worldism. She told Minute Women: "Of course, they want us to go to work so they can take over the indoctrination of our children—making them into one-worlders and zombies. JFK has one surprise coming if he thinks all American women want to be 'released' from the burdens of the kitchen. Wild horses could not drive this woman to work!"[142] Minute Women seamlessly folded feminism into a larger conspiracy toward world government. A conspiracy that they had tracked and researched for years had opened a new front, and they prepared accordingly.

The first national media event of the second-wave feminist movement, Women Strike for Equality Day on August 26, 1970, marked the fiftieth anniversary of woman suffrage and directly connected first- and second-wave feminism, but that was not the context within which Minute Women understood the celebration. The September issue of the *Minute Women of the U.S.A., Inc.* newsletter began by framing the movement as an attempt to "con" women into demanding rights that were forced upon communist women and a "gimmick to garner women's votes" by the Kennedy administration.[143] The newsletter listed the names and organizations of those the Minute Women believed important in creating the strike, including politicians and activists like Shirley Chisholm, Kate Millett, Gloria Steinem, and Beulah Sanders, as well as Joan Rivers (a "comedienne?") and modern art collector Ethel Schull, a "socialite who likes to throw parties for weirdos." The bulletin described the left-wing background of "radical" Betty Friedan and Bella Abzug, whose work on behalf of peace and civil rights the Minute Women considered a "communist front record." Minute Women condensed the goals of the feminist movement to three: equality in education and employment, free twenty-four-hour day care centers, and "free abortions on demand," although they believed these goals to be "just the beginning of a much more far-reaching revolution that included gay marriage."[144] By 1970 Frankston was no longer the editor of the Minute Women's newsletter, but Anita Phiston, who took her place, warned that enlarged definitions of human rights would bloat the state even further. She ended her coverage of Women Strike for Equality by quoting Dr. Charles Malik's 1947 speech to a meeting of the United Nations Commission on Human Rights that the new tyranny of the postwar era would be the "tyranny of the masses" embodied by the "tyranny of the state."[145]

Right-wing literature on the threat of one-worldism exploded in the 1970s as pamphlets and newsletters circulated essays with titles like "Metro: Federal Rule by Bureaucrats," "Beware! The United Nations Plans a One-World Government for You," "Say No to the New World Order," "The 'Regional Governance' Conspiracy," "The Contrived Evolution of Regional Government," and "The Path to Regionalist World Government."[146] Pro America, the Minute Women, and the JBS publications ascribed to a conspiracist worldview that had culminated by the 1990s into a pattern of conspiracy known as the "New World Order."[147] The New World Order includes, among other facets,

> the systematic subversion of republican institutions by a federal government utilizing emergency powers; the gradual subordination of the United States to a world government operating through the United Nations; the creation of sinister new military and paramilitary forces, including governmental mobilization of urban youth gangs; the permanent stationing of foreign troops on U.S. soil; the widespread use of black helicopters to transport the tyranny's operatives; the confiscation of privately owned guns; the incarceration of so-called patriots in concentration camps run by FEMA; the implantation of microchips and other advanced technology for surveillance and mind control; the replacement of Christianity with a New Age world religion; and finally, the manipulation of the entire apparatus by a hidden hierarchy of conspirators operating through secret societies.[148]

One-worlder ideas have proliferated since then and are especially evident today. There are those who believe that the Common Core's purpose is to create "global citizens"; others subscribe to the North American Union (NAU) conspiracy, which anticipates that the United States will surrender its sovereignty in a merger with Mexico and Canada, replacing the dollar with "Amero" currency.[149]

In his 1966 bid for governor of California, Ronald Reagan infamously denounced Robert Welch for his conspiracy beliefs but welcomed Birch members to join his campaign.[150] The support Reagan had among the grassroots Right, however, did not mean that they agreed with his dismissal of Welch or conspiracy theory—conspiracy belief has only grown since then. The Minute Women and Pro America had died as national organizations by the 1980s, but the JBS lives on in the twenty-first century with the mission of "less government, more responsibility, and—with God's help—a better world."[151] Beyond connecting anticommunism to antifeminism, the JBS appears to have been one avenue through which the Tea Party movement grew in the early 2000s.[152] The group continues to support conspiracists and varied conspiracy theories, leading one reporter for the Southern Poverty Law Center to conclude: "Name a right—wing conspiracy theory of the last 60 years and chances are the John Birch Society was sitting near the front of the bandwagon."[153]

In 2014 Rick Biondi and Alex Newman compiled historical sources into a self-published reader called *World Federalism 101.*[154] The book consists largely of transcriptions of primary sources taken from presidential speeches, books, conference proceedings, and the *Congressional Record*, but it frames the sources around the theme of "globalization without representation."[155] According to its authors, the book proves that there was an "'open conspiracy' to create a world government [that] existed in the Congress," of which world federalists and Atlantic Unioners were a part. Ultimately, Biondi and Newman were left with the same question that eluded previous conspiracists, namely, "Who were the actual drivers of these movements?"[156] In the final chapter, cleverly titled "New World Disorder," they borrow heavily from Robert Welch's argument about how American saboteurs planned Vietnam as a trap to sap US strength, only Biondi and Newman focus on the threat of Islamic fundamentalism: "America's adversaries hope to bleed the U.S. out financially by encouraging us to pursue costly wars and interventions while they advance alternatives to the existing new world order. It should be noted that this stage could set the pretext for a revival of the Atlantic Union idea."[157] While Biondi and Newman fail to mention the Minute Women, they credit opponents of the Bricker Amendment for having stopped "world government based on Keynesian economic theory" from taking complete hold in the twentieth century.[158] Christian Gomez, writing for the *New American*, an online news website of the JBS, lauded *World Federalism 101*, saying, "No bookshelf of anyone deeply committed to or staunchly opposed to the goals outlined in this book should be without it."[159] According to Gomez, the book makes clear that "there is now less openness on the part of the one-world schemers" and more stealth.[160]

One Minute Woman reported her observations on the twenty-fifth anniversary of the United Nations in 1971, explaining that between supporters and opponents of the UN there could be no common ground: "The differences between the two factions are irreconcilable; no common meeting ground; philosophies diametrically opposed. The Pro's include those who, to quote Eleanor Roosevelt's words, have 'caught the vision.' The Antis believe in the doctrine of constitutional limitations imposed upon unbridled governmental power."[161] Most historians cite Welch as part of the vanguard of thinkers who transitioned the anticommunism of the McCarthy era into the fire-and-brimstone Armageddonism of Pat Robertson, minister and chairman of the Christian Broadcasting Network, and separatist militia groups of the nineties; few recognize that female conspiracists and women's anticommunist organizations were part of the movement that helped create and proliferate anti-one-worldist ideas.[162] For two decades, the Minute Women, Pro America, and the JBS warned right-wing women of "planners" and the conspiracy of one-worlders who were attempting to pave the way for a global government, and by the early 1970s conservative women believed little could come from debate. The work of anticommunist, countersubversive women formed a schoolroom for female politics that later became an important site of support for antifeminist effort. Through their activities in anticommunist groups, women learned how to construct and mobilize a movement, and they asserted that this effort was the particular prerogative of women. Conservative women used gender difference and all its implicit assumptions about motherhood, moral superiority, and domesticity, but they also used their celebrated status as housewives to advance a political agenda. Right-wing women responded to the second-wave feminist movement in ways feminists could not comprehend because they failed to grasp the long history of countersubversion that linked anticommunist women's organizations to an ideology that saw the growth of the federal government, the UN, human rights, and feminism as part of a one-world conspiracy.

CHAPTER 3

The Battle over the ERA

When you first hear these things, I agree with you, it sounds ridiculous. It sounds like nonsense. But is it? I ask only that you direct your attention to things that have happened in recent events in America.

—Representative Robert L. Jones, Jr. in a speech opposing the ERA[1]

OVER THE COURSE OF THE 1970S, conservative women's arguments about feminism coalesced, drawing the separate themes of gender sameness, federal usurpation, liberalism, humanism, and internationalism together so that feminism became the new front in the decades-old threat of totalitarian one-worldism. In challenging feminism, conservative women adapted anticommunist organizations, rhetoric, and tactics to modern concerns. Like Minute Woman Dorothy Frankston, Hoosier women of the late twentieth century highlight how conservatives organized against an increasingly globalized, technological, bureaucratized world.[2] Noting the connections between anti–Equal Rights Amendment (ERA) and anti–International Women's Year (IWY) activism and conspiracism does not mean that all women who opposed such initiatives were conspiracists. What is clear is that conservative women were motivated by a broad range of impulses and beliefs, which for some women included belief in the threat of one-worldism. These women scrutinized National Education Association literature, popular magazines, and right-wing tracts to find answers, and, in that way, they, like other conspiracists, sought to find meaning and make order out of confusing events and ideas.[3] Regardless of whether they believed in one-worldism, all Hoosier conservative women found in feminism an accessible target, one that they, as women, seemed particularly suited to fight. Like earlier twentieth-century conservative women who believed "it takes women to fight women," Hoosier antifeminists mobilized to stop the threat of liberalism, especially feminism and the ERA.[4]

Just as the varieties of postwar conservatism cover a number of beliefs, loosely held together by their distrust of federal government and anticommunism, postwar feminism encompasses a range of different, even competing, ideas about women's rights and women's identity, so much so that Benita Roth argues that there is no one feminism but distinct "feminisms" of the twentieth century.[5] Feminists can have a reformist agenda in that they seek, for example, to increase the number of women in leadership positions in the Republican or Democratic Party or on the boards of Fortune 500 companies. Feminism can also be radical. Feminists may seek to challenge the very structure of society and its institutions; their goal is not to gain more power and authority within the current system but to tear down economic and political systems because they are hopelessly flawed—patriarchal, racially discriminatory, and geared to the betterment of the few at the expense of the many. The Redstockings, a radical feminist group that began in Boston, coined the phrase "the personal is political," which signifies that all aspects of a woman's "personal" life are touched by power dynamics.[6] Radical feminists see patriarchy and inequality as so pervasive, so embedded within the ebb and flow of daily routine, that they require mindfulness and discussion with other women through "consciousness-raising" sessions to identify, study, and figure out how to resist them. Feminism emerged from the idea of gender sameness, or the idea that men and women are inherently similar. These feminists believed that while there are differences of sex and biology, more differences abound from socialization, and it is primarily socialization that is responsible for perceived female inferiority. Feminism also emerged, however, from ideas of gender difference, even female superiority, as the crusading women of the nineteenth century demonstrated in the temperance movement and antiprostitution campaigns. These women believed that the category of woman, perhaps because of female culture or because of something innate to the nature of women, was morally superior to the category of man. Women, they believed, were more altruistic, more peaceful, more caring—often, maternalism, or the belief that motherhood is the essence of womanhood, is associated with this kind of thinking. White, black, and Chicana women created feminisms from within diverse social movements and tailored organizations to speak to their particular problems. The result is a diverse array of feminisms, but also feminists who do not always have much in common or shared interests.[7] Feminist coalition building was not easy, because twentieth-century feminism, like conservatism, was no monolith.

The "first wave" of women's rights activism in the twentieth century achieved suffrage with the Nineteenth Amendment in 1920. Alice Paul's National Woman's Party then turned its attention to an equal rights amendment that would cement women's equality before the law. This effort divided suffragists, however, since many worried about how such a law would affect labor legislation and other policies geared toward social justice ends and the protection of working mothers. As women's rights activists divided, they also came up against the female Right, newly empowered through suffrage to enter the political arena directly and challenge progressive women's goals.[8] The fight for an equal rights amendment continued for the next fifty years.

In 1972 Congress passed the ERA by large margins due in significant part to the burgeoning second-wave feminist movement, which emerged in the late 1960s and early 1970s.[9] The language of this ERA did not create caveats, exclusions, or exemptions to women's equality:

> Section I: Equality of rights under the law shall not be denied or abridged by the United States or by any State on account of sex.
>
> Section II: The Congress shall have the power to enforce by appropriate legislation the provisions of this article.
>
> Section III: This Amendment shall take effect two years after the date of ratification.[10]

In order to complete the ratification process, three-fourths of state legislatures or state ratifying conventions (thirty-eight states) needed to approve the amendment. Within the first year, twenty-two state legislatures signed on, and the ERA looked certain to succeed, but significant opposition began to coalesce in 1973, and anti-ERA activists worked vigorously at the local level to stave off ratification throughout the decade.

Indiana Senator Birch Bayh ushered the ERA through the US Senate, and feminists in the state were determined to add Indiana to the quickly lengthening list of legislatures to approve the ERA. Support of the ERA was something all Hoosier feminists—radicals and reformists—could agree on. Even so-called woodwork feminists, or those who had been unwilling previously to commit to the movement, supported the premise that "equality of rights under the law shall not be denied or abridged by the United States or by any State on account of sex." The differences among feminists are still very important to explaining the ERA story, however, and tie directly to the Indiana scene, because distinctions between "radical" and "liberal" were made within a local context.[11] Stephanie Gilmore argues that while the National Organization for Women (NOW) is understood as the classic example of liberal feminism, Memphis NOW was "simultaneously liberal and radical" because it blended support for the ERA with public efforts to raise awareness of rape and domestic violence and engaged in public protest.[12] Melissa Estes Blair agrees with the primacy of place in understanding the radical/liberal divide, arguing that while NOW was considered reformist or liberal in places like Chicago and New York, it was considered a radical feminist group in Indianapolis.[13] Judith Ezekiel's study of Dayton, Ohio, feminists shows that although they were always affiliated with liberationist politics that would transform, as opposed to reform, society, they also "saw no contradiction in supporting the NOW campaign to end sex-segregated classified ads, or other liberal feminist demands."[14]

Despite blurring at the grassroots level, the categories "liberal" and "radical" remain useful constructs because they provide a way to distinguish between distinct ideologies and approaches. Alice Echols's characterization of liberal feminism as a reformist effort geared toward "bringing women into the mainstream" by addressing public sphere discrimination remains apt, as does her description of radical feminism as an assault on "the sex-class system," including the elimination of exploitation within personal relationships.[15] Structurally, too, the two constructs remain distinct because liberals favored the creation of organizations like NOW, while radicals favored small groups, as Jo Freeman describes, with "a conscious lack of formal structure, an emphasis on participation by everyone, sharing of tasks, and the exclusion of men."[16] Studies of grassroots feminism add to these distinctions, however, an appreciation for what Gilmore calls "the vast space between" dichotomies and a challenge to previous chronologies.[17] Like grassroots activists elsewhere, Hoosier feminists overall maintained the "two-strand movement" model.[18] Chapter 4 will detail how a focus on the ERA affected the Hoosier feminist movement and feminist coalitions, but it is clear that Indiana housed diverse feminisms, including liberationist enclaves in Indianapolis, Bloomington, and Fort Wayne, and that diversity was challenged by the ERA campaign and the decision to deploy a "low-key" feminism.

Anticipating the need for greater intrastate cooperation, feminist activists began to combine already existing local groups, like those of Indiana NOW, and create entirely new organizations, such as the Indiana Women's Political Caucus, to ensure ERA success in the state. Existing liberal groups, moreover, formed a coalition that called itself the ERA Coordinating Committee (later renamed Hoosiers for the Equal Rights Amendment [HERA]) in the early seventies. Isolated NOW chapters existed in the state prior to Congress passing the ERA, but mobilization and coordination among chapters were prompted by the desire to ratify the ERA. The first chapter of NOW in Indiana formed in Muncie in April 1970, with Betty Newcomb acting as president.[19] Newcomb began her career at Ball State University as an English instructor and later served as the university's first director of affirmative action. At the twentieth-anniversary dinner of the Muncie–Delaware County NOW, Newcomb described that she became interested in the feminist movement after a friend loaned her a copy of *The Feminine Mystique*. Though national media coverage often portrayed feminists in a negative light, Newcomb sought to organize a local group to address the same issues as those uncovered in Betty Friedan's work. Newcomb and Virginia Jackson-Adams, who cofounded the first NOW chapter, chose to affiliate with NOW over other women's rights and feminist groups because they believed NOW appealed to a broader range of people with varied interests. The chapter thrived; the initial Muncie NOW meeting included forty-two persons from a cross section of the campus community.[20]

By the end of 1972 NOW had ten chapters in the state, and Newcomb agreed to become state coordinator to spearhead an effort to increase communication among the established chapters and at-large members.[21] In her first letter to Indiana NOW members in July 1972, Newcomb explained why statewide coordination was necessary: "It's especially important that we attempt to encourage growth in membership and participation in Indiana because ratification of the Equal Rights Amendment will be introduced in the General Assembly this January."[22] Within ten months, Newcomb told her fellow NOW members, "I feel guilty doing *anything* that is not related to ERA."[23] The connection between the growth of NOW and agitation for the ERA was a national one. Janet Boles argues that the national NOW's annual budget increased from $700,000 to $8.5 million from 1977 to 1982, and membership rolls increased from 55,000 to 210,000.[24] In October 1972, when NOW held its first statewide conference, hosted by Indianapolis NOW, the ERA emerged as the top priority. The state program included a discussion of no-fault divorce, childcare, abortion, and the Federal Communications Commission; however, the resolutions made passage of the ERA the first priority of the organization, and it would continue to be Indiana NOW's top priority until state ratification in 1977.[25]

Shortly after the formation of the National Women's Political Caucus in Washington, DC, nineteen women met in Indianapolis on 12 October 1971 to form the Indiana Women's Political Caucus (WPC).[26] Rae Ginger (Republican) and Virginia Dill McCarty (Democrat) cochaired the event and were assigned by the national organization as temporary state coordinators.[27] Rae Ginger represented the Republicans as cochair, but Mary Anne Butters, then a staff member for Mayor Richard Lugar and a former reporter for the *Indianapolis Star*, recruited other prominent women Republicans to attend the event, and she, along with Betty Blumberg, headed the Republican roster of the group.[28] The national WPC sought to "awaken, organize, and assert the vast political power represented by women," and the Indiana WPC dedicated itself to a reformist agenda by promising to work within existing major political parties to "advance the status of women" and to help women express their views so that "the talents of Indiana women will be fully utilized in the future."[29] Among the priorities set at that meeting, passage of the ERA was first, followed by equal pay for equal work and an effort to get more women into policy-making positions.[30] Unlike NOW, WPC did not have multiple locals within the state prior to the statewide organizing effort. Rather than pull together disparate locals, the WPC's challenge would be to create them. That the Indiana Women's Political Caucus was a successful bipartisan organization in the early seventies speaks to the bipartisan appeal of feminism before the Republican shift right on social issues—a shift the ERA propelled.

Indiana feminists understood that ratification would require organization and strategy, and they were prepared to work hard in order to put their state on what they understood to be the right side of history.[31] Betty Newcomb, acting as NOW state coordinator, created a strategy proposal for organizations supporting ratification in the state that outlined the creation of a coalition and mapped out legislative strategy through the November elections of 1972. Coalition organizations could publicly support or campaign for individual candidates, but the coalition would act more as a central clearinghouse for information on legislators and educational materials to inform legislators.[32] Newcomb submitted the proposal to the League of Women Voters Indiana, who approved of the plan after changing Newcomb's use of "coalition" to "coordinating committee." The League wanted to avoid being "backed into the position of having one person testify for the coalition," feeling more comfortable with a loosely structured committee that would allow individual organizations to "lobby at will."[33] State organizations interested in the ERA met in Indianapolis on 28 June 1972 and founded the ERA Coordinating Committee, with Betty Newcomb as the first chair. Roughly twenty-five people representing twenty liberal organizations attended, including NOW, WPC, Indiana Civil Liberties Union, American Association of Women Deans and Counselors, Indiana Business and Professional Women, Greater Federation of Women's Clubs, Indiana State Nurses Association, Church Women United, Women's International League for Peace and Freedom, United Auto Workers, Women's Equity Action League, American Association of University Women, and Indiana State Teachers Association.[34] After the first defeat of the ERA in the 1973 legislative session, members of the

ERA Coordinating Committee met to officially change the name of the group to Hoosiers for the Equal Rights Amendment and transformed the committee into a more grassroots organization.[35] By 1974 HERA included virtually every liberal or feminist organization in the state. The group was explicitly bipartisan and worked to cultivate that image, and with supportive Republicans like Indianapolis mayor Richard Lugar as the honorary chairman of HERA's Men for the ERA, Republican support was more than lip service.[36]

While not initially partisan, the ERA became a pivotal issue on which the trajectory of Republican politics hinged. Indiana saw increasing numbers of Republicans elected to the House of Representatives between 1966 and 1978.[37] In the state senate, Republicans held the majority in all but two election cycles (1966 and 1976).[38] The makeup and trajectory of the Republican Party mattered enormously to feminist hopes of ratifying the ERA, but throughout the twentieth century, the ERA sparked deep division within the Republican Party, a division that only intensified as the ERA moved on to the state legislatures. Second-wave feminists called on the nation, its leaders, and the parties to discuss and support women's rights and women's participation in politics. Those debates, Catherine Rymph argues, "were not simply layered on to existing party factions" but instead played an important role in shaping the conservative/liberal realignment of the parties.[39] During the postwar era, the battles at the state level were important to how conservatives took control of the GOP, and, at least in Indiana, the ERA was critical to that fight.[40] The task forces, commissions, and preexisting women's organizations like the League of Women Voters created, as Estes Blair described, an "aura of respectability to feminism" and allowed women a place from which to begin discussion of women's issues, organization of projects, and political mobilization.[41] In Indiana these "respectable" voices were often Republican, and while they sought to forward feminism, they might also defer to men who dominated the party.[42] Republican feminists were not the sole purveyors of what became the low-key strategy, but their tenuous position as liberals in a party that was increasingly shifting right made other feminists wary of pushing too far for fear of losing Republican feminists and the coalition's bipartisan appeal.[43] Ensuring that Republican women felt comfortable within the fold was an important part of why more radical voices were asked to remain silent or, worse, openly mocked by reformist feminists.

The ERA Coordinating Committee agreed early on a low-key ratification strategy.[44] Leaders adopted the strategy for a variety of reasons, including because they believed legislators might approve the amendment quickly without raising public awareness of the ERA. Newcomb intended to slip the ERA through the state legislature early in the 1973 session "before the general public know what is going on."[45] Hoosier feminists believed ERA ratification would be quick and that prioritizing the ERA would be expedient.[46] By working "extra hard now" on the ERA, they might be able to get "this thing over with" and move on to other issues.[47] As the ratification struggle dragged on into the late 1970s, feminists began to question the degree to which they were willing to downplay all their other demands. The contours of the meaning of "low-key" involved prioritizing ERA, silencing advocacy on controversial issues like abortion and sexuality, and projecting an image of feminism that prioritized respectability and moderation. While Democratic and Republican women adopted the low-key approach in 1972, Republican women remained committed to the strategy long after others in the coalition turned to more assertive measures.

The low-key ratification strategy ultimately worked to discourage public protest like that employed by liberationists in the state who entered the public sphere for all types of actions before the ERA battle heated up, challenging a local radio disc jockey they considered to be insulting to women or handing out radical feminist literature at local fairs, to name just two. HERA leaders called for an "underground" campaign that "worked behind the scenes" to contact legislators and candidates while asking feminist organizations to avoid agitation on issues that might be considered controversial and to refrain from public protest.[48] Two HERA lobbyists, McCarty for the Democrats and Blumberg for the Republicans, would engage in "vigorous campaigning" "on an active person to person basis" with legislators, but HERA specifically agreed there would be "no big publicity campaign until absolutely necessary" and concluded that the organization's letter writing would try to "minimize newspaper publicity" by only writing editorials to refute an opposition letter, and then only "factual, rational" letters.[49] Newcomb justified the low-key strategy to NOW chapter presidents as necessary because proponents faced "about the most conservative legislature in years."[50] Liberal feminists believed that they were subject to rules of decorum that required deference to male legislators, which often left them without a voice in public space. "Don't act up" was the instruction proponents received from legislators willing to vote for the ERA. However, what constituted "acting up" was unclear, which meant that, as Newcomb explained, the agreement was tantamount to "gentle blackmail" in that it restricted feminists' range of action in exchange for legislative support of the amendment.[51]

Throughout the five years that it took feminists to get the ERA ratified in Indiana, the low-key strategy became contentious, but feminist coalitions and organizations remained committed to the approach. State HERA organizers reminded members in 1974 that "the image we are trying to project as part of our strategy is one of the 'soft touch,'" so "play-up equality for all" but "keep a sense of humor" about it.[52] Not to be outdone by the opposition in the housewifery department, HERA leaders urged feminists to present a wholesome image to the media, particularly television reporters, to remind the public that "we are mothers and wives too."[53] The next chapter of this book describes the difficulty feminists encountered in maintaining a unified, nonthreatening explanation of feminism, but it is clear that many within their ranks felt stifled and unwelcome because of the approach. The results were somewhat contradictory: successful ERA ratification at the expense of long-term viability for feminist coalitions.

Unlike feminists, when conservative women began to organize on the ERA in early 1973, it was from within an anticommunist and countersubversive milieu. Phyllis Schlafly visited the state in January 1973, invited by the United Conservatives of Indiana, and her organization STOP (Stop Taking Our Privileges) ERA marked the beginning of an anti-ERA movement in the state.[54] Schlafly already was well known to many Hoosier women. Beulah Coughenour and Joan Gubbins had attended Schlafly's anticommunist "school" for politically minded conservative women, where participants learned how to project a good image, including how to dress professionally, how to speak in public, and "how to smile" even when talking about "life and death" issues.[55] Many conservative Hoosier women were already mobilized in groups like Campus Crusade for Christ and Dr. Fred C. Schwartz's Anti-Communism Crusade. As Gubbins recalls, "Phyllis came along with the ERA," and "we all joined," but "there was a whole group of people by then who were in one of these groups or another or several of them."[56] Coughenour explained, "She made us aware of what it [the ERA] was . . . where it was headed, the purpose, the motivations, and they weren't what we wanted to see."[57] Schlafly helped focus attention on the ERA, but Coughenour and Gubbins, like others, had been involved politically for some time. Jean Harvey, Rolena Jackson, and Coughenour served as state director of STOP ERA over the course of the decade. Hoosier women affiliated with Schlafly thought very highly of her, but their agenda was their own.[58]

Joan Gubbins joined the Indiana Senate in 1968 (and was the only female member of that body at the time), and she would lead conservative women in their fight against feminism, the ERA, and the International Women's Year (IWY) until she left the state senate in 1980. Her activism continued under the Reagan administration, where she served on the Intergovernmental Advisory Council on Education.[59] Born in White Plains, New York, she attended the University of Illinois for two years before marrying Dale G. Gubbins, a research engineer for General Motors Corporation, and having two children.[60] She and her husband helped charter Heritage Christian School in Indianapolis before she began a career in politics. Early political associations included participating in the Barry Goldwater campaign for president in 1964 as a local researcher; serving as a delegate to the Indiana Republican Convention in 1966, 1968, and 1970; and belonging to Pro America, the National Federation of Republican Women, Campus Crusade for Christ, and the Citizens Forum.[61] The group of women who volunteered at the Indianapolis Campus Crusade for Christ and held a Bible study there in the early 1960s formed the "nucleus" of support for Gubbins and her later anti-ERA activities.[62] In her time in the state senate, she pushed for legislation that dismantled child abuse laws in order to protect the rights of parents to whip their children; removed Christian schools from control of the Indiana superintendent of public instruction; removed state licensing accreditation requirements for day-care centers; and supported other bills representing the New Right agenda, from legislation that sought to limit sex education in schools to encouraging more active enforcement of sodomy laws.[63] During the 1970s she came to see feminism and the ERA as part of a larger effort to pollute morality with support of gay marriage and homosexual rights, sexual promiscuity, and abortion rights, which would ultimately work together to end gender difference and challenge national sovereignty by promoting global citizenship.[64] In her fight against the ERA and IWY, she worked closely with other antifeminist leaders, like Rosemary Thomson of Illinois.

Beulah Coughenour, another important conservative female leader in the state, explained that she joined STOP ERA because she feared communism imperiled her way of life and believed proponents sought to eliminate gender difference in an attempt to propel advancement toward socialism.[65] Coughenour was the daughter of an Iowa minister and received a bachelor of arts degree in biology from Taylor University, an evangelical Christian school located in Upland, Indiana, where she met her husband, a physician.[66] She worked as a medical transcriptionist before her election as a Republican to the Marion County City-County Council in 1976, a position she held through 2003.[67] Coughenour's political consciousness was sparked in the 1960s after attending a workshop series by Dr. Schwartz's Christian Anti-Communist Crusade in Indianapolis. She managed to juggle babysitters for the whole week and felt transformed by the school, especially the exercises that required attendants to create three-minute speeches on assigned topics. She recollected being "very shy then; it was interesting, because I'm not at all shy anymore and I haven't been for a long time." "That week changed my life," noted Coughenour. While at the workshop, she met Nell Aumann, a woman who was then in her midseventies and who held a weekly study group for women interested in researching the communist threat. Aumann contacted Coughenour to join the group after Coughenour wrote a public letter protesting policies at a local hospital. Coughenour was flattered by Aumann's interest in her and participated in their weekly sessions throughout the 1960s. "She tutored us on communism and studied, and read, and did all this. And we learned so much," remembered Coughenour.[68] Aumann and the operation of informal study sessions conducted in women's homes hint at how anticommunist ideas were transmitted from generation to generation.

Just as HERA joined proponents, STOP ERA acted as the antiratification umbrella organization under which varied groups worked to oppose the ERA. Anticommunist organizations like the Minute Women, Pro America, and the John Birch Society contributed to the cause of antifeminism in Indiana in different ways. The Minute Women were active in Indiana in the mid-1950s, but they disappeared from the historical record after Marguerite Dice opened her home for the founding meeting of the JBS in 1958. The lasting effect of the organization can only be sensed through the ideological and rhetorical links between its activism and anti-ERA activists. JBS members provided important support to budding antifeminism in Indiana and elsewhere. Nationally, the society opposed ratification as early as March 1973, and the JBS *Bulletin* and the *American Opinion* encouraged members to work against the ERA.[69] Local JBS chapters cohosted anti-ERA events, like the 1976 event at the Pilgrim Inn where Nancy Rider, an Ohio member of STOP ERA and author of the booklet *The ERA Con*, spoke in Indianapolis.[70] JBS influence in Indiana was perceived to be so strong that one proponent leader stated that "the [antiratification] effort from the top is being directed by the JBS."[71] Of the earlier anticommunist organizations, including the Minute Women and the JBS, only Pro America directly or publicly affiliated with anti-ERA work, and in Indiana it was Pro America that most consistently offered conspiratorial explanations of feminism.[72] It is unclear how active Pro America was in the state before the ERA, but on 20 July 1973 Jean Harvey of Monticello reorganized Pro America and led the group throughout the seventies, including during the anti-IWY campaign at the end of the decade.[73] Pro America women came from all over to attend the summer 1973 meeting, including Fort Wayne, Indianapolis, Connersville, Lafayette and West Lafayette, Wabash, Delphi, Brookston, and Monticello.[74]

Leaders and participants in the Indiana anti-ERA campaign wet their feet in politics through anticommunist organizations and came to understand the contemporary political scene through the lens of anticommunist conspiracism. Over the course of the five-year ERA ratification struggle, their argument coalesced around several key points: (1) gender difference and a heteronormative family unit organized around such difference were ideas and institutions created and blessed by God; (2) the ERA would eliminate gender difference; (3) the elimination of gender difference connected to a larger impulse or movement to eliminate national sovereignty, heteronormativity, and individualism. This last idea could be expressed as simply as arguing that the ERA, with its federal enforcement clause, would challenge state authority and lead to increased federal oversight. The last idea could also extend to the argument that feminists were lesbians and internationalists, or that feminists, lesbians, and internationalists were all working together to forward the creation of a single world government that would eliminate national sovereignty and individual rights.

Initially, many described the ERA as part of the communist conspiracy. In a study of Indianapolis newspapers in 1973, the most often cited reasons for disapproval of ratification in letters to the editor were that the amendment violated biblical dictates requiring female subservience and suspicion of the ERA as a "communist plot."[75] The connection was noted elsewhere in the country. According to a study of anti-ERA women in Texas, nearly two-thirds reported that American communists were a "very great danger," and 88 percent agreed that "in the past 25 years this country has moved dangerously close to socialism."[76] Lorena Martin, who wrote an editorial to the *Indianapolis News* about the threat of the ERA, spoke for many when she protested that so few people seemed to understand that "the destruction of the family," which the ERA hastened, was "one of the foremost goals of the Communists in taking over a country, and [that] this bill, if ratified, would be another great step forward for the worst enemy this country has ever faced."[77] They created examples in the experience of women in communist countries like the Soviet Union and Cuba who were "liberated" of their children and forced to work as manual laborers while their children stayed in state-controlled schools and nurseries.[78] Across Indiana, women wrote letters expressing their belief that the ERA was part of a communist or totalitarian plan.

Antifeminists often reported agreeing with the equality of the sexes but adamantly disagreed with any notion that hinted at gender sameness. Gubbins told an interviewer in the midnineties that when she entered the state senate, she "totally believed in equality for women."[79] At that time, she described her resistance to feminism as resulting from its being redundant at best and taking away the rights and privileges of femininity at worst.[80] Laws already existed to protect women from blatant discrimination, and she believed they were sufficient.[81] Women were inherently different from men, and antifeminists sought to preserve gender distinction in law and social practice.[82] Conservative women did not always agree on how they understood female privilege or how they understood work outside the home, but there was agreement that women's foremost responsibility was family support (in all ways but financial) and cohesion. Their literature is replete with descriptions of how "husbands would not be required to support their families, while wives would be forced to work and supply a minimum of half the family support" as a result of the ERA.[83] In 1976 Nancy Rider told the Indianapolis audience that the ERA "would promote federally funded and comprehensive child-care centers[, which] would tax the family unit and literally force women out of the home and into a job."[84] This idea was not new or simply an Indiana phenomenon. Phyllis Schlafly explained to conservative women across the nation that "in America, a man's first significant purchase is a diamond for his bride, and the largest financial investment of his life is a home for her to live in. American husbands work hours of overtime to buy a fur piece or other finery to keep their wives in fashion, and to pay premiums on their life insurance policies to provide for her comfort when she is a widow."[85] In this worldview, men support their wives, and that prerogative would be lost if the ERA was ratified. In 1975 Gubbins made a clear distinction between "benefits women desire and deserve such as equal job opportunity [that] are already guaranteed by law and Constitution and backed up by the Civil Rights Commission and our courts"—all of which she supported—and the ERA, which would "take away from women many protections and benefits that most women want to retain."[86] What was at stake for conservative women was the meaning of gender identity, and for them being female was inherently different from being male. As Rep. Robert L. Jones Jr. stated, "What this bill [ERA] gives you, ladies and gentlemen, is not equality. It gives you sameness, and I think we have to vote against it."[87]

Conservative Hoosier women built their lives around the heteronormative, so-called traditional family, and they sincerely believed that maintaining that ideal was and should remain American womanhood's primary goal. In promoting "the family," they promoted gender distinctiveness and wanted the cultural touchstone of women's experience to remain, as they believed it had been in the 1950s, a woman dedicated to her husband and children as a housewife and stay-at-home mom. Rebecca Klatch describes the perspective of conservative women: "Ironically, this same fear is voiced by feminists in recognizing that all women are just one man removed from welfare. Yet while feminists see this as the economic dependence of women, and therefore seek security through encouraging women to be independent, to be able to earn their own livelihood, social conservative women seek the same security through trying to ensure women's rights and entitlements within marriage, thereby binding men to a stable family unit."[88] Conservative women acknowledged that not all women had a "good marriage" or one that allowed a woman to stay at home, but the fact that their family ideal did not apply to all Americans did not mean that it *should not* apply or *would not* in the future—the further the actual reach of the "traditional family" ideal, the more Americans achieved "the American Dream." This would seem to indicate, as Michelle Nickerson notes, that the imagination of conservative women was thoroughly white and middle class.[89] But to them gender difference and the heteronormative family supported by a father who worked outside the home and a stay-at-home mom presented a beautiful picture of life—one that they were deeply committed to in their own lives and as a religious and social goal for others. Pro America summed it up by describing the ERA as a "giant hoax" supported by "an extremely vocal but small segment of women, assisted by certain state and federal commissions on the status of women" who used taxpayers' money to eliminate women's privileges, like protective labor legislation, dower rights for widows, and the "primary responsibility for support of their wives and children from husbands and fathers," in favor of a gender-sameness vision of equality that would require "compulsory military service including combat duty" for women.[90]

Conservative women struggled enormously with the postwar reality that women worked increasingly outside the home. While this did not immediately lead to a restructuring of the social value of the homemaker, over time it did challenge the notion that women's economic function was entirely supplemental, and it led many women to push for equal pay and more educational opportunities so that they might advance in their jobs and careers.[91] While in the 1950s a third of all American women worked (and only half of that number full time), by 1975 nearly half worked, and more than 70 percent worked full time.[92] Even by the 1960s women who did not work for any wages were the exception.[93] But the pressure to work did not come only from feminists; it was economic imperative that drove women to work. Keeping women at home would have required major changes in the way Americans lived, and fewer families wanted to alter their lifestyle to accommodate a stay-at-home mother than ever before.[94] This was not the perception of conservative women at the time, however, who often blamed feminism for the advent of working women. Linda Kerber points out that conservatives refused to acknowledge that "feminists were as much the *namers* of change as they were the *makers* of change."[95] Many conservative women simply could not understand or accept society's increasing focus on working women, seeing it as a slight to homemaking and their life choices. They resented feminists and working women, as one woman stated, for making "me feel guilty because I enjoy staying at home just taking care of my husband and kids."[96] Klatch explains that to conservative women, feminism "*implicitly* degrades homemakers by calling for women to seek fulfillment outside the home, which discredits those women who are fulfilled by being wives and mothers," and "belittles homemakers by labelling their work as drudgery, as mundane, as ungratifying, and as glorified babysitting."[97] As a younger generation of women asked why they should be "only" housewives and mothers, conservative women took umbrage and held fast to their vision of the "traditional family" built on gender difference as the purest, most important expression of the American Dream.

It is interesting to note that many conservative women in the movement worked, and they could be more or less sympathetic to working women depending on their personal experiences. Coughenour remembered a debate over the ERA during which her opponent, a female professor from Indiana University, broke down crying. She later learned that the woman was in an abusive marriage at the time and suffered many personal hardships. "There, but for the grace of God, go I," Coughenour remarked. Still, she thought that working women should not be celebrated: "It [the ERA] really was against the things that we believed in, for [the] family, because we really were family-oriented people. We had nothing against women working if that is what they wanted to do or needed to do, and many people have to do, but we didn't think you should glorify that kind of a woman over one who spends her time raising her family to be productive citizens."[98] Work might be necessary for the good of the family, in which case wives and mothers would have to work, but work should not be central to a woman's life and mission, and work outside the home should not define womanhood.

A belief that gender difference should correspond to distinct social roles was only one reason conservative women were devoted to staying at home. They also believed that the family unit was part of the sacred in their lives. Hoosier women saw the ERA as a tool to destroy the heteronormative family, which they saw as created and blessed by God.[99] Conservative women understood that good marriages involved those in which the husband and wife performed very different gender roles and in which women were largely responsible for maintaining peace and happiness. Citing a *Redbook* magazine survey, Rosemary Thomson, a leader in anti-ERA and anti-IWY activities in Illinois, pointed out that "the strongly religious woman" reported her marital relationship as "very, very good" and that she was "happy most of the time."[100] It is clear that while right-wing women might criticize men for failing to live up to the role of breadwinner and protector, that their husbands supported their politics was important to them personally and to their understanding of family. Coughenour noted that she attended the Christian Anti-Communist Crusade event in Indianapolis because her husband was too busy. So "*we* decided that it would be nice if I could go," she recalled.[101] STOP ERA in Indiana had the full support of husbands, since its budget depended entirely on "how much our husbands would give us."[102] Thomson pointed out that while feminists demanded "marriage contracts" of their husbands to ensure that household duties were shared equally, Jim, her husband, "probably helped me scrub more floors in twenty years of marriage than any liberated man."[103] That men and women were different did not keep them from helping each other, but their roles and responsibilities needed to remain distinct.

Feminists were the ones with unhappy marriages, said conservative women, and it was because of their professional ambitions and political sensibilities. Some conservative women encouraged others not to satisfy personal ambition or "the problem that has no name" but consider suppressing it or expressing it through traditional venues like motherhood and housewifery. The desire for self-gratification was strong, Thomson noted, and only a woman "firmly grounded in Biblical principles" could fight the superficial promise of "equal pay for women and personal fulfillment."[104] *The Feminine Mystique* got it all wrong, but Thomson acknowledged that many women read it and thought, "Betty Friedan understands me!" "Without investigating the real motives of Women's Lib," Thomson noted that women—even Christian women—joined state and local governments to sign up and dole out money to support feminist initiatives.[105] For Thompson, employment outside the home was a choice women made that depended on whether they sought personal aggrandizement and accolades or the simple pleasures of home and family. Working women were "being lured into full-time employment outside the home—distracting them from the nurture of their own children" by the "siren song of Women's Lib."[106] In this way, feminists were part of the new narcissism of the Me Decade. Klatch explains: "Feminism is a threat, then, because, when women pursue self-interest, not only is the family neglected but also ultimately women become like men. . . . [I]f everyone pursues their own interest, no one is left to look out for the larger good, that is, to be altruistic, to be the nurturer, the caretaker, the mother. In short, the underlying fear expressed in this critique of Feminism is the fear of a total masculinization of the world."[107]

Conservative women also did not agree on whether gender inequality was real. Some women saw wage gaps, wealth gaps, and career gaps as indicative of women's different choices and preferences to those of men. According to Schlafly, that so few women served in Congress (at the time, 18 out of 535) was not evidence of discrimination.[108] Women were underrepresented in government because "most women do not want to do the things that must be done to win elections."[109] This explanation of women's place in the public sphere meant that Schlafly could acknowledge the differences in women's status but insist that those differences were evidence of women's privilege, which she rooted in a Christian tradition of respect for Mary, the mother of Jesus Christ.[110] Contrary to Schlafly, Coughenour acknowledged the existence of gender inequality ("I know women have a higher standard to be held to"), but she believed it natural or at least inevitable: "You have to do everything the hard way, and I think that's true for [all] women, and it's going to be true for a long time." "But that didn't bother me," she noted. Inequality had not stopped her progress; she learned to fight back early on: "I grew up with five brothers." "Some of those people had a horrible life," she recognized, and that made them advocates of gender equality, "but I don't think it will help them," she concluded; "I think it will hurt them."[111] Kathryn Nikou, who helped organize anti-IWY activities at the end of the decade, did not think the ERA was necessary, because "nobody wants to keep the girls down," but there was real danger in a new constitutional amendment. "In the name of compassion, in the name of equality, in the name of all kinds of things, somebody comes up with some loony idea," and that idea eventually would go to the Supreme Court for interpretation, a body she feared would be "activist" and dependent on the whims of even a single president.[112] None of the conservative women interviewed for this book explained their opposition to feminism in conspiracist ways; they largely agreed that their movement was built around their commitment to the heteronormative family and their belief that the family and women's role in it were sanctioned by God.

While opponents of the ERA encouraged women to stay at home, they were not without a college or university education. Antifeminist women came from a variety of backgrounds, although, like proponents of the ERA, they tended to be white and middle class, but anti-ERA activists were even more homogeneous than their feminist counterparts (although Indiana's IWY delegation included two black conservative antifeminist women who will be discussed in the next chapter).[113] Empirical data on antifeminists challenged contemporary observations that conservatives were motivated by socioeconomic angst and frustration or by their personal dependency on men. Sociologist Jerome Himmelstein summarized the local studies of anti-ERA activists conducted in Texas, North Carolina, Pennsylvania, Virginia, and Maryland and argued that although anti-ERA activists were more likely to be married, housewives, less educated, and less wealthy than their pro-ERA counterparts, they were not necessarily frustrated or vulnerable because of increased dependency, since they also reported long histories of political activism and "fairly high levels of personal competence and political efficacy." These women were no "shrinking violets" driven by personal fear and anxiety, he concluded; nor were they distinguishable by socioeconomic status or related factors.[114] Conservative women active in Indiana, including Gubbins, Nikou, and Coughenour, had college and work experience; they describe their life choices, however, as rooted in serving the interest of their families. "The stereotype of a conservative woman is one who is barefoot and pregnant in the kitchen—that wasn't true in our house," said Nikou.[115] But maternalism was the root of most conservative women's politics—as Gubbins described, her only political ambition was to "ensure a goodly heritage for my children and all Indiana children."[116]

While women like Gubbins made a career out of championing the politics of traditional gender roles (that women should act as stay-at-home wives and caretakers of children and men act as breadwinners), they saw their activism as necessary to help *other women* in their desire to stay at home and feel good about that choice.[117] In championing motherhood and domesticity, conservatives actually pulled women out of the home and blended their work in the private and public spheres. While conservatives recognized that they could be seen as hypocritical for doing the same thing they criticized feminists for doing, Ronnee Schreiber notes in *Righting Feminism: Conservative Women & American Politics*, "They consider their actions to be politically necessary and thus bank on the likelihood that such behavior will not damage their credibility."[118] Both conservatives and feminists acted in the public sphere "in the interests of women" but differed entirely on what being male and female meant and what the best interests of women were. It is not a question of sincerity (even if there is often the question of strategy), as both conservatives and feminists seemed to believe their arguments.

Running throughout conservative women's anticommunist and antifeminist belief is their commitment to evangelical Christianity. Studies on supporters and opponents of the ERA agree that church membership distinguished pro- and anti-ERA ranks more than any other factor. Sociologist Kent Tedin analyzed data from the Texas study and reported that "nonaffiliates," or women who described themselves as "atheist, agnostic, no preference, none," accounted for 51 percent of the pro-ERA activists, while fundamentalists accounted for 66 percent of the anti-ERA activists. Nonaffiliates, Jews, and liberal Protestants made up 61 percent of proponent women, and conservative Protestants, fundamentalists, and Mormons comprised nearly 80 percent of the opponent women in Texas.[119] Since conservative Protestants stressed traditional gender roles and a literal interpretation of the Bible, both of which they believed the ERA threatened, Tedin argued that religious affiliation was a "very strong predictor" of anti- and pro-ERA activism.[120] Himmelstein agreed that "church attendance is generally more strongly related to antifeminist beliefs than are education, income, occupational status, class, age, residence, and most other social traits," but disagreed that denomination was an important distinguishing factor.[121] He found continuity across the denominational divide, arguing that, regardless of doctrine or creed, the more religiously involved a person was, the more likely that person was to be against the ERA.[122] Religious involvement—not denomination—constituted the "crucial factor" for distinguishing antifeminists from their opponents.[123] While proponent activists tended to organize through professional and political networks, Gubbins recalled that conservatives in Indiana often communicated and spread the word at church events.[124]

For some, communism, feminism, and internationalism connected to another dangerous "ism": secular humanism. While humanism dates back to the Greek philosopher Protagoras, it is more commonly associated with the Enlightenment, which prioritized human reason and the belief that through scientific inquiry the organization, purpose, and structure of the natural world might be understood.[125] Conservatives tended to focus on more modern manifestations of the humanist movement, including *Humanist Manifesto I*, published in 1933, and *Humanist Manifesto II*, published in 1973.[126] The first manifesto was a short statement of fifteen affirmations, beginning with the belief that the universe was "self-existing and not created" and denying belief in "any supernatural or cosmic guarantees of human values."[127] It called on traditional religion to acknowledge fundamental shifts in the modern organization of life away from ways of the past: what was needed was "a heightened sense of personal life" and "a cooperative effort to promote social well-being."[128] According to signers of the manifestos, religions should address themselves to human needs and quality of life in order to be relevant in the modern world.

The second manifesto, created by the American Humanist Association and signed by liberals like Betty Friedan and A. Phillip Randolph, recognized global problems of the last half of the twentieth century. Nazism, racism, sexism, poverty, "police states, even in democratic societies, widespread government espionage, and other abuses of power by military, political and industrial elites"—all these and more prompted the signers to create *Humanist Manifesto II*, "an affirmative and hopeful vision" for the twenty-first century. The second manifesto is more pointed in its criticism of "salvationism" and "traditional theism" for "diverting people with false hopes of heaven hereafter" than dealing with the problems society faces.[129] The manifesto charges that "traditional moral codes and newer irrational cults both fail to meet the pressing needs of today and tomorrow. False 'theologies of hope' and messianic ideologies, substituting new dogmas for old, cannot cope with existing world realities. They separate rather than unite peoples. . . . Humanity, to survive, requires bold and daring measures. . . . The ultimate goal should be the fulfillment of the potential for growth in each human personality—not for the favored few, but for all humankind. Only a shared world and global measures will suffice."[130] Criticism of monotheistic traditions and theism generally, along with a focus on global solutions to the problems of humankind, made humanism a top priority concern for conservatives in the 1970s. Leaders of the New Right, including Jerry Falwell and Tim LaHaye, denounced secular humanism as part of the "continuing infiltration of socialism" and humanists as "a small but very influential cadre" intending to "turn traditional moral-minded America into an amoral, humanist country."[131]

Conservative Hoosier women agreed; humanism was related to communism and feminism because all three challenged a way of life rooted in tradition and religious meaning. "Equal Rights like Human Rights are very charitable words," explained Joanne Reynolds of Madison County STOP ERA. "It's easy to understand how churches and ministers can be taken in by these words. But remember Satan isn't going to label slavery by its real name! We have all under-estimated the cunningness of the 'Women's Liberation Movement.'"[132] Reynolds found the real root of feminism in a humanist conspiracy that used "equal rights" as a "façade" for a much more insidious agenda:

> What is *Humanism*? Humanism is a fast growing cancer. It feeds on materialism and apathy. Its goal is enslavement. It is elusive, permeating every facet of our lives destroying as it goes Christian charity. . . . Humanism produced wife beating, rape, child abuse, murder, homosexuality, pornography, robbery, drug abuse, divorce, unhappiness and suicide! After producing these evil results it seeks to find solutions through law and law enforcement! In effect the Humanists feel that man and man alone must solve the problems that threaten his existence on earth. In 1973 the 4,000 word document called the 'Humanist manifesto' was signed by those who believe that the Universe is self-existing and not created. The Humanists believe that Communis (man responsible to man) is to be preferred to the American way of life (man responsible to God). They reject the Ten Commandments. They deplore the division of humankind on nationalistic grounds and they support and look to a system of world law and of world order. The Manifesto affirms a right to birth control, abortion, euthanasia, divorce, sexual freedom and they reject the family as the basis of society. In the area of sex they believe that intolerant attitudes often cultivated by orthodox religions and puritanical cultures unduly repress sexual conduct. According to the Humanist, "sin" is an old fashioned word. They say that good and evil are indisputable categories depending upon circumstances and that any act, including the killing of thousands, could be good or bad depending upon class ideology, defined by a handful of people.
>
> There are many who believe that the Women's Movement was not, in the beginning, a radical movement involving women with such extreme philosophies. That Homosexuality, abortion, sexual freedom, etc. wasn't a part of it and that

> the Equal Rights Amendment would not legalize the cancerous sores. But I would like to remind these people that the leaders of this movement have not changed. They still support and have always supported these social extremes. We are only kidding ourselves if we think that they had any other goal in mind.[133]

Reynolds would go on to be an Indiana delegate to the national International Women's Year conference in 1977, and she spoke for many social conservatives within the Hoosier antifeminist fold who denounced the low-key explanation of feminism as inaccurate and deceitful.

Rosemary Thomson picked up this theme in the IWY battles in the following year. In an exchange with Gubbins, Thomson argued that the root of the problem was John Dewey's educational reform movement of the Progressive Era. His "humanist philosophy" sought to restructure society; to eliminate nationalist divisions in favor of one-worldism; to reduce discrepancies in wealth across the world; and to deny the existence of God and replace the Ten Commandments with a moral code that accepted "the right to abortion, divorce, sexual behavior between consenting adults . . . euthanasia and suicide."[134] "Ms. Steinem incorrectly assumed that feminism leads to humanism," but Thomson argued that "humanist education produced an entire generation of women without moral absolutes who voted for IWY's National Plan of Action without a second thought. Humanism left a God-shaped vacuum which Women's Lib filled. . . . All we like sheep have gone astray. We have turned everyone to *her* own way (Isaiah 53:6)."[135] In a world without biblical Truth, wayward feminists subverted God's plan by challenging men in the bedroom and in the workplace; they encouraged sexual liberation, gay rights, and abortion; they dismantled the interdependency of the family with their focus on gender sameness. They rejected the old loyalties of family, nation, and religious orthodoxy and instead forwarded a cosmopolitan worldview that demanded global cooperation and pluralism.

Feminism and gender sameness, secular humanism, and communism collapsed into the threat of one-worldism for many right-wing women. Antifeminists heralded the state's acceptance of gender sameness through the ERA as the first step toward an androgynized world that would include totalitarian government. Wrapped within right-wing women's fear of homogenization of the sexes lay a connected fear of a distant global government. As June Sterman explained in her anti-ERA editorial, "When human beings under the law have no identifiable roles of discriminate sex, human beings then become nothing more than human resources to a government." Inevitably, feminist policies would make American women cogs in a global government that did not allow for individuality and personal difference. Ultimately, Sterman argued, "Equality of sex is only desirable to a one world or totalitarian form of government."[136] Jan Buechler of Kokomo also described the situation: "The Equal Rights Amendment will prevent us forever from making reasonable differences between men and women based on factual differences, and will force upon us a rigid, unisex, gender-free mandate enforced by the Federal government and the Federal courts."[137] "They (feminists) were not interested in equality before the law," Gubbins explained. "They are interested in a sex same society—they are interested in societal change."[138] Conservative women might support some measures of equality—such as equal pay and the equal right of women to participate in the political process. Indeed, they tended to think that women's participation in politics was essential, not because women were equal to men but because they were different. Riffing on this theme of gender difference, conservative women distributed fresh bread to legislators ahead of the 1973 legislative vote to counter the "expensive luncheon" being offered by proponents and distinguish the efforts of opponents who approached male legislators as endearing wives and mothers with gifts "homemade in our kitchens from our own resources, and they come to you from the heart."[139] But the ERA would eliminate gender difference and socially distinct roles based on that difference, and for some, this was part of a larger impulse or movement by feminists and others toward a globalized, uniform, state-centered world. "The fear is that once the feminist agenda is in federal hands, the essential differences between the sexes will be eliminated, replacing diversity with uniformity," Klatch explains.[140] Ultimately, conservatives connected feminism to a "leveling" quality they associated with collectivism, whether under the auspices of a too-powerful federal government, communism, or one-worldism.[141] Feminists were part of a plot to take women out of the home, and in their place would be "our 'Father' in Washington, D.C."[142]

Just as conservative women fought any action to eliminate gender difference, they acted against any attempt to consolidate, merge, or regionalize government entities. When Republican mayor Richard Lugar forwarded a plan for a consolidated metropolitan government in Indianapolis (Unigov) in 1969, conservatives denounced his "power grab" and worked against adoption. Unigov promised to combine governmental services and departments in the city and Marion County, eliminating inefficiency and simplifying government functions. Even if it looked appealing, as a similar program had in 1963, when Congress signaled an intention to increase federal aid to state and local police, a Pennsylvania Minute Woman warned that the true intention was to "take over as much local government as possible."[143] Around Indianapolis, conservative opposition surfaced at public hearings where locals argued that Unigov was part of the communist plot. Gubbins distinguished herself as the lead opponent of

Unigov, insisting that consolidation should be put to a vote of the people affected.[144] Unigov passed, to the consternation of many conservatives, and proved once again that "planners" were actively at work in local communities.

Criticism of the ERA could be as mainstream as linking the ERA to expanding federal authority. Evelyn Pitschke was an important voice among right-wing Hoosier women, and she lent considerable time and energy to opposing ratification in Indiana and around the nation. She focused her criticism on how the ERA would further concentrate the power of the federal government away from states, fusing an antistatist opposition to "big government" with states' rights rhetoric.[145] As an Indianapolis lawyer admitted to the state bar in 1945, she was an ideal spokesperson on the ERA and its impact on the law.[146] In fact, she considered herself legal advisor and spokesperson for all "citizens [wh] o oppose the equal rights amendment" and gave free legal counsel to groups that solicited her help.[147] She gained notoriety by appearing on local television programs and was a skilled public speaker.[148] In late January 1973 she debated the pro-ERA's leading lawyer, Virginia Dill McCarty, at a YWCA event and cemented her title as a "chief spokesperson" for the opposition movement.[149] As the national spokesperson for STOP ERA and a lawyer, she traveled extensively throughout the nation expounding on the ERA threat. In 1973 alone, four of the six state legislatures she spoke before followed her advice and rejected the amendment.[150] Her major complaint against the ERA centered on its expansion of federal oversight—a theme she described at length in an article for the *Phyllis Schlafly Report*, as well as in flyers, letters, and speeches to legislators.[151]

Pitschke described herself as a "modern day minuteman" who became involved in the ERA issue because of "reverence for the constitution" and her belief that the ERA would create, ironically, a "federalized government."[152] She focused her criticism of the ERA specifically on the Section II federal enforcement provision: "*ERA's Section 2* is an *outright grant of power to the Federal government,* allowing it to exercise more control over our personal lives. *Section 2 allows state legislatures to hand over to Congress the power* to pass all laws relating to the sexes and the relationship between the sexes. This includes laws concerning divorce, inheritance, sex crimes and *even building codes.* Hidden within this seemingly beneficent little amendment is a rip-off of states' rights—*a sell-out* of a *part* of *our liberty.*"[153] She challenged conservative women not to "let feminism outweigh patriotism!"[154] The theme was picked up by others. In the 1973 statehouse forum, one Indiana senator warned Hoosiers that any "legislative intent to give equality" would be misinterpreted "in judicial interpretation and administrative edicts coming out of a Federal Bureau."[155]

Pro America took that antistatist impulse to a more conspiratorial end. In a flyer circulated during the ERA ratification debates, Pro America explained that behind feminist calls for childcare centers and public school reform lay "Marxist concept[s]" and a "humanistic and socialistic one-world point of view," with the combined intent of these influences seeking to "convert our children to the status of trained animals conditioned to serve the elite in a one-world socialist state."[156] Feminism was at the center of this conspiracy, according to Nola Meredith: "THE WOMEN'S LIBERATION MOVEMENT, WITH THEIR EQUAL RIGHTS AMENDMENT, WORK HAND IN HAND WITH OTHER MOVEMENTS THAT INTEND TO OVERTHROW OUR TRADITIONAL AMERICAN SYSTEM BASED ON A FREE ENTERPRISE SYSTEM OF ECONOMICS AND A REPRESENTATIVE FORM OF GOVERNMENT. HISTORICALLY, BULLETS, BOMBS AND MISSILES HAVE BEEN THE MEANS OF GAINING CONTROL OF PEOPLE AND THEIR NATIONS. TODAY'S ULTIMATE WEAPON IS CONTROL OF THE MINDS—OR CONSCIOUSNESS—OF MANKIND."[157] Recent events were very disturbing to Pro America women. Americans had been "led away from our principles as a republic with a free enterprise economic system which gives opportunity to all with the will to improve their lot to do so, into a partial democracy where the State and vested interests, even criminal conspiracies and ideological misleaders have increasingly put restrictive and reactionary burdens on us as individuals, regardless of race, creed or color. We recognize this as retrogression into slavery to the State."[158] Conservative women were "progressive" because they rejected "tenets of Socialism, Communism and World Government just as our forefathers rejected them two hundred years ago, in favor of the only truly new concept of government in the thousands of years of human development."[159] Given their heightened awareness of the threat of one-worldism, it is not surprising that Pro America took the lead in anti-IWY and anti-UN activities.

Conservative women's criticism of the size and scope of the federal government varied, with one-worldism on the far end and advocacy of state's rights and local autonomy on the other. Women did not have to choose between the two impulses but could tailor their approach and argument to their audience. To the wider public, Gubbins might focus on the idea of protecting state authority, but in communication with supporters, her language and message were more strident: "A careful reading of this report will have shown the reader how diligently members of our society have planned for the eventual takeover of the rearing of our children. . . . I have proven that an intricately woven pattern exists, both in Indiana and the Nation, to create a new age, a global society, as envisioned by the behaviorists and Humanists, using the schools as surrogate parents, in order to perpetuate their philosophy and worldview."[160] By 1978 Gubbins had openly described ERA support as an "umbrella" of "radical groups," including "homosexuals and Marxists who want to destroy American society."[161] She was treading a well-worn path by the late 1970s on themes such as progressive education and one-worldism popular with Minute Women and Pro America in the two preceding decades.

With the defeat of the ERA in the Indiana Senate in April 1973, the ERA Coordinating Committee regrouped to assess its weaknesses and discuss strategies for future success, ultimately sticking with lobbying and educating as its mission through 1976. Although Republican Party leaders organized the 1973 state senate defeat, proponents did not understand the ERA as a partisan issue. While more Republicans than Democrats objected to the bill, bipartisan support encouraged activists to work within their respective parties on educating the electorate and legislators until 1976. Indiana had long held to the notion of the state legislature being a "citizens' assembly" of nonprofessionals and held a short session (sixty-one days) every other year.[162] The short session in 1974 provided little opportunity for coordination on controversial issues like the ERA.[163] On Valentine's Day in 1975 ERA supporters faced a tremendous disappointment as the legislature again failed to pass the measure. As will be discussed in the next chapter, at that point feminists turned on the Republican Party and looked to the election of 1976 to rid the state senate of enough Republicans to pass the ERA, leaving Republican feminists with a difficult decision to make between loyalty to party or to the feminist cause.

Efforts to change (even incrementally) the makeup of the 1976 state legislature proved successful the following year when the Indiana House of Representatives passed the measure 54 to 45. After a failed attempt by Senator Gubbins to vote down the committee report favoring ratification, a few Republicans broke party ranks and joined the Democratic majority to pass the measure in the state senate 26 to 24.[164] Indiana was the thirty-fifth state to ratify the ERA in 1977, but also the last. The clock for national ratification ran out, and the ERA died just three states short. Across the nation, anti-ERA activists scored repeated victories throughout 1977 by defeating the ERA in Missouri, Illinois, Oklahoma, and North Carolina, and, although resting on dubious legal grounds, rescission efforts gained popularity, with Idaho, Nebraska, and Tennessee leading the way.[165] Despite a 1981 Gallop poll that reported that 63 percent of Americans supported the ERA, the ERA time clock ran out in 1983, stalled in large part because of weak support in the South and Midwest and mixed support among Republicans.[166] The year 1980 saw a series of setbacks for proponent forces, most importantly, the Republican Party's repudiation of its forty-year commitment to the ERA at the national convention—the same convention that nominated Ronald Reagan as its presidential candidate.[167] Phyllis Schlafly had lost the chairwomanship of the National Federation of Republican Women (NFRW) because of the more liberal element in the party, who supported Gladys O'Donnell in 1967, but by 1980 the party increasingly reflected Schlafly's politics.[168]

Conservative Hoosier women failed to defeat the ERA at the state level, and they were deeply disillusioned, but they had crafted an argument about feminism that bridged the political activism of anticommunists to the needs of the present. They successfully articulated a role for modern women that stood in opposition to feminism, creating, paradoxically, a new "traditional" womanhood that supported national sovereignty to the exclusion of global cooperation and evangelical Christianity to the exclusion of religious pluralism, especially secularism, and that prioritized gender difference. They embraced conspiracist understanding of the one-worlder threat and explained feminism as a tentacle of the larger beast of collectivism, and they had awakened women around the state to the need to engage in political work. Hoosier feminists also mobilized for action but adopted a very different approach toward more radical voices in their midst. As the next chapter explains, through HERA and other feminist coalitions and organizations, Hoosier feminists "low-keyed" their explanation of feminism, crafting an antiradical, nonthreatening version that denied lesbianism, a critique of capitalism, and the idea that "the personal is political" had a place in the movement.

CHAPTER 4

Low-Key Feminism as a Strategy

The opposition really believes that they are attempting to save the world for God!

—Betty Newcomb in a letter to the ERA Coordinating Committee[1]

OVER THE COURSE of the 1970s, right-wing women articulated an explanation of feminism that connected to Cold War conspiracy theories about one-worldism and totalitarianism along with a commitment to the heteronormative family. While Hoosier feminists anticipated a political culture resistant to feminism and adopted the low-key approach to make the ERA and feminism palatable to the public, feminists never understood the real meaning of the charges against them. The low-key approach mandated decorum and private, behind-the-scenes lobbying. By pressuring feminist organizations in the state to refrain from advocacy on controversial issues and public protest throughout the five years the Indiana statehouse considered the ERA, Hoosiers for the Equal Rights Amendment (HERA) sought to present a single feminist identity that eschewed radicalism, specifically projecting a "'Mom and apple pie' image."[2] Feminists hoped that low-key feminism might appeal to Republican lawmakers, and Republican feminists were important proponents of the low-key strategy within HERA. Clearly, however, it also stifled many liberationists and radicals within the ranks. Indiana ratified the ERA in 1977, but over time HERA's commitment to low-key feminism also worked to discredit and discourage a feminist coalition. And the low-key strategy did not protect feminists from being understood and labeled by conservative women as dupes (at best) and conspirators (at worst) in a collectivist scheme that promoted world government.

Although the state National Organization for Women (NOW) and the Indiana Women's Political Caucus (WPC) led the effort to ratify the ERA, they were not the first second-wave feminist organizations in Indiana. Indiana WPC cofounder Virginia Dill McCarty recognized that by the time the state caucus formed in 1971 the women's movement "was in full swing" already.[3] By the early 1970s, Indiana housed pockets of liberationists active in scattered enclaves around the state. They existed in university towns such as Indianapolis and Bloomington, as well as Fort Wayne, but little is known of their collective history beyond the fact that they were early examples of radical and liberationist feminism. The state NOW especially was aware of the existence of what it called "old women's liberationists" groups, in part because NOW local chapters welcomed so many liberationists into the fold. The Indianapolis NOW chapter grew out of the older Indianapolis Women's Liberation (IWL), and Betty Newcomb, the state coordinator for NOW, met with a liberationist group in Fort Wayne in the fall of 1972 that was trying to decide whether to "go NOW or not."[4] Liberationists from around the state testified at a public inquiry on sex discrimination held by the Indiana Civil Rights Commission in November 1972, one of the first statewide public forums for feminist issues. The agenda for the day records that Nancy Brand spoke for Bloomington "Women's Liberation," Joan Uebelhoer for "The Feminists" of Fort Wayne, and Diana Sider for IWL.[5]

Bloomington Women's Liberation grew out of the New Left movement on the campus of Indiana University (IU) and the battle to end "women's hours," or the in loco parentis rules that regulated women's life on college campuses.[6] After meeting with University of Chicago sociologist Marlene Dixon, feminist and leader of the Women's Caucus of the New University Conference, in February 1969, IU women began to hold informal meetings weekly where they discussed personal and professional issues, "venting the steam of suppressed anger at their own and other women's burdens, both at home and in their working lives."[7] IU liberationists focused on women's access to high-quality and affordable day care and began operation of the Bloomington Cooperative Day Care Center in 1969. They actively participated in campus politics and formed splinter groups, including Concerned University Women, which challenged the university administration to implement nondiscriminatory hiring and salary policies and a branch of WITCHes (Women's International Terrorist Conspiracy from Hell), who protested a dinner meeting of male administrators at the Pic-A-Chic Ranch.[8] IU liberationists spurred the formation of gay rights groups on campus. Mary Ann Wynkoop argues that "women's liberation was the beginning of gay liberation," and in 1970 Bloomington Gay Liberation sponsored an All Campus Liberated Multi-Everything Halloween Party.[9]

IWL brought New Left tactics to the capital city with a protest at the War Memorial in the downtown Circle on 26 August 1970 as part of the national Women Strike for Equality Day.[10] Women Strike for Equality was the first significant media event of the second-wave movement, and it was meant to draw connections between the first-wave movement and second-wave feminist activism of the postwar era by staging a national strike on the fiftieth anniversary of the ratification of the Nineteenth Amendment.[11] IWL repeated the march the following year, and newspaper cameras captured women holding handwritten signs that read "Equal Job Opportunities," "Abortion on Demand," "Legalize Abortion Without Fear of Penalty," and "Free Ourselves Free Our Sisters."[12] IWL hosted the first women's liberation state conference on 22 April 1972, entitled "The Ecology of Women," as a joint celebration of Earth Day and women's liberation.[13] Evident in the workshop titles are the "wide-ranging leftist interests" Melissa Estes Blair attributed to the group.[14] Sessions revolved around four themes: "Arts and Interests," which promised a speaker from the Chicago Graphics Collective and discussion of history and literature; "Community Relations," focusing on newsletter publications and how to establish speakers' bureaus; the "Political Action" sessions, which discussed welfare, childcare, and abortion reform; and "Lifestyles," which included discussion of "collective living, lesbian life, the nuclear family AND MORE."[15]

Topics related to lesbianism were frequently discussed in IWL newsletters, and analysis of IWL and the Gay Liberation Front—Indianapolis literature reveals cross-pollination and mutual support. An article covering the August 1971 IWL march entitled "Women's Liberation Is Our Liberation" was featured on the front page of the first issue of the Gay Liberation Front—Indianapolis newsletter and promised: "GAY LIBERATION FRONT / INDIANAPOLIS EMPHATICALLY SUPPORTS INDIANAPOLIS WOMENS LIBERATION AND PLEDGES TO WORK TOGETHER TO COMBAT MALE CHAUVINISM AND SMASH SEXISM IN INDIANAPOLIS, 'ALL AMERIKKKA CITY.'"[16] IWL newsletters featured lesbian poetry, advertised for a "gay liberation prom," and provided information about support groups.[17]

Despite its willingness to take on issues like abortion and homosexuality, IWL was neither isolated nor insular. It reported a large support base, and members read widely on feminist scholarship and maintained contacts with liberationists in Cincinnati, Ohio, and around Indiana.[18] IWL staffed a booth at the Volunteer Advisory Fair, held in Indianapolis on 27–28 March 1971, during which over twenty-five volunteers distributed three thousand pieces of literature, including tracts about "daycare, a history of women's liberation, a fact sheet on how far women have not come in the last fifty years, a sheet giving a brief explanation of the concept of the support group . . . a sheet on what committees and other activities we have been involved [with] here in Indpls, free copies of '[The] Politics of Housework' by Pat Mainardi . . . buttons, bumper stickers, and women's lib magazines." One participant reported that "so many things were great about working at *OUR* Women's Liberation booth. . . . We were all together in an effort."[19] The newsletter noted that some fairgoers were hostile to IWL, but "most were thirsty for information and face to face talk with women, who had decided no longer to accept the shitty limitations of our sex roles."[20] Even when IWL merged with Indianapolis NOW in 1973, IWL's issues, strategies, and vigor remained visible, pushing Indianapolis NOW further left than other state chapters. In 1973–74 Indianapolis NOW protested a bridal fair (distributing six hundred copies of Pat Mainardi's "The Politics of Housework"); held a prochoice rally; protested feminine hygiene sprays; boycotted Folgers coffee for promoting stereotypes in the media; appeared on the local WIFE radio station to protest crude and sexist jokes; developed a referral service of sympathetic doctors, lawyers, and marriage counselors; and worked to ratify the ERA.[21] Along with local liberationist groups, like those in Indianapolis, Bloomington, and Fort Wayne, women were involved in women's organizations like the League of Women Voters, and increasingly they were taking a feminist turn.[22]

Republican women were key participants in creating a feminist movement in Indiana. In 1972 Audra Bailey, a high school counselor and teacher, and Mary Anne Butters, a reporter for the *Indianapolis Star*, encouraged Republican Richard Lugar, mayor of Indianapolis (1969–76), to create the Mayor's Task Force on Women and the Woman's Anti-Crime Crusade, on which both of the Republican women served.[23] Bailey wrote the proposal for the women's task force after studying guidelines laid out by President Richard Nixon's Task Force on Women's Rights and Responsibilities, and she and Butters presented the idea to Lugar.[24] Butters, who became a staffer in the Lugar administration, led the task force. By 1973 the group had spurred the creation of Women Against Rape. Within a year Women Against Rape operated a rape crisis center that served nine Indianapolis hospitals and encouraged the training of female police officers and prosecutors to handle rape cases, improving the treatment of rape victims and evidence collection procedures.[25]

In the spring of 1973, when Governor Otis R. Bowen (1973–80), also a Republican, founded the Governor's Commission on the Status of Women to coordinate local efforts, Gary, Indianapolis, Columbus, and Tippecanoe County already had such commissions in place, with Evansville and Fort Wayne set to announce the formation of commissions shortly thereafter.[26] The Governor's Commission on the Status of Women in the spring of 1973 sought to coordinate local commissions on the status of women and provide women a forum to discuss important issues.[27] Throughout the 1970s, the commission held meetings around the state and primarily sought to research discrimination with regard to women's access to the public sphere, particularly workplace discrimination and women's access to advanced degrees. Overall, commission literature outlines that the group sought to provide women "an opportunity . . . to improve their relationship with their government and to assess their political potential."[28] The commission promised that its weekend retreat in February 1976, called "Win, Place, or Show," at Saint Mary-of-the-Woods College would be an "intellectual get-away for women" with a program that included a "feminist film festival and rap room," an audiovisual presentation entitled *Win with Women—Indiana* put on by "political women," and a finale with leaders from WPC, the League of Women Voters, NOW, and "Dem. and Rep. Women."[29]

Prompted by Governor Otis Bowen's creation of the statewide Commission on the Status of Women (SOW) in 1973, Fort Wayne mayor Ivan Lebamoff (Democrat, 1972–76)) established a mayoral SOW the same year. Fort Wayne councilwoman Vivian Schmidt and Norma Roembke chaired the Fort Wayne SOW, and within the year the commission recommended the creation of a women's bureau within the municipal government to forward the interests of women at the local level.[30] It took Lebamoff two years to act on the suggestion, but the Women's Bureau officially became part of the city government in 1975. The move sparked heated opposition, especially when the Human Resources Department allotted the new bureau a budget of $16,250.[31] After beating Lebamoff in the 1975 election, Mayor Robert Armstrong (Republican) stripped the bureau of many of its functions and resources. Harriet Miller, who served as the executive director for the bureau from its inception in 1976 through 1995, encouraged the women's bureau to become a nonprofit organization to accomplish its mission, and in 1976 the Fort Wayne Women's Bureau (FWWB) severed ties with the city government and began operating independently. Miller was defiant in an interview with the *News Sentinel* regarding the bureau's decision to go nonprofit: "Even if it's only one person in one room, we'll be out there. It's not the first time we have had to struggle, and it won't be the last. But when you're working for a just and right cause, you just have to keep at it."[32] Criticism and opposition changed the direction of the FWWB, but no one seemed to mind the attention. Persons contacting the bureau almost doubled due to the publicity.[33]

Like the SOWs, NOW, and other second-wave feminist organizations, the FWWB drew on the support of radical feminists coming out of the New Left. The year before Lebamoff created the Fort Wayne SOW, which would go on to create the FWWB, a special issue of the *Fort Wayne Free Press* celebrated the accomplishments of the women's movement in the city. The issue included discussion of feminist goals and tactics and reported local meetings for interested women. The range of topics mark the groups as more radical than reformist, including "women's studies—action" to encourage more women's studies coursework at area universities, "consciousness-raising" sessions throughout the week, an all-day "Women's Teach-In" scheduled at IU-Purdue, and lots of counseling available for abortion and birth control services, consumer counseling, even "radical therapists," including psychologists, psychiatrists, and gynecologists.[34] The Fort Wayne Feminists were distinct from the FWWB, at least in the first year.[35] There was also the Women's Political Caucus in Fort Wayne, headed by Vivian Schmidt and Betty Meazell, active by 1972, which hoped to get women elected to the state Democratic Convention.[36] The ERA gave new purpose to these organizations and changed the nature of their interactions, although as Fort Wayne activists will make clear, not everyone prioritized the ERA.

Liberationists in scattered enclaves and liberal, usually professional women working within political parties and unions formed the core of the second-wave movement in Indiana. Their activism predated the ERA. Liberationists provided a starting point for statewide organizations like NOW and the WPC by offering a ready forum for feminist discussion and welcomed liberal women interested in statewide coordination to their events. At IWL's "Ecology of Women" workshop in 1972, NOW leaders from Gary, Indianapolis, and Lafayette came together to plan the first panstate conference for Indiana NOW, to be held in the fall.[37] In Bloomington the "old feminists" contributed their records to NOW concerning contacts and members in the Indiana Abortion Repeal Coalition.[38] At liberationist events and within liberationist groups, state organizers began their push for an intrastate feminist movement, coordination that they believed ERA ratification required.

The ERA Coordinating Committee, later renamed HERA, coordinated the activities of feminist organizations and individuals in the ERA struggle. It enacted the low-key strategy because of feminist understanding of the state's political conservatism, which transcended both the Democratic and Republican Parties. Mary Anne Butters recorded the crowd's response to the August 1971 IWL downtown march as ranging from "passive antipathy to angry hostility." Mayoral candidate John Neff addressed the assembled feminists with "Hi, girls.

I even took off my bra for the occasion." One man shouted at the protesters, "You're all a bunch of nuts!"[39] Virginia Dill McCarty explained in an oral interview that she considered it a liability to use radical methods or activists in trying to appeal to conservative legislators.[40] Linda Gail Seward, in her study of the ERA argument in the state, concluded, "Generally organizations and individual members sublimated their personal goals to those of the majority."[41] Because HERA believed that "women's lib turns people off," the low-key approach was meant to forward women's equality without calling up images of radicals.[42] In order to streamline feminism and make it as palatable to the general public as possible, HERA argued that the ERA was "a matter of simple justice," and Indiana WPC used the notation "W:M" to explain the movement.[43] Both sought to nullify conservative women's argument that the ERA symbolized many of the dangers that threatened their families, including abortion, collectivism, and the growth of the federal government. HERA argued that the ERA would not radically alter women's place but would "simply" cement women's equality; feminists were centrists, even traditionalists, just average "wives and mothers" who wanted only equal opportunity. In an Indiana NOW cartoon entitled *Who Opposes Equality?* the artist identified "radical extremists" of the Right *and* Left as the opposition, making support of the ERA the moderate choice.[44]

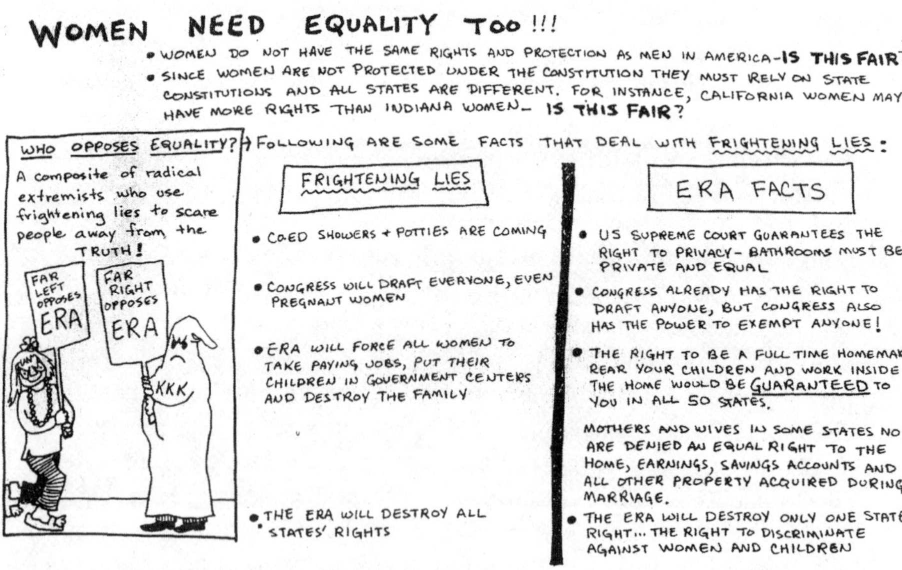

FIGURE 1. "Women Need Equality Too!!!" Flyer, folder 15, box 2, M0583, Indiana NOW Records, Indianapolis, IN. Courtesy of the Indiana Historical Society.

It is important to note that the low-key strategy does not appear to have been prompted by specific interaction with the opposition but was adopted early by ERA proponents to preempt criticism by framing the ERA in an unambiguous context of justice and securing the equality of all individuals, including women. Proponents accumulated information concerning antifeminists throughout the 1970s but understood very little about the mindset or nested politics of conservative women (and vice versa). In the fall of 1972 McCarty wrote Newcomb that she had yet to get a complete assessment of where legislators stood on the ERA. Even Senator Joan Gubbins was only presumed to be against ratification.[45] At the time, a Phyllis Schlafly newsletter from the previous spring and antiratification letters to the editor constituted McCarty's basis of knowledge concerning conservative women's arguments.[46] Proponents observed that antifeminists drew from a number of sources, most prominently Schlafly's STOP ERA and the John Birch Society, with important aid from fundamentalist churches.[47] By the end of 1972 McCarty warned activists at the local level that there was "a deliberate conservative campaign" operating in the state.[48] However, nowhere do activists mention the need to create or maintain the low-key strategy specifically because of the nature of anti-ERA arguments. The approach seems to have been a way to preemptively and strategically nullify potential counterarguments in what feminists must have believed was a skeptical, if not hostile, political climate.

The thinking of Hoosier feminists and proponents of the ERA is not entirely clear, but it would seem that the low-key strategy was a way to make feminism "nice" and palatable to midwesterners and Republicans. While exceptions to the midwestern culture of politeness existed, Indiana feminists implicitly understood that feminism, especially street protest, would be unpopular and perhaps seen as too demanding, too confrontational to be acceptable to midwesterners invested in notions of consensus, moderation, and conformity. As late as the 1990s, when Iowa was considering a state-level equal rights amendment, an editor of a small-town newspaper wrote, "All men and women are by nature free and equal[; however,] Iowans usually vote the way they feel, and some consider women's rights as too pushy, too demanding, and creating suspicion."[49] James Madison argues that the "Indiana way" is to make "evolutionary rather than revolutionary" change—well summarizing the conservatism that had permeated the state's politics since the 1940s.[50] Indiana saw competitive races in presidential elections in the twentieth century, but since the presidential election of 1944 Democrats only twice secured Indiana's electoral votes: Lyndon Baines Johnson in 1964 and Barack Obama in 2008.[51] If feminists wanted to pass the ERA or any other feminist initiatives in Indiana, they would need Republican support. Respectful of Indiana's Republican and traditionalist leanings, reformist feminists intent on statewide acceptance of ERA asked for liberationists' silence on controversial issues and shunned public protest until ratification was achieved. While at the grassroots level Indianapolis and Bloomington liberationists followed the Dayton Women's Liberation approach of holding "no single feminist philosophy," an approach that promoted coexistence between liberals and liberationists and "complementary" activism, at the next level up, the state, just the opposite occurred as liberals enforced the "soft touch" or low-key approach.[52]

The low-key strategy was not without early detractors. A. Reed McFarlane, speaking for the Indiana Civil Liberties Union, told HERA leaders in December 1972, "Frankly . . . I am very disappointed that you have continued to re-affirm your 'low profile' position. I think it is a mistake. . . . [I]t is foolish to remain quiet." He urged HERA to "come out in the open and soon."[53] Even for supporters of the low-key approach, it was problematic. When in early 1973 national NOW encouraged the "Blood Money for ERA" publicity campaign, in which NOW members would sell their blood and donate the money to support ratification efforts, Newcomb hesitated to enact the plan. She doubted that HERA would respond warmly to such action, believing that the blood drive might "jeopardize the effectiveness of [HERA] and NOW status with that group."[54] Publicity associated with the drive would likely "create waves" that she would rather avoid.[55] Newcomb worked "diligently and diplomatically" to put HERA together and reported that she would not "rock the boat or [disturb] the feeling of well-being" that characterized HERA meetings.[56]

Feminists were not the first to try the low-key approach. In his investigation of civil rights activism in Indianapolis, Richard Pierce characterized African American demands for equality throughout the twentieth century as "polite protest."[57] This choice to pursue a policy of "protracted negotiations" with the city's power elite rather than public protest reflected what African Americans understood as the political reality of their city and state.[58] Black Hoosiers pursued racial equality continuously in the postwar era, but because Indianapolis African Americans were "reluctant to jeopardize their gains through active, disruptive civil disturbances," they "regularly eschewed radical, abrasive forms of protest."[59] Pierce argues that the strategy yielded little success. He avoids being dismissive of their political calculations; nonetheless, he is "critical of their choices because they were unable to increase their fortune significantly."[60] Pierce's study does not consider gender or feminism, and the activists he uncovers do not figure in the policy decisions within HERA. However, it is interesting that both sets of postwar activists, civil rights activists in Indianapolis and liberal feminists from around the state, anticipated a hostile reaction from the legislature and public and tempered their approach accordingly. In this way, we can catch a glimpse of the kinds of decisions activists make in order to adapt their political message to a specific time and place—in this case, to meld civil rights or feminism to a midwestern culture that celebrated respectability and the status quo. But the existence of that regional culture does not mean the politics of respectability made for a happy consensus. Indeed, the decision to subdue feminism created conflict within feminist coalitions.

Liberationists provided crucial support for HERA, but increasingly their interests became antithetical to those of statewide groups bent on generating broad public support for the ERA. After attending an Indiana WPC workshop, Vonda Metzger of Indianapolis sharply criticized the event in a letter to Virginia Dill McCarty, president of the WPC, describing much of the day as a "disgusting waste of time."[61] Though liberationist groups had "paved the way for the Caucus," Metzger argued, WPC leaders "put down" liberationist perspectives and approaches. Most distressing for Metzger was the way the WPC attempted to control participation in the workshop, using a hierarchical structure wherein speakers talked at attendees instead of the more common approach among radicals in consciousness-raising groups that relied on women sharing their personal histories and experiences. "Preoccupation with hierarchy and positions should have been dispensed with," Metzger argued, asking, "Do none of the women in the Caucus worry about their young children, or the resistance of husbands? Have they been so courageous and indomitable as to not ever be bothered by such things?" Instead of interaction and discussion, the workshop amounted to "a lot of women doting on posts they have achieved [and] setting them[selves] apart from the group . . . [when we] should be united in the same purpose as equals."[62] In her response, McCarty focused on the generational divide, neglecting to engage Metzger's criticism related to the structure of the conference and lack of person-to-person interaction. Younger feminists like Metzger needed to be patient with women McCarty's age. "I ask your indulgence," she wrote, "until such time as you have had the opportunity to discuss this with them [older feminists] over a period of time," and then she asked Metzger only to do so "in a friendly way."[63] McCarty agreed that liberationists helped establish groups such as the Indiana WPC, but she asked Metzger to use "cautious judgment" in assessing those "not yet ready" to accept radical ideas and tactics.[64]

Not everyone in the Indiana NOW appreciated the priority accorded the ERA or the limits it placed on activism, but even most critics begrudgingly accepted the decision.[65] As early as the fall of 1973, Newcomb admitted that her work toward ratification disallowed work on other important state matters, but her successor, Lynn Schrum, continued the approach, reminding members and chapters to "low key our abortion fight until ERA passed."[66] Bloomington NOW cancelled a statewide prochoice rally in 1974 after "more moderate members" of the feminist community argued it would send the wrong image of prochoice activists; chiefly, it would identify feminists as students and "radical activists (like us)."[67] Through 1975 NOW chapters avoided the public protest that they (and the liberationists before them) had been so committed to early in the decade.[68]

By the end of 1973, major unions in the state—the Indiana State Teachers Association and the United Auto Workers—supported the ERA, and the American Federation of Labor switched its position to favor the ERA as well. HERA efforts continued throughout 1974 and 1975 through the low-key approach.[69] On Valentine's Day in 1975, eight Republican senators voted against releasing ERA out of the Senate Subcommittee on Governmental Affairs and on to a full vote. Frustrated by the senators' stonewall, the first cracks in HERA's low-key approach emerged. Though the official HERA press release after the Senate block pledged to continue efforts to inform legislators of majority support of the ERA, HERA's private letter to Senator Philip Gutman excoriated the Senate leadership (and Gutman in particular) for having "killed" the ERA.[70] Gutman's actions left HERA little choice, but instead of threatening to work against him in coming elections or target his district with more "education," HERA warned Gutman that it could no longer protect him from the organization's members: "We promised you before this session began that we would make every effort to use low key in-Senate lobbying for your convenience and the convenience of other senators. We believe . . . that we have succeeded in that dignified effort remarkably well. To our knowledge no Senator was ever harangued or harassed in the State House by HERA people." McCarty and Blumberg concluded their letter by adding that though they found it regrettable, they would be unable to "guarantee such lobbying techniques in the future."[71] The "gentle blackmail" Newcomb described became explicit; in return for the ERA, HERA agreed to shield legislators from more assertive elements of its movement: the women who would harangue and harass. HERA applied pressure to legislators by convincing them that it saved officials from radical, and implicitly less desirable, feminist contact. In addition to using the language of emotionalism to separate themselves from the opposition, HERA leaders used similar language to separate themselves from liberationists and radicals on the left.

Despite McCarty's and Blumberg's threat, HERA continued to control feminist contact with legislators and the wider public. In the lead-up to legislative action in 1975, Senator Thomas Teague, sponsor of the ERA, told the HERA policy council that he wanted the group to streamline its advocacy into a single lunch or dinner with representatives so as not to take up too much of the legislators' time. Although Representative Clifford Arnold noted at the same meeting that the intense lobbying effort of the opposition was eroding ERA support, especially among freshman legislators, Roberta Simons recorded that "HE [Teague] WISHES TO HAVE CAREFULLY CONTROLLED CONTACT."[72] Teague agreed to lobby senators individually so long as HERA funneled communication and interaction through a few carefully chosen spokespeople. HERA encouraged women to join the statehouse lobbying effort under the direction of McCarty and Blumberg, but an internal report encouraged HERA leadership to keep to the "carefully devised legislative strategy designed by the legislative sponsors."[73]

The February 1975 disappointment shattered HERA as internal dissent increased. No longer satisfied with the low-key approach that asked activists to quietly work behind the scenes to effect change, some within HERA, NOW members particularly, argued the time had come for more assertive measures, including targeting the reelection of opposition legislators. The month after the Business and Professional Women's Club (BPW) withdrew its monthly donation toward HERA expenses, Dorothy Steinmeier, the BPW representative on HERA's organizational council, excoriated the low-key strategy: "Sweet pussyfooting, sugar love-notes, and being scared to talk-up isn't going to get us anywhere in this fight. I think we proved that."[74] Speaking to other NOW leaders of the Great Lakes region, Sue Errington of Muncie explained that the chapters "realized [in 1976] that Indiana would not ratify ERA without organized grass-roots support," and they believed "NOW was the only state group capable of such an undertaking."[75] Insolvency threatened HERA as president Audra Bailey pleaded with members for donations, reminding them that she had personally signed the rental agreement, telephone, and tax documents because HERA had no access to credit.[76] Despite the financial and legislative setbacks of 1975, the HERA policy council still refused to consider more assertive tactics, like funding a group within the organization that could take political stands and endorse candidates.[77]

The turn against the low-key strategy coincided with a turn against the Republican Party, hinting further at a relationship between the two. Sydney Goddard, the NOW state legislative coordinator, explained to members that their problem was Republicans: "We know the Republican party in Indiana *is* the enemy, the identifiable enemy, but we need to get the ERA to committee so they will help us prove it."[78] By 1976 both ERA Indiana and NOW had agreed that ratification was a partisan issue that would be determined in November, not January, and both worked to ensure a Democratic majority in the Senate.[79]

National NOW targeted Indiana with money and personnel for the ratification effort, which allowed the state group to implement the strategy some had long desired.[80] Indiana NOW continued its efforts to educate the public at the local level, as the Muncie chapter demonstrated by staffing a pro-ERA booth at a local mall complete with ribbons, buttons, petitions, and postcards.[81] The second facet of NOW's plan, however, marked its real break with HERA strategy. Indiana NOW targeted key Senate races in an effort to change legislative leadership and organized public rallies across the state.[82] While acknowledging that "Demo[crat]s and Pro-ERA are not synonymous," internal NOW documents explained that "the goal in the Senate race[s] is to simultaneously elect a Pro ERA majority while electing a Democratic Senate."[83] During the late summer months, Indiana NOW directed the ERA Caravan, which traveled throughout the state and provided speaking opportunities to local proponent candidates. The caravan also allowed Indiana NOW to "cultivate grassroots," but the real goal was to ensure a November victory for Democrats in the Senate.[84]

Republican feminists were Republican and feminist for a variety of reasons, and they represent a broad range of experiences, of which Audra Bailey is one example.[85] She had a long history of professional activism when she joined the Greater Indianapolis Women's Political Caucus as a charter member and served as treasurer and president of HERA. For years Bailey taught mathematics at Arlington High School, Indianapolis, and before that worked at Roosevelt Junior High, Kokomo. By the end of her career, she boasted a decades-long membership in the National Association of Women Deans, Administrators, and Counselors. In her time in the public school system in Kokomo, she established an American Field Service chapter to encourage the exchange of students internationally and to foster world peace. As the only female in an otherwise all-male department, she felt driven to prove that she and, by extension, all women "might have some capacity for the subject of math," and personally she survived an abusive marriage that ended in divorce.[86] She helped Richard Lugar's mayoral campaign in 1968 by serving on a teacher committee and from there took an active part in the founding of the feminist coalition to support the ERA and the ongoing business of HERA. It was Bailey who spoke for Republican women in HERA and within the feminist fold, especially about her growing unease with how some feminists came to see the Republican Party as the problem.

Feminist Republicans continued their activism in the ERA struggle but increasingly felt out of place within the feminist fold. Republican HERA members felt the tension of dual loyalty as they struggled to restrain HERA from a full assault on the Republican leadership but also to reprimand the Republican leadership for its failure to recognize HERA's cause. In a letter to state senators, Bailey, then president of HERA, explained that many members felt they had been "put-down" and "treated as inferiors" by legislators, and as a result some in the group "have taken on a degree of militancy," including plans to make "changes in voting booths, come next election."[87] Bailey followed that observation with the story of a North Carolina senator who acknowledged that his no vote on ERA cost him the reelection. She concluded ominously, "We'll see you in 1976!"[88] Privately, however, Bailey, Blumberg, Anita Burrous, and other Republican women resisted the call to "go after" targeted GOP candidates.[89] Bailey's ties to state Republicans, especially Lugar, were strong, and she hesitated to attack her party. Possibly in an effort to quell the demand for a more aggressive strategy, Bailey asked the executive board to consider a separate committee within HERA for Republican women. She pointed out to the board that the few Republican women involved in the organization were placed in different committees that diluted their power, allowing Democrats control of all policy decisions, even those concerning Republican representatives, by sheer force of numbers. Bailey asked the HERA executive board not to make the situation any more difficult for them by asking them to target Republicans: "It seems to me that we should sit down very unemotionally and decide what organizations are going 'after' certain Senators to replace them, and then Republican women might try to salvage things in certain districts. I don't believe we can produce results with one hand saying 'we are out to get you,' AND another saying 'we would like to have your vote.'"[90] Bailey worked with other HERA Republicans to create the Task Force of Prominent Republican Women for the ERA, which sought to increase the power and voice of Republicans within the organization, but the larger membership seemed bent on a more assertive strategy.[91]

While Bailey tried to paint her Republicanism as an asset in her reelection bid later that summer, she clearly represented a minority opinion concerning strategy after the February defeat. Bailey's Republicanism and commitment to the low-key strategy distanced her from an increasingly frustrated membership.[92] Her replacement as HERA president by Laurie Scholl prompted a new direction for the organization. One HERA member wrote of the new direction that had taken place by late 1975: "In the past, the opposition has been highly vocal and visible, and it has proven to be very effective. The HERA Organization fully intends to employ those same tactics from now on." Gone was the low-key approach. Now HERA claimed, "We look at ourselves . . . to be there in the foreground."[93] By 1976 Indiana feminists in NOW had concluded that the Republican Party had deserted women's rights and that alliance with Republicans in HERA was stifling their ratification efforts.[94] HERA's largely Democratic membership turned away from the low-key strategy it had employed for the previous three years; the tenuous HERA coalition collapsed and left dedicated Republican women with few outlets for feminist activism.[95]

In 1976 the feminist vanguard in the state shrank further when the WPC evaporated.[96] The last contribution the WPC made was to help launch ERA Indiana, the state branch of ERAmerica. In an effort to ensure ERA success in unratified states, over 130 prominent national groups created ERAmerica in 1976, seeking to provide "political leadership at the national level and to unify existing ERA programs."[97] ERAmerica strategists believed that if Indiana did not ratify in 1977, it never would, because political roadblocks were likely to increase as Senate Democrats elected in 1974 came up for reelection in 1978. The 1977 legislature presented the "only realistic hope for ratification," and then only if ERA Indiana could secure six additional pro-ERA Senate seats in the upcoming election.[98] ERA Indiana eventually faced the same challenge regarding the low-key strategy that destroyed HERA.[99]

Hoosier feminists in HERA and ERA Indiana achieved their primary goal in January 1977, which was state ratification of the ERA. In that way, the low-key strategy was successful. The sense of accomplishment Hoosier feminists felt in realizing ratification was evident still in 2010; "I've done my job," said Beth Van Vorst Gray, "along with my generation."[100] Following ratification and perhaps in deference to the help given them by Republican leader Kermit Burrous, feminist leaders again reached a "tacit agreement" with legislative leaders to lie low on all issues relating to the ERA. Feminists agreed not to "start anything" and only respond to anti-ERA attacks and efforts.[101] For this reason, the leader of the Religious Committee for the ERA in the state begged to be excused from holding a pro-ERA rally before the national ratification deadline in the early eighties. She wrote United Methodist Women leaders that since "this is such a mixed up and confusing time," a pro-ERA rally would do "no good and might cause great damage not only in Indiana but elsewhere."[102] Indiana NOW allowed that it did not regret joining ERA coalitions, but if it had it to do over, Indiana NOW would not have relinquished its contact with legislative leaders and ERA sponsors of coalition forces.[103] Ruth Adams, campaign director of ERA-Indiana, cautioned her colleagues in unratified states that too often "the ego" of member organizations gets in the way of the issue at hand. She acknowledged that having a single voice moving the bill through the legislature was tempting, but the single-issue nature of proponent coalitions resulted in little "political clout" when compared to the historical involvement of ongoing organizations. Use "the strongest political forces within the coalition," she concluded.[104] By spring ERA Indiana was dead, leaving women's and feminist organizations in the state without any tangible ongoing connection to one another. The path to ratification had not been easy and left lingering reservations about coalitions among some feminist organizations.

After ratification, Indiana NOW took a more unilateral approach to conducting its work in the state. Sue Errington reported that Indiana NOW prepared for the International Women's Year (IWY) state meeting in June 1977 without other feminist groups' oversight. NOW relished the fact that "there was no one on the steering committee whose arm could be twisted into making our strategy more low key"; however, her report on IWY concluded by noting a conservative victory.[105] These developments might have been related. By late 1977 the Indiana situation was dire. Frances Dodson Rhome, feminist Republican and presiding officer for the state IWY coordinating committee, reported that "women's rights are under strong, vicious attack and ERA under violent assault." Feminist coalitions, she reported, were defunct.[106] In Indiana the failed IWY state conference in 1977 marked a political turning point as feminists met a fully mobilized New Right that obliterated their Unity Coalition. Despite HERA's and ERA Indiana's history of marginalizing the Left, Rhome charged that it was extremism of the Right *and* Left that hurt the movement. "Women feminists who represent the moderate liberal view are being pulled apart and undermined by extreme positions of both the right and left," she charged. She asked women on the state IWY coordinating committee to stay active, since they represented "a very important stance—that of credibility and of responsibility—and yes, maybe of a more moderated and acceptable view," coming as they did from "both parties, in leadership positions of numerous fine organizations, and of wide geographical diversity."[107]

While feminists meant to create broad-based support for the ERA, making the ERA the top priority for the statewide feminist movement limited the appeal and meaning of feminism.[108] Evidence suggests that whites predominated among liberal Hoosier feminists, and many proved unwilling to tackle issues of racial discrimination and social hierarchy. To comply with the national affirmative action program, Indiana WPC begrudgingly surveyed its members in 1972.[109] While African Americans accounted for 8 percent of the membership, which constituted a higher percentage than the black proportion of the general population, the lack of participation of black women was a problem.[110] Black women in the caucus did not take an active role in the organization, adopting instead a "wait and see attitude."[111] The caucus struggled to interest women of color, likely because they refused to include in their objectives any discussion of racial issues or any issues specifically pertinent to minority communities. "Concerning the problems of blacks and Chicanos," McCarty observed, "other groups can and should solve these; the Caucus would get lost trying."[112] When

Pat Forhan suggested that the WPC find out what racial and ethnic groups the caucus was not appealing to and why, McCarty and Pat Kane countered that they "simply weren't ready" to handle minority issues.[113] The discussion carried over into following meetings. Rhome reminded her colleagues that "we not only want blacks, but we need them"; however, minutes reveal no discussion of the possibility that inclusion of black women might require revisiting the established priorities. The conversation ended with Connie Green asking that the Indiana delegation to the national conference in February not be "totally white."[114] In the affirmative action report issued in February 1973, Indiana WPC described briefly its efforts to attract black members and focused instead on its work to protect and promote Republicans as the significant minority group in the caucus.[115]

The Indiana WPC discussion of race provides further evidence that while white feminists believed their "'I' was 'we'" with regard to black women, they refused to acknowledge, as Winifred Breines argues, that racism "is not only a matter of personal intention" but a "social structural system that works subconsciously in individuals," including themselves.[116] Paula Giddings points out that while Aileen Hernandez tried to get NOW to deal seriously with issues of concern to minority women, NOW instead chose to focus on creating chapters in minority communities. Hernandez called the response a "totally inappropriate approach." NOW was attempting to "indoctrinate minority women" on the ERA as opposed to opening the agenda to shared concerns.[117] Black women and Chicanas focused on the "intersectionality of inequality," according to Benita Roth, which created tension with white feminists who saw feminism as a "universal sisterhood" built on a collective identity.[118] Work throughout the decade brought black and white women in the WPC closer together, and by 1977 feminists had elected Sita Keith Miller, an African American woman and former secretary of the WPC, as an official delegate to the IWY National Conference in Houston.[119] However, white feminists' focus on the ERA for most of the 1970s did not seem to mirror that of minority women, and while liberationists like those in IWL had employed a more "ecumenical approach" in the creation of a feminist agenda, Indiana NOW and the WPC believed they could afford no such flexibility.[120] The panstate feminist agenda was built around the understanding that the ERA was paramount; nothing could challenge that priority, and all other efforts were sublimated to achieving it.

While Indiana NOW focused attention on the ERA, the FWWB did not. It is difficult to pinpoint why trajectories differed, why certain feminist organizations zeroed in on the ERA and accepted the low-key strategy while others did not. Partial explanation may lie in the particular makeup of individuals active in Fort Wayne. Critics of a reformist agenda surfaced early in Fort Wayne. Mary Doherty, writing in the *Fort Wayne Free Press* in 1972, noted that the recent Women in Politics series, hosted by the Women's Workshop of the Fort Wayne Folk School, included a diverse understanding of political action. While she acknowledged that she would support some reformist goals—for example, she would sign a petition to get women into positions of authority in party politics—she argued that "a woman at the Democratic State convention, or in a political position, is [not] going to make much difference when the system that exists is so much more powerful than any individual." Doherty encouraged New Left women to cast their lot with the radicals, "the minority of the woman's movement who are developing a political strategy that will become a system that can replace our so-called democracy."[121] Part of the explanation may also lie in the individual inclination and priorities of important leaders. The experience of Harriet Miller, who worked with the FWWB for over two decades, is instructive. Her early experience with the statewide SOW proved disheartening, as the Bowen administration failed to provide direction or resources to the group.[122] In the fall of 1973 Miller described to a friend feeling "frustrated" with "the inability of this Commission to be active." She identified miscommunication, lack of follow-through, lack of funding, and an overall "low profile level" of functioning as the problem.[123] Already in 1973 she planned to turn her attention to other avenues of feminist activism. Because her work in the commission seemed to have hit a "stalling stage," she spent "the time and energy I might have been using to develop an active Speakers Bureau [for the SOW] elsewhere." She was not without guilt over the decision but noted that she was "very impatient." "I know that is a bad trait[,] for something this big does take time and carful study," but she wrote that she wanted to be part of a movement that she could feel and see moving.[124]

When Lebamoff lost reelection in 1975, the new Republican mayor cut resources and left the fledgling Women's Bureau dying on the municipal vine. Miller led the Women's Bureau out of the city government and into nonprofit status. It is clear that in the next two decades, the FWWB supported the ERA, but engaged activism in that effort surfaces only briefly in FWWB records. Perhaps because of lessons learned about the slow pace of change and the fleeting nature of change when working within existing government institutions or directly with the parties, the FWWB developed a range of goals that were not centered on ERA.

Within HERA the "feminisms" present in Indiana at the grassroots level were sacrificed to the goal of broad appeal and bipartisan support for the ERA. In this way, Hoosier women add to the discussion of why feminist coalitions of the second wave were difficult to maintain.[125] Liberals believed the ERA ratification required bipartisan support, which in turn necessitated a low-key strategy, making liberationists and advocates of more radical tactics the enemy, albeit one that was closer on the spectrum of "social distance and social advantage" than conservative women but dangerous to the progress of their feminism nonetheless.[126] This was in keeping with a national trend. Berenice Carroll finds that the failure of the ERA was due in part to a problem of "strategy (not organization)" and specifically argues that it was a "failure to incorporate tactics of civil disobedience and nonviolent direct action on a substantial scale."[127] NOW, she concludes, "never endorsed civil disobedience or other militant actions" in the push for the ERA and, in fact, viewed efforts shading toward militancy in the 1980s with "much doubt, if not hostility."[128] Feminists outside the state saw the benefit of a "big tent" approach; as a Dayton liberationist described, "You need the wild-eyed radical people to make it possible for the milder—viewed as the more reasonable—organizations to make any progress."[129] Indiana liberals, however, did not agree. The promise of a constitutional amendment gave feminist political activism very high stakes; liberal women did not want to lose the chance to achieve what suffragists before them had tried (and failed) to accomplish.

The problem with a low-key strategy as Berenice Carroll sees it is that only through public protest or direct action are public officials exposed to public scrutiny, confronting on "a face-to-face basis, those who are seeking to hold them accountable by a public, bodily witness." Only direct action "makes highly visible and urgent a conflict or demand that has been obscured by silence, indifference, timidity, conformity, apathy, or despair, and impresses upon [the public and office holders] the depth of commitment to the cause on the part of its adherents," she explains.[130] In their effort to achieve ERA ratification, HERA leaders adopted the values of a more conservative political power structure and in so doing might have blunted their own effectiveness. Jo Freeman agrees: "Movements that conform themselves to the norms of behavior in order to participate successfully in political institutions often find themselves forsaking their major goals for social change. Long-range ideals are warped for the sake of short-range gains."[131] In this way, it is possible that Hoosier feminists fell victim to the paradox of political organization Freeman warned against. "Without the more flamboyant and/or extremist groups," she suggests, "organizations like NOW and WEAL [Women's Equity Action League] would have been open to being dismissed as too far out." Social movements need a "radical flank," she argues, if for no other reason than it encourages the public to recognize centrists.[132] Marginalizing the radicals and liberationists did not keep HERA's moderate demands and deferential approach from being labeled radical or conspiratorial.

By focusing on a single state, we can better see how feminist coalitions dealt with issues of identity and difference and how diversity and cooperation at the grassroots level could be lost when personal connections could not alleviate or mitigate conflict, as they often did at the local level.[133] In part, what the Indiana story tells us is that when feminists sought to accomplish goals through the political process it fundamentally changed the nature of their movement—its organizations, strategies, and trajectory. Low-key feminism suited a particular strategic goal (ratification of the ERA at the state level), but that kind of feminism was exclusionary in many ways, even if it was well fitted to the task. Indiana feminists created an identity based largely on a strategy, not a theory. The only problem with this, as Gayatri Chakravorty Spivak argues, is that a good strategy should match "the trick to the situation," and as such it can be fleeting, while a theory is good in all possible cases. She warns that users of strategic identity (like low-key feminism) must be quick to grasp when a strategy is no longer helpful or when it misfires, thereby tethering those who adopted it to something potentially harmful to the cause.[134] A study of the second-wave feminist movement in Indiana further proves that understanding place and regionality is necessary to understanding feminist ideological development and movement strategy. While Dayton Women's Liberation pursued a genderless society and rejected notions of equality as too limited, Indiana liberationists supported the ERA. For Hoosiers, the ERA represented an intersection of radical and liberal efforts—liberals who supported working within the two-party political system favored its promise of equality between the sexes, and radicals saw in the ERA its potential to eliminate social hierarchy—but the division between them centered on how to accomplish ratification in the state.[135] The split in HERA was less over ideology than strategy, since most feminists, radical and liberal, agreed that the ERA was an important contribution to the movement.

The low-key explanation of feminism never satisfied or pacified conservative women who firmly believed that feminism was a radical movement—something with which many feminists would have agreed but that the low-key approach of reformists required they deny. Radicalism and lesbianism were part of the movement in Indiana and around the country, and denying it created problems of its own. Toni Carabillo, reporting to ERAmerica on right-wing efforts in California, spoke of the strategy of denial among liberal feminists in that state. She encouraged feminists to recognize gay men and lesbian women as allies in the fight, calling them "a new activist constituency in support of ERA." She acknowledged that openly supporting homosexuality was a "liability," but "if the traditional organizations can't bring themselves to handle the gay issue at least with equanimity as a human rights issue, both gay rights and the ERA may be doomed—and the right wing reactionaries will be riding high—more disasters will surely follow."[136] Even as the conservative argument tightened to explain feminism as evil and traitorous, Hoosier feminists did not abandon the low-key approach or directly counter the accusations of their opponents. But to their opponents, feminists did not go far enough to silence the radicals. Years after the ERA struggles, Gubbins suggested that it was the radicals who were the greatest liability to the ERA and that HERA's use of belligerent lobbyists hampered the feminist movement.[137] Feminists "berated" Congress to pass the specific language of the ERA, and Indiana feminists attempted to do the same thing in the ratification effort.[138] While the Right in Indiana embraced conspiracist narratives, the Left marginalized radicals and liberationists in their midst; HERA's moderate demands and deferential approach became radical by default.

What argument could feminists possibly have made to convince the opposition they were not evil or conspirators, given that right-wing women already believed them to be duplicitous? There is no easy answer. Deny the conspiracy, and you may only succeed in convincing conspiracists that they are right. The more strenuous the objection, the more assured conspiracy theorists become. Michael Barkun explains: "The belief must be true *because* it is stigmatized."[139] What seems clear in the case of Hoosier women is that denying difference or division in the ranks or downplaying it through low-key strategies did not lessen the divide or calm the fears that one-worldism through feminism conjured. Despite the chasm between conservatives and feminists, women's historians and scholars continue to hope that discussion across the divide might be possible. In the epilogue of *Women of the New Right*, published in 1987, Rebecca Klatch pleaded: "The very existence of multiple meanings, the fact that our world views do *not* coincide, makes it all the more imperative that we listen to the voice of the other, that we begin by respecting those who are different from ourselves. For only by realizing that differences is *not* a sign of weakness, that pluralism is *not* the same as relativism, that there is *not* simply one way to live, to act, or to think, does hope remain for common symbols that truly unite us ever to be forged."[140] Ronnee Schreiber, too, tries to find a path forward, suggesting that both feminists and conservatives need to "be more specific in their interest-based claims" and recognize, at least, that neither or both speak for "women," since "women" do not share "a homogeneity of interests and experiences."[141] Historian Glen Jeansonne advised that "the key" to getting along might be "dissipating people's anxieties about those who happen to be different."[142] Given the twenty-four-hour news cycle, the proliferation of fear-driven arguments, and increasing accessibility of conspiratorial narratives on the internet, the question of how to lessen our anxiety about difference in the modern world remains.[143] How to do so in the Midwest, a place known for its commitment to traditionalism and politeness, presents an even greater challenge.

When facing an inhospitable political climate, Hoosier feminists attempted to sublimate other demands in favor of pushing the ERA. The result was state ratification of the ERA and a feminist movement that worked at times to mute its own activists. At the moment of victory, with state ratification of the ERA, feminists looked forward to a new era in Indiana, one in which the public and leaders would recognize feminists' commitment and hard work in the political arena and accept them as dedicated professionals. But ERA ratification cost them much, and beginning in the spring of 1977, conservatives launched a full-scale attack on IWY that caught feminist activists in the state by surprise and capitalized on their battle fatigue. IWY proved to be the fulcrum on which the political fortunes of the Right and Left turned. In late 1977 Jane Fribley, writing to feminists in Church Women United, described the state IWY conference as a "fiasco." Conservative women attacked feminists as "anti-family, anti-life, anti-God, and anti-America"—all this despite the fact that "left wing groups cooperated and were very low key." Failing to understand the connection between a vibrant left wing and centrist acceptability, Fribley wondered, "Is there no place for the 'middle of the roaders'?"[144]

CHAPTER 5

The International Women's Year as a Fulcrum

You know, when we started it was almost a disgrace to be a member of the Birch Society. We're quite respectable now.

—Robert Welch, founder of the John Birch Society, 1978[1]

FEMINISTS IN INDIANA BELIEVED that the state's International Women's Year (IWY) conference, coming so quickly on the heels of their ERA victory, would reaffirm the state's commitment to women's equality by approving the feminist agenda laid out by the National Commission on the Observance of International Women's Year in 1976. They quickly discovered, however, that antifeminist conservatives in the state had no intention of conceding the fight. Instead of the ERA deciding the direction of state or national policies concerning gender equality, it proved to be the opening bell for another round. As feminist coalitions in the state disintegrated, conservatives emerged from the ERA battle determined to reclaim their state's affiliation. Antifeminists launched a concerted and vigorous campaign in the spring and summer of 1977 in Indiana and at other state meetings in an attempt to dominate the National Women's Conference, scheduled to take place in Houston later in the year. In both the national and state IWY meetings, women's rights and antifeminist delegates contested the meaning of gender and citizenship for modern women and fought the first battle in what would come to be called the "culture wars" of the 1980s.

The United Nations' IWY celebration ultimately included three international conferences, the first held in Mexico City in June 1975, followed by Copenhagen (1980) and Nairobi (1985). National conferences were held around the world during the UN Decade of Women from 1975 to 1985.[2] The United States held the second National Women's Conference in its history (and the first to be federally funded) in Houston from 19 to 21 November 1977, but prior to the national conference, the IWY included a series of state and smaller regional (intrastate) conferences, most held between January and July of 1977, totaling more than 150,000 participants.[3] IWY's position as an international, national, state, and local series of events made it a centerpiece for building conservative women's political consciousness not only because of the confluence of issues it embodied but also for the "accessible target" it provided.[4] As such, the events surrounding IWY in the United States throughout the summer and fall of 1977 present historians a special opportunity to understand how grassroots women responded to and influenced the national conservative agenda.

Because of its overt connection to the UN, IWY was a coalescent event that proved the long-held belief that liberalism and feminism were part of a one-world conspiracy. Using now familiar logic, right-wing women explained the IWY and its top priority, the ERA, as a global conspiracy to androgynize the sexes and pave the way for a totalitarian world government directed by the UN. For many of these women, IWY was an eschatological battle between the forces of Light and Darkness. As a result, this confrontation was a religious one, but one set within two decades of anticommunist activism that had long understood the UN to be bent on "a gradual approach to world government."[5] Building on the work of previous grassroots anticommunist women, like the Minute Women, right-wing Hoosiers imparted a sharp anti-internationalism to their antifeminism, and anticommunist ideology prompted them to understand IWY as the fulcrum of a conspiracy decades in the making. Anticommunist rhetoric also had long associated sexual anxieties, particularly homosexuality, with political threats and domestic subversion, and IWY cemented the connection between feminism, lesbianism, and totalitarianism for many. Although much of the anticommunist and anti-internationalism sentiment was downplayed at the Pro-Family Rally in Houston organized by Phyllis Schlafly and her STOP ERA organization as a way to present a favorable image to the press, a close examination of the grassroots women who came to the Indiana IWY conference reveals a larger world of international conspiracy than expressed by national conservative leaders at the time. The IWY platform calling for the global and national extension of women's rights and demands for homosexual rights confirmed for many antifeminists that something more was afoot than just a movement for women's equality. This is not to say that all or even most antifeminists who attended the Pro-Family Rally or any IWY event were one-world conspiracists. Yet to ignore the anti-internationalism that motivated part of the antifeminist movement prevents a full understanding of a turning point in the history of feminism as it entered the conservative decade of the 1980s.

Although the IWY was a "watershed event" for the second-wave feminist and conservative movements of the late twentieth century, historians have only lately begun to understand the conference's legacy and meaning. Historians Marjorie Spruill and Martha Sonntag Bradley have pioneered studies of the conference and describe the IWY national conference held in Houston in November 1977 as the decade's political tipping point, marking a high point for feminists and an insurgence of antifeminist right-wing activism.[6] While feminist leaders successfully passed all major aspects of their agenda, conservative leaders and delegates (who accounted for 20 percent of state delegations) also boasted a victory. By making their presence known throughout the affair and staging a wildly successful alternative, the Pro-Family Rally, which attracted over fifteen thousand participants, conservative women effectively stole the spotlight. Spruill argues that the Houston conference signaled a "right turn" in American politics and marked the beginning of a national conservative ascendancy.[7]

The UN designated 1975 International Women's Year and called upon the international community to improve the status of women. At the first international conference, held over the summer of 1975 in Mexico City, delegates crafted the "World Plan of Action for the Implementation of the Objectives of the International Women's Year" and related resolutions, which called for women's participation in creating and developing policy and for women to be integrated into the political systems under which they lived.[8] But as historian Judith P. Zinsser argues, "the Plan" ultimately left women in "passive roles" by prioritizing the transformation of economies over the goal of making women equal participants and "active agents" in society.[9] IWY received bipartisan support domestically, as US presidents Richard Nixon, Gerald Ford, and Jimmy Carter demonstrated their commitment to the celebration. In January 1975, through Executive Order 11832, President Ford appointed a thirty-five-member national commission to create "an agenda for the future." President Carter later expanded that commission to include forty-five members headed by Bella Abzug.[10] Not to be outdone, Congress responded with support of its own. Public Law 94-167, passed in December 1975, called on the national commission that Ford had created to organize and convene a national conference, preceded by state conferences, to broadly "recognize the contributions of women [and] set goals for the elimination of all barriers to . . . equal participation," as well as recognize women's contributions to strengthening world peace.[11] Congress appropriated $5 million for the project and set a deadline of March 1978 for the final report. In 1976 the national commission published the 394-page report *". . . To Form a More Perfect Union . . .": Justice for American Women* to serve as an agenda for state conferences. The national commission created the report to guide the work of state coordinating committees and included potential themes such as employment, health, childcare, rape laws, female offenders, legal status of homemakers, and international interdependence; in addition, it provided helpful bibliographies and suggested possible films and speakers state committees might utilize. Although the report included resolutions, such as the ERA, that far exceeded the modest demands of the "World Plan of Action," Sonntag Bradley explains that the national commission believed the agenda reflected a "national consensus on the most urgent items facing women during the 1970s."[12] State coordinating committees, however, were ultimately responsible for the planning, staging, and content of conferences, and all state conferences had in place procedures to accept resolutions from the floor.[13]

In March 1977 the State Department confirmed sixty-three appointments to the Indiana IWY coordinating committee.[14] Chosen from over fifteen hundred applications, the members of the Indiana coordinating committee, headed by Frances Dodson Rhome, affirmative action officer for Indiana University, represented a spectrum of women's politics and organizations, but absent were any specifically anti-ERA, antifeminist women's representatives.[15] Late notice from the national commission that Indiana had to have state IWY celebrations completed by 10 July 1977 left the coordinating committee little more than four months to plan and execute the regional meetings, as well as the state conference. Undeterred, members of the coordinating committee and their army of volunteers announced their effort to make the state conference, a true "coming together," the beginning of "a more visionary state community in which loving and amenable understanding of our various differences erase conflict, hatred, and alienation."[16] They would be sorely disappointed.

Nationally, anti-ERA activists and Phyllis Schlafly supporters formed the Citizens' Review Committee for International Women's Year (CRC), a coalition that united a number of conservative organizations, most often drawing on STOP ERA, the Eagle Forum, and the John Birch Society, but the specific makeup of the coalition differed from state to state.[17] The national CRC advisory board included state leaders of STOP ERA, such as Elaine Donnelly of Michigan and Rosemary Thomson of Illinois, along with Nellie Gray, president of March for Life. While the majority of state IWY conferences resulted in delegations and resolutions that supported the national agenda, the CRC racked up an impressive showing at Houston—eleven states sent a majority antifeminist delegation, and 20 percent of national delegates reported opposing the ERA.[18] Indiana antifeminists in the CRC proved particularly successful at organizing, and they formed a coalition to protest IWY using elements of the world government conspiracy, which had deep roots. In May STOP ERA reported that representatives from various conservative groups were working to form an Indiana Citizens' Review Committee.[19] "Non-feminists" needed to speak out, said STOP ERA literature, and coordinate their activities to "neutralize the women's lib 'propaganda' which will surely bombard us before, after and during the Indiana Conference."[20]

STOP ERA reported that representatives from various antifeminist groups were working to form an Indiana Citizens' Review Committee in May 1977.[21] Fundamentalist church groups formed a core of support in states where antifeminist conservatives dominated state meetings.[22] Diane Edmondson, CRC chairman in Oklahoma, mobilized scores of church groups ahead of the Oklahoma conference and spearheaded a winning strategy that CRC leaders effectively copied in subsequent meetings throughout the country. Edmondson recorded an appeal on a cassette tape that circulated in Oklahoma. The tape alerted churches of IWY intentions and encouraged attendance, a tactic that antifeminists in other states borrowed and used in their own efforts.[23] Before the Oklahoma conference, Ohio and Missouri had elected anti–"World Plan" delegates, but with the winning Oklahoma strategy the CRC piled up victories.[24] Throughout the summer of 1977, CRC activists contacted church leaders, "right to life" organizations, and friends in the anti-ERA network. Much credit for the success of the Indiana CRC, however, must go to evangelical and fundamentalist churches, which provided crucial aid at the state meeting.[25] Beulah Coughenour noted, "We bussed in, we alerted all the people we had contacts with throughout the state, which we had because of ERA, and a lot of them were in churches."[26]

Like the coordinating committee, many leaders in the Indiana CRC (who later became Indiana delegates to the national conference) had vast experience in women's organizations and partisan politics; however, IWY also excited new recruits to antifeminist politics. Leaders in the anti-ERA campaign such as Evelyn Pitschke, Beulah Coughenour, and Joan Gubbins marshaled antifeminist support in state and local government. Nonetheless, it was Kathryn Nikou, a senior student at Indiana University–Indianapolis, who became the chairperson of the Indiana CRC. Although she lacked organizational or leadership experience, Nikou proved a skilled public speaker, and as a former Miss Indianapolis, she had undeniable poise and charm.[27] Raised in South Bend, Indiana, she attended Butler University before Indiana University, where she majored in music. While at Butler, she wrote a number of editorials against the ERA and feminism, "rabble rousing" generally, as she described it.[28]

Nikou well represents the 35 percent of women at the state conference who listed their occupation as homemaker and claimed few political or organizational affiliations.[29] A survey of IWY participants revealed that 12 percent of respondents belonged to Pro America, and 2 percent claimed membership in the Eagle Forum, while 36 percent marked no affiliation with any women's organization.[30] Partisan loyalties were evenly split, with Republicans and Democrats nearly tied at 24 and 26 percent, respectively, but again, the independents stood out with a little over 43 percent. These figures suggest that many of the women attending the meeting saw themselves as political outsiders, unaffiliated with and unrepresented by existing women's groups and political parties.[31] The convenience of regional and state meetings and the clear understanding that the conference was women's territory encouraged women, even those invested in notions of gender difference and separate spheres, to claim the event as theirs. Coughenour told STOP ERA members that the state IWY conference presented a "unique, important occasion" for conservative women to "speak up in defense of our own opinions and values."[32] In the process of planning coalitions, operating headquarters, and managing supporters, women became skilled political operatives, so much so that participation in IWY amounted to a "crash course" in the practicalities of political organization.[33] "We organized for that [IWY] probably more than anything we'd done," recalled Coughenour.[34] The mass mobilization of conservative and right-wing women proved to be the single greatest achievement of the CRC coalition and represents the most significant outcome of IWY in Indiana.

Indiana CRC efforts belied conservatives' claim that, in fact, they were not organizing ahead of the state meeting. In the lead-up to the state conference, the CRC, Pro America, and STOP ERA acknowledged alerting members to IWY and encouraging attendance but denied planning a coordinated response. "We're not planning anything like that," Nikou explained when asked whether Indiana women would follow the example of efforts in Michigan and Illinois, where conservatives disrupted meetings by walking out. "Nor are we mobilizing the anti-ERA or anti-feminist forces," Nikou claimed. Jean Harvey, president of Indiana Pro America, described her preparation efforts to the *Indianapolis Star* as limited to sending out one thousand fliers urging conference attendance. "We are encouraging people to attend the meeting," said Rolena Jackson of STOP ERA, but not to disrupt the state conference, because "our society is sick of violence and disruptive influences and it would only hurt our stand."[35] Spruill notes that the CRC utilized a "stealth approach" in states across the nation;

however, that theory overestimates the degree to which CRC leaders in Indiana knew of conservative support.[36] Although they worked tirelessly to galvanize women's groups and church members, antifeminist leaders genuinely appeared as surprised as others to see the turnout for the state conference. As Earl Powers, the minister of Grace Baptist Church in Darlington, explained to a reporter, his congregation learned of the conference only the night before, when state representative Donald Boys, a Republican from Greenwood, showed up at the church and urged attendance. "He's got hundreds here backing him," Powers boasted.[37] The strategy of the CRC coalition at the state meeting implied that they anticipated being a minority; from blocking tactics to the time-consuming affidavits they asked their voters to sign, it is clear they had not planned to dominate the state convention as they did.[38]

Hoosier conservatives and feminists alike connected the IWY conference to their previous battle over the ERA; however, feminist organizations like NOW did not respond quickly or warmly to the IWY movement. Feminist activists cheered the triumph of ERA, but with that victory they lost the issue that drew them together, and even then their cooperation often reflected more an awkward bargain than a shared perspective. ERA ratification had the ironic effect of fostering a burgeoning conservative movement while dividing feminists in NOW from women's rights activists like those in the League of Women's Voters and liberationists active in urban collectives such as Indianapolis Women's Liberation and Fort Wayne Liberationists.[39] Pro-ERA spokesperson Russell Lloyd begged proratification forces to attend the IWY state meeting and warned that any negative action taken there on the ERA would bolster rescission efforts. He also reminded supporters that it would be a "major embarrassment" to proratification legislators if the largest women's conference in the state's history voted against the ERA only months after the General Assembly approved it.[40]

Less than one month before the state conference, Indiana NOW alerted NOW members and friends to the growing threat posed by conservative activists and the likely IWY coup. With ERA Indiana gone, no other state coalition dedicated to women's rights existed to pull liberals together in its immediate wake, and this, in part, explains why feminist groups responded late to IWY.[41] Whether feminists assumed like-minded delegates and sympathetic proposals would carry the day or because they felt IWY was "too establishment oriented," Sharon Boothby, NOW state coordinator, acknowledged that feminists had been "somewhat apathetic" concerning IWY.[42] In her "State of the State" report at the NOW Great Lakes Regional Conference in April 1978, Sue Errington made clear that Indiana NOW chapters felt spurned by HERA and ERA Indiana, noting that despite NOW's prominent role in securing state ERA ratification, no one in NOW was appointed to the IWY state steering committee.[43] Errington explained that this was "another case of NOW being accepted when there's work to be done but left out when pay day came around." The state NOW also hinted at continuing frustration with HERA and ERA Indiana's dedication to the low-key strategy. Despite being left out of the planning of IWY, Errington reported: "As it turned out, we were better off because when it became obvious that someone had to organize feminists around the state to oppose the right wing coalition, we assumed that role and with no hassle from anyone. There was no one on the steering committee whose arm could be twisted into making our strategy more low key."[44] Since opposition plans amounted to an "antifeminist blitzkrieg," quick action had to be taken to prevent an entirely "right-wing, anti-rights" Indiana delegation. NOW led the effort to create the feminist coalition, but this time with a clear mission to avoid those who would entangle NOW in a low-key strategy.[45] After intercepting some of the opposition's mailings, Boothby described their degree of organization as "mind boggling." The contraband documents outlined "a sophisticated plan of action, with detailed instructions on appointing poll watchers, floor leaders, etc."[46] Belatedly, the Unity Coalition led by NOW sought to organize any and all "pro–women's rights groups and individuals" interested in attending the state conference. While Errington was pleased with the performance of the Unity Coalition, her report to NOW members concluded that the IWY ended in defeat: "Unfortunately for the state IWY, we didn't have the numbers to outvote the 100's of robots mustered by the right wing coalition."[47]

The two-day Indiana conference began Friday, 15 July 1977, with the workshops and elections scheduled for Saturday.[48] Preregistration a week before the conference numbered 1,537, but by the close of business on Saturday, coordinators counted 3,712 registered participants, amounting to almost 2,200 walk-ins, along with an unknown number of nonregistered observers.[49] While an overwhelming majority (86 percent) of participants were white, the actual number of whites in attendance was probably higher, since the largest reported nonwhite contingency was an apparent mistake or ruse. Almost 9 percent of IWY survey respondents claimed they were Native American—a significantly larger number than their percentage in the overall state population—representing either some confusion as to the meaning of the category or a symbolic statement of nativism.[50] The committee planned fifteen workshops with themes taken from those suggested in "*. . . To Form a More Perfect Union . . .*" Workshop attendance averaged nearly 220 per session, but some workshops proved more popular than others; with issues like abortion and reproductive rights on the agenda, the health workshop was the largest, accommodating nearly 600 people.[51] The Unity

Coalition proved true to its name, with no dissent reported within its ranks; that solidarity, however, yielded little success at the end of the day.[52] The state meeting officially concluded at eight o'clock, with no resolutions passed at the business session and the delegate vote count ongoing, but all indicators suggested that the state conference was a total victory for the CRC.

Nonregistered participants roamed the convention center throughout Saturday, setting a confrontational and hostile tone even before participants began deliberation of the agenda. Evangelist ministers George Smock and Max Lynch of the Terre Haute Temple added the most drama to the day, excoriating state convention planners for being "whores, prostitutes and lesbians" and encouraging participants to reject the wicked ways of liberationists.[53] The two wandered the front lawn of the center, as well as the escalators and hallways, and delivered classic political theater borrowed in part from the "generation of rebels" they despised, as one of the men illustrated his point of a world turned upside down by preaching while walking up the descending escalator and vice versa.[54] Reporter Jean Lamm of Indianapolis spoke for many when she said that the conference resembled nothing so much as a Fellini film.[55] Although Rhome complained about the ministers' disruptions and harassment to convention center security and the Indianapolis police force on the scene, it was to no avail; in fact, she noted that the response of male officers to her request could only be described as "openly belligerent."[56]

That conservative women seemed to be following male leaders "unquestioningly" proved particularly galling to Hoosier feminists.[57] Sonntag Bradley notes that Indiana and five other states included "men with walkie talkies" who monitored the conferences, and all six of those conferences saw the national resolutions fail.[58] According to *Indianapolis Star* reports, men made up roughly 10 to 12 percent of participants, and the official report of the coordinating committee put that number at 15 percent.[59] Possibly to demonstrate their commitment to patriarchy and the established gender order, conservative women chose men to marshal and lead antifeminist forces at the state meeting. In addition to Lynch and Smock, Greg Dixon, pastor of the Indianapolis Baptist Temple and later cofounder of the Moral Majority, led participants in workshops and added his substantial congregation's support to antifeminist efforts. Daniel Manion, lawyer and son of Clarence Manion, renowned conservative radio talk show host, acted as a CRC floor watcher in the business session.[60] Ruth Cartwright, columnist for the *Marion News Herald* and Indiana delegate to the Houston conference, noted in her feature that "downtrodden Hoosier housewives" saved the day, "with encouragement from their husbands."[61]

The shouting and name-calling within the workshops and hallways of the convention center deeply disappointed feminist participants, but it was the way that antifeminists appeared to follow orders that feminists found "terrifying." Jane Fribley attended the meeting with others from Church Women United and lamented that the historic conference, which "could have been the most constructive experience ever for women[,] was misused by the extreme right wing conservatives," many of whom admitted that "they did not know what the meeting was all about but they were voting as instructed."[62] Utah feminists noted the same trend among opponents who protested at the state meeting with signs that read "IWY Asked for Women: You Send Sheep."[63] This in part explains why years after the state meeting, Molly Rucker, a member of the Indiana coordinating committee, continued to be haunted by the experience. "No one can completely describe the intensity of the emotions that were felt during that brief period immediately before the Indiana meeting and certainly the mere recollection of those two days is extraordinarily painful," she explained.[64]

For the most part, the business session crowd was orderly, although one man was ruled out of order for breaking a microphone, and a minister disrupted the proceedings by loudly condemning "women who wear men's clothes."[65] The official IWY resolutions recommended in "*... To Form a More Perfect Union ...*" were defeated either in workshop or by vote in the business session.[66] With no resolutions passed, elected state delegates to the Houston meeting would create the slate of official Indiana resolutions.[67] At a press conference the following morning, Rhome announced the names of the thirty-two women selected as Indiana's official representatives. Only one, Sita Keith Miller of Anderson, secretary for the Indiana Women's Political Caucus, was not affiliated with the CRC. Indiana, along with ten other states, had elected a majority antifeminist delegation.[68] Rhome expressed the apprehension of many feminists, saying, "We don't know if these delegates will reflect accurately the interests of most women in Indiana."[69] Nikou triumphantly told the local media at a press conference held at the Indiana Right to Life office that "we are not surprised at the outcome, as we have always known that given the opportunity to speak, this is what would be heard." With militaristic rhetoric and an Agnewian sense of phrasing, she warned that her supporters would give any other "feminist fiascos financed by federal dollars" the same thrashing.[70] The CRC delivered a "Pearl Harbor to the feminist movement," proclaimed Nikou and promised to do it again if provoked.[71] In the aftermath of IWY, CRC leaders reveled in the victory and prepared for the national conference in November, but for most participants the state conference completed their IWY experience. Ruth Cartwright told readers the following day that the state conference vindicated "Hoosier pride and prestige." "Hoosier women," she explained, "came to their state capitol and turned chaos into beautiful order."[72]

Certainly part of the appeal of IWY to right-wing Hoosier women lay in its timing with ERA ratification. While the January 1977 success of the ERA fractured feminist alliances, it riled and rallied antiratification forces. By that summer, Cartwright explained in her call to action that conservatives needed to reassert control of the state: "OPPONENTS OF ERA HAVE THIS OPPORTUNITY TO STAND UP AND BE COUNTED. . . . YOU SHOULD GRAB THIS OPPORTUNITY TO REDEEM THE REPUTATION OF YOUR STATE."[73] Indiana CRC literature described the ERA as the IWY's "top priority," with the national commission spending much of the $5 million allotted by Congress to propagandize in the states for ERA ratification and other radical issues "designed to undermine the traditional American Family."[74] Pro America writers agreed, arguing that the IWY commission's "foremost goal" was ERA ratification, followed closely by government-funded abortion facilities and government-supported childcare centers.[75] STOP ERA devoted the entire May issue of the *Indiana STOP ERA Hotline* to plans for IWY and told readers, "If you have been wondering what YOU can do to stop E.R.A., this is where the action is."[76] The CRC used the ERA and social issues closely associated with the ERA like homosexuality and abortion to mobilize already active women, and while the ERA was an important part of anti-IWY rhetoric, it was only one facet of the women's larger critique. The remarkable response of right-wing women at state conferences reflected much more than their opposition to the ERA; instead, the ERA represented to them much more than legal equality between the sexes.

For right-wing women, IWY presented the perfect storm of right-wing fears; evils they imagined combining behind the ERA were proven active by IWY. First, IWY was initiated by the UN and thereby represented the power of that assembly to reach into state and local communities within the United States. One-world government under the direction of the UN appeared even closer because IWY directives were being voted on at the Indianapolis Convention Center. The very title of the IWY agenda that came out of the Mexico City conference, the "World Plan of Action," conjured images of a totalitarian government bent on global domination. Indiana CRC literature stated without equivocation that "the World Plan of Action is actually a blueprint for the United Nations to institute its One World Government."[77] Feminism represented the newest link in a long chain of ideologies and "isms" that promoted a collective consciousness, and their systematic solutions to group discrimination and social problems looked similar as well. At best, feminists were dupes of collectivist subversives; at worst, feminists were traitors in league with an internationalist conspiracy. The ERA excited this concern, but the IWY made this connection explicit. An anonymously penned CRC flyer circulated at the Indiana meeting linked the three this way: "The Equal Rights Amendment planners are not satisfied with just creating total government in the United States. They, in fact, have made it a part of the world plan for equal rights for women, through International Women's Year."[78] The exact nature of the connection between communism, feminism, IWY, and one-worldism differed, and the identities of the conspirators themselves were often vague, but the implication was clear: IWY promoted an internationalist perspective and global cooperation and therefore implicated feminists as one-worlders, possibly even traitors.

Spruill argues that the threat of "Godless Feminism" smoothly and easily replaced "Godless Communism," but feminism was only part of the new threat.[79] The real issue for Hoosier women was internationalism and collectivism. While this certainly represents right-wing attempts to paint liberals as communists, something the "respectable" or "responsible" Right tried to squelch, it also represents the real fear of women that their authority in their families and local communities would be lost in an increasingly global world.[80] The forces pushing globalization and androgyny were myriad and at times must have seemed an overwhelming opponent for right-wing women. Pro America's list of resolutions for 1977 called on women to fight public schools in their effort to push "unisex views" and "convert our children to the status of trained animals conditioned to serve the elite in a one-world socialist state," to be on guard against "subliminal techniques which are used to convey actions or messages beyond the threshold of normal awareness" in television programming, and to speak out against electronic fund transfers by their banking institutions, since they "would eliminate the check book and substitute for it a plastic card, carrying a number assigned to one owner only."[81]

In 1978 Rosemary Thomson, national leader of the CRC, published an account of her experience at the National Women's Conference in Houston entitled *The Price of LIBerty* through Creation House Press of Carol Stream, Illinois. Senator Jesse Helms wrote a foreword, and the book's cover included Schlafly's praise. Thomson argued that feminists were only the newest driving force behind evil in the world, but the ultimate goal was centuries old—feminists worked steadily and constantly to hasten the Second Coming.[82] Thomson connected feminism with Satan on a number of occasions, employing leading questions like "Where do IWY's sympathies lie? Is this philosophy the spirit of the antichrist? And is it moving the earth toward the prophesied One World Dictator? How far down the road of humanism will feminists take us under the guise of 'equal rights'?"[83] After describing a host of ills that ratification of the ERA would provoke, Thomson concluded, "Surely the stage may be set for an authoritarian dictator.... Could the rise of humanism, be the real identity clue [pointing toward the reign of Satan]—God discarded, man deified?"[84] The connections between the various "isms" of the twentieth century were so thoroughly familiar to right-wing women that Thomson saw little need to distinguish between them: "The entire global community has adopted the view that there is no living God; therefore, there are no absolutes, no right or wrong. Call it secular humanism, progressive education, behavioral science, socialism, internationalism, communism, liberalism or feminism—the aim is diabolically synonymous. No wonder Scripture teaches that Satan is the prince of the world. He is, indeed, alive and well on planet earth, urging its sisters to unite!"[85] For CRC activists, the IWY goals specifically and feminism generally subverted a traditional focus on woman's role as wife and mother and connected to a much more amorphous collection of fears expressed in the one-world conspiracy.

Androgyny and authoritarianism melded together as conservative women conceived a feminism directed by the UN. Explaining her interest in IWY, Maryanne Dolan told an interviewer, "I am very much afraid of big government.... I see a trend of even social welfare and things like that being taken out of the hands of individuals and becoming mass-produced, where we lose our identity."[86] Gaye Steele, who attended the IWY national conference in Houston, pleaded for the preservation of "the eternal difference between men and women" and asked, "in the name of God," that state legislators not force upon her "the tyranny of federal dictatorship."[87] Right-wing women likened the state's power to strip them of gender difference, which they believed the ERA and other IWY resolutions would achieve, to a world government's ability to strip them of nationality and even identity. This argument, which stressed gender difference and connected homogenized sex roles and the federal government, had been hinted at before in the struggle over the ERA, but in the debate over IWY, with its connection to the United Nations and globalism, it becomes prominent in the discourse of conservatives. Feminists took note. Toni Carabillo described an anti-ERA and anti-IWY pamphlet she encountered:

> The first part is of course concerned strictly with their arguments against the ERA—which we've all heard before. It was the second part that I found both startling and enlightening because of the way it links up consciousness-raising, NOW, the Commissions on the Status of Women, Socialism, Communism, Humanism and the whole Human Potential Movement into one giant "conspiracy." Over the years we've all had glimmerings of these perceptions from the "anti's"

> but I've never before seen it all laid out at one time, nor did I understand how they had made the ERA the focal point of all these fears.[88]

For some right-wing women, the IWY was proof of the one-world connections of feminism that many had long surmised.

At the state conference, Indiana women in Pro America drew heavily on the theory of "federal regionalism" in developing the connection between the growth of the federal government and a totalitarian world government. Federal regionalism holds that diverse forces seek to eliminate county and state governments by creating federal regions, complete with their own regional capitals, that, according to author and speaker Archibald Roberts, ultimately intended to "seize control of property and production facilities, change the form of government, and reduce Americans to the status of economic serfs on the land which once was theirs."[89] The Minute Women publicized the threat of federal regionalism to conservative women throughout the 1960s and early 1970s.[90] A 1963 national newsletter explained that "those of us who are cognizant of the long-range plans of the enemy to establish a socialist world government with all the rights of the people destroyed are alert to and interested in all the organizations that are constantly cropping up with the aim of creating regional unions."[91] Despite the myriad forms federal regionalism might take, Minute Women warned that ultimately it represented "clandestine UN power" to violate the "natural law of individual sovereignty belonging to citizens of each nation under God."[92] IWY proved that American feminists were agents and dupes of the power-hungry UN, but by the late 1970s that hardly qualified as a revelation to conservative women.

Building on the argument of the Minute Women and others, Pro America spearheaded the anti-internationalist campaign at the state meeting. Their literature outlined how the UN, through the IWY "World Plan of Action," intended to institute a "New International Economic Order" intent on restructuring the American system of federated government into new territorial regions, administered from Washington, DC.[93] With the closest (or geographically nearest) government to the people usurped, federal domination could easily morph into international domination, headed by the UN. The international interdependence motions submitted from the floor at the state conference explain how seamlessly the United States could move from federal usurpation of local and state sovereignty to global government. Motion 4 passed by the International Interdependence workshop argued:

> Whereas there is a form of government called Federal Regionalism structured alongside of our constitutional form of government, which is at the same time

> unconstitutional, and as it is, its ultimate goal will result in international interdependence, [and] [w]hereas this unconstitutional form of government called Federal Regionalism is socialistic and totalitarian in structure, and will destroy our constitutional free enterprise system, [and] [w]hereas the unconstitutional Federal Regional structure will serve as subregions in one world government under the United Nations; LET IT BE RESOLVED that any American citizen, be he man or woman, who knowingly works toward international interdependence be called a traitor to his country . . . and be treated as such according to the law of the land.[94]

The androgynizing effect of the ERA to eliminate sex difference coupled perfectly with the homogenizing effect of global government to obliterate local, state, and national sovereignty, and right-wing Hoosier women left no doubt where they stood on the issue. Quite simply, they called on Congress to preserve gender difference and "do away with the United Nations."[95]

Although they had been stripped of any specific reference to federal regionalism or the systematic plan of subregions, the international interdependence resolutions presented by anti-IWY delegates at the national conference in Houston demonstrated the influence of Hoosier conspiracists. In their minority report, "To Establish Justice," anti-IWY national delegates argued that "this World Plan of Action, among other untenable proposals, calls for the establishment of a New International Economic Order to create 'uniform' and balanced development of the international community to 'insure a more equitable distribution of income among all sectors of the population,' a system which could exist only under a totalitarian world government."[96] To counter this influence, conservative women called for "a return to the local level of government, which is most responsive to the needs of the people."[97] By ignoring the conspiratorial theory of federal regionalism, the national delegates' resolution held broader appeal; however, both sets of resolutions make explicit that the forces driving homogenization of gender and the state were linked.

Just as it had in the 1950s, the prospect of world government in the 1970s drew a heated response from millennial evangelicals. Ruth Schiller, a retired math teacher, explained to the Indiana coordinating committee that Satan, "the big liar," had many paths to one-worldism: "The Illuminati, communists, Bilderbergers, Trilateralists, [the] Council on Foreign Relations, Common Cause, etc." had "been duped into furthering his very subtle purposes." A global government controlled by the UN, which IWY hastened and symbolically represented, fit perfectly into a worldview that anticipated global domination by the Antichrist. Schiller, like other millenarians, was not without hope that human beings could affect the course of world events, and she argued that it was women who would make the difference.[98] Because "knowledgeable women can be very effective," she strongly encouraged the Indiana coordinating committee to get educated, especially since only fifty years remained before "complete take over."[99] Evelyn Pitschke also described IWY as a religious battle and reported that she and fellow delegates prepared by "having observed certain days of prayer and fasting."[100] This preparation was necessary because, as Lillian Steele explained, conservative women at Houston represented a "Christian minority" who "stood proudly for God" against the power of "ten thousand satanic spirits."[101] The "apocalyptic paradigms" of millennials contributed mightily to the urgency Hoosier women felt in responding to IWY, and through the mobilization of grassroots conservative networks, IWY further explains how an evangelical worldview became part of the political mainstream.[102]

The intersection of eschatology and the anticommunist fear of global government provoked an impressive showing among evangelicals at the state meeting. National planners agreed that fundamentalist and evangelical church groups formed core support in states where conservatives dominated state meetings, and Indiana coordinating committee members credited most of the two thousand walk-ins to church bus caravans.[103] Protestants made up nearly 83 percent of survey respondents at the state meeting, but of that group, 24 percent marked "Other" and wrote in "Born Again Christian" rather than lump themselves together with other Protestants.[104] Sociological studies on opponents of the ERA show a marked connection between antifeminism and religious fundamentalism, and Hoosier anti-IWY participants bear out that association.[105] Using Oklahoma CRC chairperson Diane Edmondson's technique of circulating cassette tapes that warned of the IWY threat to evangelical church networks, Kathryn Nikou obtained crucial support from conservative churches.[106] The bus caravans worked so well that Greg Dixon expanded the fleet to include over fifty buses by 1980, which he used to transport his congregation across the country to protest taxation of Christian schools, pornography, and abortion, beginning an era Dixon called "the decade of confrontation."[107] Using evangelical and fundamentalist churches as a recruiting ground became de rigueur for Republican hopefuls in the state, and religious conservatives represented a core of support that in 1980 helped Dan Quayle unseat US senator Birch Bayh, longtime spokesman and symbol of Indiana liberalism.[108] In her description of the political scene after IWY, Molly Rucker explained that right-wing women in Pro America and elsewhere had become "extremely active in the 'hate campaigns' which have gone on in Indiana in all of our elections since that time."[109]

It is important to remember that not all conservative women at the state or national conference agreed with the conspiratorial turn of some within their ranks. However, the rhetoric of some delegates and participants carried the seed of the older conspiratorial thinking promoted by Dorothy Frankson and Robert Welch and further demonstrates how women performed "bridge labor" in connecting the Right across generations.[110] Hoosier women aligned against IWY exemplify how a conspiratorial belief in world planners can live alongside a more mainstream critique of the growth of the federal government without dissonance breaking the movement. Furthermore, right-wing Hoosier women confirm that despite the efforts of William Buckley and others to police the Right and cull extremists from the ranks, the ideas forwarded by those discredited sources did not disappear; indeed, they continued to feed the larger conservative movement. Throughout the postwar era, conspiracy may have had particular appeal for women because it required some reading up on issues and administrative work in filing and keeping an organizational system to retrieve information, but it was work they could do in their homes and share with one another. It did not require resources or political power to enact, just women's "common sense" and collective experience as mothers and guardians of the home.

Conservative women believed that feminists were dangerous and capable of anything, including violence. The vote on the minority women's resolution in Houston was a powerful, poignant moment for feminists. A coalition of minority delegates, made up of African American, American Indian, Asian American, Pacific Islander, and Hispanic women, forged a substitute motion that met with overwhelming approval by the IWY body. The consensus generated an "emotional demonstration" that proved to Coretta Scott King that "when we [minority women] are divided, we can be conquered; when we are united, we can achieve. With this kind of unity, we cannot lose."[111] The minority resolution received even the unanimous approval of the conservative Utah delegation, members of which joined hands with black women of the Texas delegation to celebrate. The acceptance of the minority plank represented the high-water mark of cooperation at the conference and symbolized the camaraderie and spirit of inclusiveness that the event meant to inspire.

Within the Indiana delegation, most delegates abstained from the vote on the minority resolution, including Mattie Coney, one of the three Hoosier African American women to serve as delegates. Two of Indiana's white CRC delegates broke ranks and voted for the resolution, as did Sita Keith Miller, an African American delegate and the only non-CRC delegate in Indiana's delegation. Gertrude Dishman, however, voted with Indiana's other opposition delegates against the resolution. Because Dishman and Coney were black women, their actions surprised many. Coney defended her abstention, saying, "All of the things included in the minority women's report are needed for all women." Exasperated, she declared, "I am so sick of separate identities that I could cry."[112] Dishman's vote against the measure provoked an even more heated response. She reported that a stranger hollered at her to "act like" she was black, and several people threatened to "cut [her] to pieces."[113] Dishman left the conference unharmed, but Indiana delegates reported that menacing women repeatedly threatened her.[114] Even after returning to her Anderson, Indiana, home, Dishman continued to fear for her safety and called on the local police force to provide security around her house.[115] If Dishman's and Coney's conservatism surprised their Houston colleagues, it was not without precedent. Dishman and Coney, like JBS speaker Julia Brown, challenged the unity of identity politics just as such politics were becoming increasingly important on the national scene; as a result, they were seen by some as betrayers of their race and gender.[116]

IWY politics got uglier still after the national women's conference in Houston ended. Upon returning to Indiana, state delegates, led by Gubbins, opened the sexually explicit display in the rotunda of the statehouse that caused a local sensation. Hoosier feminists, long committed to a low-key approach that sought to deny the radical implications of feminism, were left with little recourse: to affirm the connection between lesbianism and feminism would be to acknowledge that feminist initiatives were more than "simple justice" and that within feminism there existed a profoundly radical critique of the social and political status quo and public institutions. Both sides accused the other of radicalism in a way that clearly meant that being "radical" was wrong, but it would seem that the Left alone used the charge of radicalism against allies—all part of HERA's and ERAIndiana's commitment to the low-key strategy.

The pointed barbs, intemperate language, and repeated attempts to portray feminists as lesbians provide further evidence that right-wing women often perform the "dirty work" of politics, allowing male conservatives to appear moderate by comparison.[117] Despite their reliance on separate-sphere notions of female dependency and male protection, right-wing women of the late twentieth century considered themselves warriors, not angels, as they entered the political field. Others could develop the New Right's positive image; right-wing Hoosier women considered their opponents to be "snakes in a pit," and their rhetoric reflected that belief.[118] The vitriol of conservative women's rhetoric astounded feminists, but it fits within the larger context of literature on conspiracism and countersubversion. Melissa Estes Blair notes that in cities across the country feminists used the language of emotion to describe the argument of conservative women.[119] Juxtaposing the "emotional" response of conservatives, they positioned their arguments as fact based and nonpartisan.[120] Another explanation for the "emotion" of conservative women was that they believed feminists to be not only different and wrong but evil. Robert Alan Goldberg explains in *Enemies Within: The Culture of Conspiracy in Modern America* that "conspiracism demonizes opponents and makes struggle internecine."[121] Michael Barkun agrees that in the polarized world of conspiracy believers, their opponents are not "merely misguided" but "thought to be at best the conspirators' dupes and at worst their accomplices. Hence the alternative reality sees itself as a fighting faith that must obliterate its adversaries."[122] Theda Skocpol and Vanessa Williamson explain a similar tendency in the treatment of in-group and out-group persons among right-wing women today. Of right-wing women in the twenty-first century, they noted:

> Another paradox of Tea Party citizenship is the sharp bifurcation between generous, tolerant interaction within the group, and an almost total lack of empathy or sympathy for fellow Americans beyond the group. As we have commented, many local Tea Parties include both social conservatives, who feel strongly about traditional moral questions, and libertarians, many who prefer to keep government and politics out of individual moral choices. That is quite a split, but in practice Tea Partiers of these different persuasions make a strong effort to understand one another and work together. For both politically pragmatic reasons and out of genuine social affection for other people in their group, they work to bridge and elide and accommodate the different outlooks within the Tea Party. We suspect that Tea Party participants usually find it difficult to stereotype and reject people they actually deal with face to face. That can also explain why Tea Partiers who dealt with us in person were invariably polite. . . . But Tea Partiers, as we have seen, freely wield demonizing stereotypes about fellow Americans in different age groups and life circumstances.[123]

Conspiracy theories give "hope, unity, and purpose in a world that often seems beyond the reach of the powerless," writes Goldberg, but they also inject anger, vitriol, and distrust into the political discourse, and that can effectively ruin any chance for cooperation and compromise.[124]

While both right-wing and left-wing women considered "the other" to be engaged in "dirty tricks," conservative women alone considered their feminist opponents evil, satanic, unpatriotic, and traitorous. The language they employed demonstrates this, and the association of feminism with sin and subversion carried with it permission to use rough treatment. Kathleen M. Fallon and Julie Moreau explain that the "process of Othering" creates social boundaries between groups, which, combined with "anti-Other" discourse to incite fear and the valorization of motherhood and the heteronormative family, constitutes the best definition of what it means to be a right-wing woman in a global context.[125] Around the world, the postwar human rights movement stigmatized racist and anti-Semitic rhetoric, but right-wing American women found the Other in their political rivals—in that sense, their heated language fits within a larger pattern of right-wing demonization of the Other, only their Other was no longer a racial or ethnic minority but a political and ideological adversary. The conspiratorial and satanic nature of their foe made anything but the most strenuous effort and bold denunciation an abdication of their responsibility to their families and country. At the national conference in Houston, grassroots Hoosier women sent "a message to the world," Linda Steele explained, and she promised they would return to their hometowns to "carry on the fight FOR A NATION UNDER GOD."[126] Rules of etiquette and common civility did not apply to enemies of the state and God, proving that the nicety, conformity, and politeness that dominate midwestern culture have limits. Conservative women desired to "wake up" the rest of the country to the threat posed by feminism. That their language alarmed their audience was exactly the point.

How anti-internationalism affected conservative women's ability to connect with other right-wing women across geopolitical borders into the twenty-first century continues to be a question for scholars. Margaret Power investigates how Phyllis Schlafly drew on the experience of Brazilian and Chilean women in Eagle Forum literature to demonstrate to American women that it was possible to stop communist subversion and infiltration.[127] But Jill A. Irvine, in her study of Concerned Women for America (CWA)—itself a conservative women's organization born out of the Houston IWY conference experience and led by Beverly LaHaye, activist and wife of evangelist and author Tim LaHaye—focuses on the difficulty organizations rooted in anti-internationalism, opposition to the United Nations, and hostility to a perceived one-world order have in participating in globalized efforts, especially advocacy within the UN.[128] New leadership in the CWA—possessed of a new mantra: "The United Nations is worth fixing"—led efforts to get official NGO status for the CWA. Today the CWA actively lobbies on behalf of women around the world *within* the UN. Irvine is skeptical, however, about the degree to which conservative women within the United States desire to reach out to women in other countries to support transnational conservatism or the degree to which the enthusiasm of CWA leaders for cooperation with the UN is mirrored at the grassroots level.[129] Hoosier women prove that anti-internationalism rooted in fear of one-worldism capably supported antifeminism and a strident nationalism, but anti-internationalism seems to have difficulty maintaining alliance or connection across geopolitical borders, even regarding common concerns like human trafficking.

The only shared result feminist and conservative women experienced in response to IWY was a heightened political and group consciousness, in part because they were politicizing one another in their struggle over the meaning of gender equality.[130] As second-wave feminists reached for equality they unintentionally sparked the consciousness of their conservative counterparts and prompted a new era of activism for many. Gaye Steele, eighteen years old in the summer of 1977, accompanied her mother to the Houston conference and upon returning to Indiana circulated a letter to friends that spoke to her newfound political commitment. "We cannot just stay in our own world and ignore this ugliness," she explained of feminist plans. Speaking particularly to people her age, she exhorted, "It's our very lives we're talking about, and it is time to put a stop to this madness once and for all."[131] Evelyn Pitschke seconded that sentiment, arguing that the greatest achievement of IWY was the heightened political consciousness of conservative women: "When all is said and done, in my opinion, the greatest result of the IWY Conference is the burgeoning awareness of American women that they must become involved in the mainstream of public life. . . . We must be alert and aware of forces that seek to destroy personal initiative, capitalism and freedom."[132] Rebecca Klatch agrees that the IWY was the beginning of the "profamily" movement of the 1980s that solidified with President Carter's White House Conference on Families in 1980. Schlafly called IWY the "boot camp" conservative women needed: "Now we're ready for the offensive in the battle for our families and our faith."[133] Indiana's IWY delegates were charged by the experience; the series of IWY conferences made them experts on the feminist totalitarian threat, and they felt their authority immediately. "We were ambassadors to Hell," they explained in a letter to state legislators, "and we can tell Hoosiers what Hell is like." "We have all worried about 'Big Brother,'" the letter concluded. "'Big Sister' would be much, much worse!"[134]

Among feminist ranks, too, IWY transformed women's understanding of their political responsibilities, although not always in a positive direction. By the fall of 1977 it was clear to Rhome that "we must face the painful fact that inadvertently we provided the staging area for ultra-conservative solidification." She urged liberal and feminist women to remain active, "regardless of which state organizations feminists chose to support," or face being "flattened by the mammoth conservative steamroller."[135] Virginia Dill McCarty and Donna Bucove tried to buoy the spirits of conference planners by pointing out that the rational and orderly presentation of material at the conference provided conservatives with "a more accurate picture about how contemporary women in leadership behave." They clung to the idea that by representing feminists as competent, dispassionate professionals, they had altered "the stereotype image they carry of 'libbers,' even if it's only at the subconscious level."[136] But many feminists only wanted to put activism behind them. In the weeks following the state conference, Barbara Zimmer expressed the feelings of many when she wrote, "I had anticipated facilitating a positive movement," but "it has been a dreadful experience and promises to get worse."[137] Hoosier feminists struggled to find their footing as the state and nation entered the conservative decade of the 1980s.[138]

Conservative Hoosier women pursued their political interests into the next decade and beyond. President Ronald Reagan appointed Joan Gubbins to the Intergovernmental Advisory Council on Education, and she continued to be active in the field of education and school politics into the 1990s.[139] She started her own nonprofit organization, Our Kids, Inc., which aimed to raise educational standards in Indiana schools and explain the danger of contemporary educational policy to the uninformed and misinformed. In the eighties, Beulah Coughenour spearheaded a citywide obscenity law that defined pornography as "the sexually explicit subordination of women" and therefore subject to regulation by the Indianapolis Human Relations Commission. The initiative was based on a similar law introduced in Minneapolis and sponsored by well-known feminists Catharine MacKinnon and Andrea Dworkin.[140] Federal courts later denounced the law as "unconstitutionally vague," but cooperation on the issue makes clear that Coughenour was willing to work with feminists when their interests aligned.[141] Looking back on her work and that of other conservatives since the 1970s, Coughenour made clear that the ERA mobilized right-wing women, and "Phyllis trained the nation."[142]

What happened in Indiana happened elsewhere. The "culture wars" of the 1980s were fought throughout the country, and the divide between feminists and conservative women over the meaning of feminism and gender equality continues into the twenty-first century, as does the question of strategy. Conspiratorial understanding of feminist initiatives as part of a larger one-world threat did not disappear in later decades but became part of the New World Order conspiracy that was popular in mainstream culture by the close of the century. The fall of the USSR did not end anticommunist efforts, because since at least the 1950s many conservatives had pivoted to the related threat of one-worldism. In 1991 television evangelist Pat Robertson prefaced his book *The New World Order* by noting that the dissolution of the USSR and the "lightning-fast" Persian Gulf War only confirmed that Americans lived in a "new world," one filled with uncertainty and doubt. Who, he asked, was "molding and shaping United States public policy toward—world government—from generation to successive generation?"[143] Robertson concluded that whether it was the Illuminati, New Age religion, international bankers, global corporations, or Old World aristocrats, there was an "invisible cord" that connected world history and events:

> There are many suspects [in the New World Order conspiracy], but little consensus. *Whichever is correct*, it is my firm belief that the events of public policy are not the accidents and coincidences we are generally led to believe. They are planned. Further, I do not believe that normal men and women, if left to themselves, would spend a lifetime to form the world into a unified whole in order to control it after it had been so unified. No, impulses of that sort do not spring from the human heart, or for that matter from God's heart. They spring, instead, from the depth of something that is evil.[144]

The New World Order was a *New York Times* best seller and a sensation—and not only because of Robertson's use of anti-Semitic sources.[145] While the publication of the book may have signaled broader accessibility and acceptability of one-worldism, by the 1990s the idea was "old news" to the grassroots Right.[146] Robertson capitalized on ideas created and polished by grassroots men and women throughout the postwar era, but conservative women had taken responsibility for battling "Big Sister" over a decade before.

"How did the political fringe become the mainstream?" Donald Critchlow and Nancy MacLean ask in their 2009 reader on the postwar conservative movement.[147] The politics of ERA and IWY help explain how that transformation occurred. Blending anticommunist concern over one-world government with the social and sexual dangers of androgyny promised by IWY initiatives like the ERA, right-wing women articulated a worldview that directly challenged feminists' call for women's equality and global cooperation. When in May 1977 President Carter told an audience at the University of Notre Dame that America needed to conquer its "inordinate fear of communism," he could not have been more out of sync with right-wing Hoosier women.[148] Not only did they absolutely believe in the global threat of communism, but that threat was connected to the homogenizing ideologies of feminism, internationalism, and homosexuality—a multifaceted, decades-old menace that IWY embodied and that only they seemed to understand or be prepared to fight.

Epilogue

> Now it's election time. Now it's in the hands of voters. And I could not be more gratified that the Midwestern good judgement, common sense of Hoosiers is going to decide the direction of this entire country, going to decide what path the Republican party goes down, what path the nation goes down. And it's now in the hands of the people of Indiana.
>
> —Senator Ted Cruz on 3 May 2016, the day of the Republican primary vote in Indiana[1]

EVEN FOR A RESEARCHER of conspiracy theory, the 2016 presidential cycle was remarkable to watch. The Republican primary and general election of 2016 saw conspiracy theory explode onto the national scene. No longer part of the undercurrent of American politics, conspiracy theory came into the mainstream with the candidacy of Donald Trump. Indiana proved to be an important battleground over the direction of the Republican Party as two candidates emerged who represented dominant threads of grassroots Right politics in the state: Moral Majority, evangelical Christian conservatism as represented by Ted Cruz and the "outsider" and conspiracist Donald Trump. Both campaigned hard ahead of the Indiana primary because everyone considered Indiana a make-or-break state for the Republican presidential hopeful.[2] By May 2016 Ted Cruz was the choice of evangelical leaders of the religious Right, and he had the endorsement of Indiana governor and social conservative Mike Pence.[3] Cruz clearly knew evangelicals would be important to his campaign, and by kicking off his run at Jerry Falwell's Liberty University, he signaled to them from the very beginning that he was their candidate. But Trump had an allure all his own. Rafael Cruz, Ted Cruz's father, had been in Indiana for days prior to the primary, meeting with ministers and asking that "every member of the body of Christ vote according to the word of God" by voting for his son, Ted Cruz. When *Fox & Friends* hosts asked Trump to respond to that request, Trump suggested that Rafael Cruz was connected to the Kennedy assassination. In a style recommended by Robert Welch, where conspiracists only ask questions and make vague suggestions—not specific or direct accusations—Trump asserted: "His father [Rafael Cruz] was with Lee Harvey Oswald prior to Oswald's being shot, you know. I mean the whole thing is ridiculous. What is this? Right? Prior to his being shot. And nobody even brings it up. I mean, they don't even talk about that. That was reported [by the *National Enquirer*]. And nobody talks about it. . . . But I think that it is horrible. It is absolutely horrible."[4] In that moment, Trump connected his political rival to one of the major conspiracist events of the twentieth century—the assassination of Kennedy—and implied that Cruz's father was somehow involved. Senator Lindsey Graham of South Carolina responded quickly, tweeting: "Any doubt left Trump is completely unhinged? His assertion that Ted Cruz's father was associated with Lee Harvey Oswald should remove ALL doubt."[5] Rush Limbaugh called Trump's idea "absurd," and Mark Salter, an advisor of John McCain in his 2008 run for the presidency, tweeted that he would not support for president "a guy who reads the National Enquirer and thinks it's on the level," finishing with the feminist Hillary Clinton slogan "I'm with her."[6] But Trump won the Indiana Republican primary in a landslide, beating Cruz by sixteen percentage points.[7] In the general election, Trump won Indiana by 18 percent, securing Indiana's title as "the reddest" midwestern state.[8] When Bill O'Reilly was asked whether he believed that Trump believed that Rafael Cruz played a role in the Kennedy assassination, O'Reilly flatly said "No." "But I believe that he puts that out there just to create mayhem," he explained, "and creating mayhem has won the election for him."[9] From leading the birther movement to calling climate change a hoax perpetrated by the Chinese, Trump's use of conspiracy theory—and his ability to simultaneously secure the Republican presidential nomination and the White House—made him what Alex Jones described as a "George Washington level" leader of the Right.[10]

Reince Priebus, chairman of the Republican National Committee, defended Trump in the days that followed the Indiana primary, noting Trump's ambiguity in making the allegation. Trump had not explicitly said that Rafael Cruz was part of the Kennedy assassination, Priebus explained: "I don't think he was ever saying this was some sort of factual piece of information. . . . It was something he referred to, he's talked about it and gotten off of it. As far as I'm concerned, we can move on."[11] Trump had "a right to talk about whatever he wants," Priebus asserted.[12] This capitulation to Trump's use of conspiracy set the tenor for the rest of the Republican primary as the party moved to align itself with the Trump campaign. Following the Indiana results, Priebus named Trump the "presumptive GOP nominee," and Priebus later accepted the position of chief of staff in the Trump administration.[13] Indiana governor Mike Pence switched allegiance from Cruz to Trump and became Trump's running mate, and even Ted Cruz eventually endorsed Trump.

From hiring Stephen Bannon of Breitbart News to implying that President Barack Obama was complicit in the Orlando shootings, Trump proved a natural conspiracist. In October 2016 a number of women came forward charging Trump with sexual misconduct that ranged from lewdness to sexual assault, speaking to a long personal history of such actions.[14] With his campaign on the line, Trump made extensive use of conspiracy to explain the situation. In a speech in West Palm Beach, Florida, he charged that the allegations against him were evidence of his mistreatment at the hands of global conspirators who were bent on shipping American jobs overseas.[15] "The Washington establishment, and the financial and media corporations that fund it, exist for only one reason, to protect and enrich itself," he explained, and "the establishment has trillions of dollars at stake in this election."[16] His candidacy menaced the global power elite, and they were responsible for the sexual assault allegations:

> It is a global power structure that is responsible for the economic decisions that have robbed our working class, stripped our country of its wealth and put the money in the pockets of a handful of large corporations and political entities. Just look at what the corrupt establishment has done to our cities like Detroit, Flint, Michigan and rural towns in Pennsylvania, Ohio, North Carolina, and all cross our country. Take a look at what is going on. They've stripped away the towns bare and raided the wealth for themselves and taken our jobs away, out of our country, never to return unless I'm elected president.[17]

Ultimately, who was responsible for this conspiracy against American workers and himself? "The Clinton machine is at the center of this power structure," Trump revealed. His proof was the WikiLeaks documents, which were evidence, according to Trump, that "Hillary Clinton meets in secret with international banks to plot the destruction of U.S. sovereignty in order to enrich these global financial powers, her special interest friends, and her donors."[18] He continued the argument to audiences in Charlotte and Greensboro, North Carolina.[19] Melania Trump supported his explanation in a *CNN* interview, saying that it was the Left, left-wing media, Hillary Clinton, female reporters, and the female victims of Trump who planned and organized the sexual assault charges against her husband—all to ruin his campaign.[20]

The reasons for Trump's appeal are still being sorted out, but there is no doubt that he made use of conspiracy belief to explain world events, saying in public and on Twitter what many at the grassroots level had been saying to one another for decades. And white women supported him—53 percent of white women voted for Trump, in keeping with the modern trend of white women voting for Republicans.[21] Republican women might not have liked the sexism of the Trump campaign, but that did not keep them from voting for him, proving that party loyalty, not gender, factors large in women's voting decisions.[22] That a conspiracy of the global elite was headed by Hillary Clinton, a feminist, and that global elites used the American women's movement and the election of the first female president as a cover for their nefarious intentions would have come as no surprise to many conservative Hoosier women who had long battled "Big Sister."

For Democrats, too, the 2016 primary cycle raised the question of how to handle challengers from the wings as Bernie Sanders, Vermont senator and self-described democratic socialist, racked up a series of state victories and threatened to win the nomination over Hillary Clinton and against the wishes of at least some officials in the Democratic National Committee (DNC).[23] In 2016, as in the 1970s, while Republicans by and large looked for ways to accommodate the Far Right, Democrats responded coldly and slowly to the Left, at least within the DNC. Democratic support had solidified around Clinton by the time of the general election, and Democrats and feminists hoped to secure the first female presidency and stop the Trump movement simultaneously. The failure of Clinton's bid and the election of Trump was heartbreaking, particularly for feminists; women's colleges around the country were in mourning.[24] Will the Women's March on Washington, DC, and related marches and protests around the country set to begin the following day be one-day affairs or Day One of a new movement? And what strategies should Democrats and feminists deploy? The question Hoosier feminists faced in the 1970s exists now for Democrats and feminists nationally as they search for a strategy that can successfully challenge a conspiracy theorist and populist conspiracism. Future success hinges on this question because the new political reality will include conspiracy theory. The longevity and flexibility of conspiracy theories indicate that they do not seem to die so much as morph, and belief is intensifying.

It is impossible to say where these trends will lead, but we have entered a political era in which what counts as a "fact" is widely debated. In the Winter 2015 *Intelligence Report* titled "Margins to the Mainstream," the Southern Poverty Law Center's Mark Potok described the country as "drowning in an even larger ocean of conspiracy theories now than in decades or centuries past." Especially concerning to him were the number of politicians, like Donald Trump, who openly endorsed and supported conspiracist understanding of the world.[25] Even Alex Jones, one of the most important voices of conspiracy theory in America today, was surprised by how close Trump hewed to his line, saying on his show on 11 August 2016: "I'll tell you it is surreal to talk about issues here on air and then word-for-word hear Trump say it two days later. It is amazing. And it just shows how dialed-in this guy is and that's why they're so scared of him."[26] Public polling supports such assessments. A 2013 telephone poll conducted by Public Policy Polling revealed that 28 percent of voters believed that "a secretive power elite with a globalist agenda is conspiring to eventually rule the world through an authoritarian world government, or New World Order." Republicans and independents (at 34 and 35 percent, respectively) believed that particular conspiracy (more than Democrats at 15 percent). Intense partisan divides were evident, too, in the question about whether global warming was a hoax (58 percent of Republicans agreed, while 77 percent of Democrats disagreed) and about whether President Barack Obama was the Anti-Christ (20 percent of Republican voters said yes, as did 13 percent of the independents, but only 6 percent of Democrats). On questions like "Do you believe the moon landing was faked, or not?," however, partisan divides disappeared (with Democrats at 6 percent and Republicans at 5 percent).[27] J. Eric Oliver and Thomas Wood concluded in 2014 that conspiracy beliefs are "quite commonplace" and may constitute an "alternative mechanism" to political ideology or race in determining how Americans understand politics.[28] The advent of the internet seems to have increased the proliferation of conspiracy belief exponentially. The explosion of online messages and memes is "*prima facie* evidence of a larger conspiracy," according to the John Birch Society.[29] Michael Barkun warns that complicity on the part of media outlets and government authorities has made conspiracism mainstream and has ruined people's trust in government and public institutions, and the situation is dire: "Without a new awareness of its character and quick intervention, countersubversion may overcome the body politic."[30]

It has been a long road to today's political reality; the 2016 election did not come out of nowhere. The extent to which Donald Trump believes that he is a warrior in the battle against one-worldism and globalists is questionable, but at the very least his election demonstrates the power of conspiracy narratives to shape American politics in the twenty-first century. The politics that motivated the Minute Women, Pro America, and the JBS continue to find resonance. "Communist" as a charge or accusation has died out because the threat posed by global communist domination fails to speak to a shared, common anxiety. But for many right-wing women it was only ever part of an idea about collectivism, statism, and globalism. Since the collectivist impulse or conspiracy could morph into any political idea or movement that its leaders sensed might be useful, anticommunism itself needed to be fluid and capable of transitioning to new threats. Given its highly adaptable nature, defining collectivism or setting down exact parameters for what was collectivist was entirely wrongheaded—just as soon as activists explained it as one thing, it might change direction. From communism to civil rights agitation to feminism, collectivism proved to them to be capable of tireless adaptation to the times. Regardless of the mechanism, any movement that smacks of "social planning"—especially any initiatives associated with the United Nations and global cooperation—continues to conjure the same suspicions that it did decades ago. In December 2016 Sarah Palin described her feelings on national sovereignty movements like the Brexit vote to *Breitbart News Daily*, saying, "This is such an encouraging time, where it's not just us, but those across the pond, too, are understanding that their nation's sovereignty and security are on the line here, with ties that bind us to interests that really don't further our agendas." In language almost identical to the old JBS slogan, Palin called for "the U.S. to get the heck out of the UN and get the UN out of the US."[31] Larry P. McDonald, a Democratic representative from Georgia (1975–83) and JBS member, was all too accurate when he explained to reporters in 1978, "If the society has had a fault, it's that maybe what we said, we said before it was popular to say it."[32] Rosemary Thomson felt the same sea change with regard to conservative women's status in the country: "We were a silent majority, now we are in the mainstream of politics."[33]

In studying second-wave feminism and the history of the ERA and IWY in Indiana, it is impossible to ignore the role of conservative women in shaping the political environment and rhetoric regarding gender ideology and women's place—one cannot study feminist choices and organization without understanding the opposition they faced and vice versa. Once conservative women enter the frame, it is impossible to ignore how collectivism and conspiracy shaped their understanding of women's responsibilities as citizens and as wives, mothers, and daughters. The deep gulf that existed between feminist and conservative Hoosier women over the meaning of equality and global cooperation suggests that the categories of "women's politics" and "women's issues" are more divergent and diverse than scholars might have previously imagined. For many women, conspiracy holds the key to understanding the world and unlocking its meaning; this belief profoundly influences their politics and complicates the concept of identity politics or even the idea that women agree on basic issues that most affect women. More study of conspiracy and its appeal, alongside efforts to improve information literacy, might help stem the tide of conspiracy belief, but ultimately those efforts will only work if they are coupled with transparency and integrity on the part of the federal government and federal officials, elected and appointed. Kathryn Olmsted warns that "if antigovernment conspiracy theorists get the details wrong—and they often do—they get the basic issue right: it is the secret actions of the government that are the real enemies of democracy."[34] Conspiracy belief feeds on the lies, manipulations, and mischaracterizations on the part of government officials, as well as the use of fear and anxiety to explain issues and motivate voters. When and if people feel afraid or that they cannot trust officials and representatives to speak and act honestly or straightforwardly, conspiracy belief will proliferate. Hoosier women's politics attest to this and demonstrate that conspiracy can be of greater significance than party, race, or gender in explaining how women perceive the nation and the world, as well as their role in it.

Notes

Acknowledgments

1. Aesop, "The Man, the Boy, and the Donkey," in *Aesop's Fables*, Lit2Go Edition (1867), accessed 3 January 2017, http://etc.usf.edu/lit2go/35/aesops-fables/648/the-man-the-boy-and-the-donkey/.

2. "Coalition and Control: Hoosier Feminists and the Equal Rights Amendment," *Frontiers: A Journal of Women Studies* 34, no. 2 (2013): 52–81; "Battling 'Big Sister' Government: Hoosier Women and the Politics of International Women's Year," *Journal of Women's History* 24, no. 2 (Summer 2012): 144–70.

Introduction

1. Martha Sonntag Bradley, *Pedestals and Podiums: Utah Women, Religious Authority, and Equal Rights* (Salt Lake City: Signature Books, 2005), 136, 237.

2. "X-Rated Display Stirs Statehouse," *Indianapolis News*, 8 February 1978.

3. Joan M. Gubbins, "News Release, Indiana IWY Delegation," 9 February 1978, Anti-ERA Materials (unsorted collection), Indiana Historical Society (cited hereafter as IHS), Indianapolis.

4. R. Cartwright, "Lesbian Pornography Displayed at Indiana State Legislature," *Marion News Herald*, 10 February 1978.

5. Jane Fribley to the State Senators and Representatives, 8 January 1978, and Fribley to the Editor, National IWY Conference, both in folder 10, box 1, International Women's Year Records, IHS.

6. Letter to Indiana Legislators, 1978, Anti-ERA Materials (unsorted collection), IHS.

7. Beth L. Bailey and Dave Farber, *America in the Seventies* (Lawrence: University Press of Kansas, 2004), 1.

8. Benita Roth, *Separate Roads to Feminism: Black, Chicana, and White Feminist Movements in America's Second Wave* (New York: Cambridge University Press, 2004), 216.

9. Jane J. Mansbridge, *Why We Lost the ERA* (Chicago: University of Chicago Press, 1986), 1.

10. Ronnee Schreiber, *Righting Feminism: Conservative Women and American Politics* (New York: Oxford University Press, 2008), 124–25.

11. Ibid.

12. Ibid., 54.

13. Ibid.; see also Rebecca E. Klatch, *Women of the New Right*, Women in the Political Economy (Philadelphia: Temple University Press, 1987), 139.

14. Schreiber, *Righting Feminism*, 41–42; Gayatri Chakravorty Spivak, *Outside in the Teaching Machine* (New York: Routledge, 2009), 3–5.

15. Kathleen M. Blee, "Troubling Women's History: Women in Right-Wing and Colonial Politics," *Journal of Women's History* 15, no. 2 (2003): 214–21.

16. Kathleen M. Blee, *Women of the Klan: Racism and Gender in the 1920s* (Berkeley: University of California Press, 1991); Donald T. Critchlow, *Phyllis Schlafly and Grassroots Conservatism: A Woman's Crusade* (Princeton, NJ: Princeton University Press, 2005); Glen Jeansonne, *Women of the Far Right: The Mothers' Movement and World War II* (Chicago: University of Chicago Press, 1996); Lisa McGirr, *Suburban Warriors: The Origins of the New American Right* (Princeton, NJ: Princeton University Press, 2001); Kim E. Nielsen, *Un-American Womanhood: Antiradicalism, Antifeminism, and the First Red Scare* (Columbus: Ohio State University Press, 2001).

17. Kirsten Delegard, *Battling Miss Bolsheviki: The Origins of Female Conservatism in the United States* (Philadelphia: University of Pennsylvania Press, 2012); Michelle M. Nickerson, *Mothers of Conservatism: Women and the Postwar Right* (Princeton, NJ: Princeton University Press, 2012).

18. Susan Goodier, *No Votes for Women: The New York State Anti-suffrage Movement* (Urbana: University of Illinois Press, 2012); Kathleen M. Blee and Sandra McGee Deutsch, eds., *Women of the Right: Comparisons and Interplay across Borders* (University Park: Pennsylvania State University Press, 2012).

19. Blee and Deutsch, *Women of the Right*, 15.

20. Ibid., 11–14.

21. Judith Ezekiel cautions us against using liberationist and radical interchangeably, arguing that it "flattens out the [radical] movement" by lumping together distinct groups (*Feminism in the Heartland* [Columbus: Ohio State University Press, 2002], 38–39).

22. I take a broad approach in applying the title "feminist" to women and organizations that were often uncomfortable with the label, connoting as it did street protest

and a radical critique of gender roles. Studying inchoate politics often requires flexibility in order to flesh out the origins of thought and action. See Nickerson, *Mothers of Conservatism*, xxii.

23. Roth, *Separate Roads*, 3.

24. Jeansonne, *Women of the Far Right*.

25. George H. Nash, *The Conservative Intellectual Movement in America since 1945* (New York: Basic Books, 1976), xviii–xxii.

26. Kathleen M. Fallon and Julie Moreau, "Righting Africa? Contextualizing Notions of Women's Right-Wing Activism in Sub-Saharan Africa," in Blee and Deutsch, *Women of the Right*, 69–70.

27. Kathryn S. Olmsted, *Real Enemies: Conspiracy Theories and American Democracy, World War I to 9/11* (New York: Oxford University Press, 2009), 3.

28. Michael J. Wood, Karen M. Douglas, and Robbie M. Sutton, "Dead and Alive: Beliefs in Contradictory Conspiracy Theories," *Social Psychological and Personality Science* 3, no. 6 (2012): 767.

29. Viren Swami et al., "Lunar Lies: The Impact of Informational Framing and Individual Differences in Shaping Conspiracist Beliefs about the Moon Landings," *Applied Cognitive Psychology* 27, no. 1 (2013): 78.

30. Robert Alan Goldberg, *Enemies Within: The Culture of Conspiracy in Modern America* (New Haven, CT: Yale University Press, 2001); Viren Swami and Rebecca Coles, "The Truth Is Out There," *Psychologist* 23, no. 7 (July 2010): 560–63.

31. J. Eric Oliver and Thomas J. Wood, "Conspiracy Theories and the Paranoid Style(s) of Mass Opinion," *American Journal of Political Science* 58, no. 4 (October 2014): 958.

32. Olmsted cites a study in which as many as 36 percent of Americans believe the Bush administration planned 9/11 or did nothing to stop it. That percentage increases to a majority when looking at those between the ages of eighteen and twenty-nine (Olmsted, *Real Enemies*, 1). Goldberg notes that as many as one in four believed the "government elite" was "involved in a conspiracy" (*Enemies Within*, 259).

33. Swami et al., "Lunar Lies," 71; Olmsted, *Real Enemies*, 11.

34. Oliver and Wood, "Conspiracy Theories," 955, 959.

35. Olmsted, *Real Enemies*, 11.

36. Oliver and Wood, "Conspiracy Theories," 952.

37. Michael Barkun, *A Culture of Conspiracy: Apocalyptic Visions in Contemporary America* (Berkeley: University of California Press, 2003), 2.

38. Olmsted, *Real Enemies*, 9.

39. Ibid.; Dana Milbank, "Bush Defends Assertions of Iraq–Al Qaeda Relationship," *Washington Post*, 18 June 2004, A09.

40. Olmsted, *Real Enemies*, 3–5.

41. Ibid.

42. Robin Morris, "Organizing Breadmakers: Kathryn Dunaway's ERA Battle and the Roots of Georgia's Republican Revolution," in *Entering the Fray: Gender, Politics, and*

Culture in the New South, ed. Jonathan Daniel Wells and Shelia Phipps (Columbia: University of Missouri Press, 2010), 164.

43. Stephanie Gilmore, *Feminist Coalitions: Historical Perspectives on Second-Wave Feminism in the United States*, Women in American History (Urbana: University of Illinois Press, 2008).

44. Andrew R. L. Cayton, "The Anti-region: Place and Identity in the History of the American Midwest," in *The Identity of the American Midwest: Essays on Regional History*, ed. Andrew R. L. Cayton and Susan E. Gray, Midwestern History and Culture (Bloomington: Indiana University Press, 2007), 148.

45. James R. Shortridge, *The Middle West: Its Meaning in American Culture* (Lawrence: University Press of Kansas, 1989), 1.

46. Cayton, "Anti-region," 149.

47. Andrew R. L. Cayton and Susan E. Gray, "The Story of the Midwest," in Cayton and Gray, *The Identity*, 4.

48. Cayton, "Anti-region," 151.

49. Ibid., 159; R. Douglass Hurt, "Midwestern Distinctiveness," in Cayton and Gray, *The Identity*, 160–61.

50. Cayton, "Anti-region," 150–51.

51. William J. Spurlin, "What?! Queers in the Midwest?," in *Reclaiming the Heartland: Lesbian and Gay Voices from the Midwest*, ed. Karen Lee Osborne and William J. Spurlin (Minneapolis: University of Minnesota Press, 1996), xvii.

52. James H. Madison, *Hoosiers: A New History of Indiana* (Bloomington and Indianapolis: Indiana University Press and Indiana Historical Society Press, 2014), 332.

53. Ibid., 213.

54. Linda Gail Seward, "The Equal Rights Amendment Campaign in Indiana: A Study of Ideas and Arguments" (Ph.D. diss., Purdue University, 1991), 87–88.

55. Madison, *Hoosiers*, 228.

56. Ibid., 231.

57. Ibid., 305.

58. Ibid., 308.

59. Ibid., 219.

60. Ibid., 222.

61. Cayton, "Anti-region," 141.

62. Ibid., 150.

63. Joanne J. Meyerowitz, *Not June Cleaver: Women and Gender in Postwar America, 1945–1960* (Philadelphia, PA: Temple University Press, 1994).

Chapter 1. Women's Experience in Cold War America

1. Quoted in Alan Brinkley, *Liberalism and Its Discontents* (Cambridge, MA: Harvard University Press, 2000), 94.

2. Paola Bacchetta and Margaret Power, eds., *Right-Wing Women: From Conservatives to Extremists around the World* (New York: Routledge, 2002), 15.

3. Brinkley, *Liberalism*, 94.

4. Lawrence S. Wittner, *Rebels against War: The American Peace Movement* (Philadelphia: Temple University Press, 1984), 134.

5. Ibid.

6. Ibid., 135.

7. Ibid.

8. Ibid.

9. Ibid., 136.

10. Quoted in ibid., 141.

11. Ibid., 141.

12. Ibid., 142.

13. Ibid.

14. Joseph Preston Baratta, "The International Federalist Movement: Toward Global Governance," *Peace & Change* 24, no. 3 (July 1999): 342.

15. Ibid., 340.

16. Ibid., 379. The Bricker Amendment was first proposed by U.S. Senator John Bricker of Ohio in 1953 and, if adopted, would have limited the president's ability to negotiate treaties. Especially of concern was the prospect of world government treaties being binding within the United States without congressional approval.

17. Wittner, *Rebels against War*, 137, 140; Baratta, "The International Federalist Movement," 342.

18. Cousins quoted in Wittner, *Rebels against War*, 137.

19. Joseph Preston Baratta, "The International History of the World Federalist Movement," *Peace & Change* 14, no. 4 (October 1989): 375.

20. Ibid.

21. Wittner, *Rebels against War*, 138.

22. Harry S. Truman, "President Harry S. Truman's Address before a Joint Session of Congress, March 12, 1947," The Avalon Project: Documents in Law, History and Diplomacy, Lillian Goldman Law Library, Yale Law School, http://avalon.law.yale.edu/20th_century/trudoc.asp, accessed 6 August 2015.

23. Baratta, "The International History," 381.

24. Ibid., 379.

25. Gunnar Myrdal, Richard Sterner, and Arnold Marshall Rose, *An American Dilemma: The Negro Problem and Modern Democracy* (New York: Harper, 1944).

26. Thomas Cripps and David Culbert, "*The Negro Soldier* (1944): Film Propaganda in Black and White," *American Quarterly* 31, no. 5 (Winter 1979): 616–40.

27. Brinkley, *Liberalism*, 102.

28. Alice Kessler-Harris, *Out to Work: A History of Wage-Earning Women in the United States* (New York: Oxford University Press, 2003), 250–99.

29. Ibid., 273–99.

30. Ibid., 299.

31. Ibid.

32. Ibid., 301.

33. Ibid.

34. Ibid.

35. Duane Tanenbaum, *The Bricker Amendment Controversy: A Test of Eisenhower's Political Leadership* (Ithaca, NY: Cornell University Press, 1988), ix.

36. Robert Alan Goldberg, *Enemies Within: The Culture of Conspiracy in Modern America* (New Haven, CT: Yale University Press, 2001), 259.

37. Ibid.

38. Elaine Tyler May, *Homeward Bound: American Families in the Cold War Era* (New York: Basic Books, 2008).

39. Stephanie Coontz, *The Way We Never Were: American Families and the Nostalgia Trap* (New York: Basic Books, 1997).

40. Ibid., 29–30.

41. Brinkley, *Liberalism*, 105.

42. Cord Meyer, *Facing Reality: From World Federalism to the CIA* (New York: Harper & Row, 1980), 55–65.

43. Ellen Schrecker, *Many Are the Crimes: McCarthyism in America* (Boston: Little, Brown, 1998), xii.

44. Ibid.

45. "Case Closed on the Rosenbergs," *Los Angeles Times*, 17 September 2008, http://articles.latimes.com/2008/sep/17/news/oe-radosh17, accessed 22 February 2016; Robin Shulman, "Rosenberg Sons Say Father Was Guilty, Mother Was Framed," *Washington Post*, 23 September 2008, http://www.washingtonpost.com/wp-dyn/content/article/2008/09/22/ar2008092202622.html, accessed 22 February 2016; Victoria Phillips, "Reflections of a Neo-liberal: An Interview with John Haynes," *American Communist History* 13, nos. 2–3 (2014): 85–152.

46. Schrecker, *Many Are the Crimes*, x.

47. John Earl Haynes and Harvey Klehr, *In Denial: Historians, Communism & Espionage* (San Francisco: Encounter Books, 2003), 231.

48. Ibid., 226.

49. Ibid., 224.

50. Ibid., 6, 82, 223; Victoria Philips, "Reflections of a Neo-liberal: An Interview with John Haynes," *American Communist History* 13, no. 2–3 (2014): 109.

51. *St. Louis Post Dispatch*, 7 November 1953, quoted in Don E. Carleton, *Red Scare! Right-Wing Hysteria, Fifties Fanaticism, and Their Legacy in Texas* (Austin: Texas Monthly Press, 1985), 121.

52. Michael Paul Poder, "The Senatorial Career of William E. Jenner" (Ph.D. diss., University of Notre Dame, 1976), 103.

53. Dale R. Sorenson, "The Anticommunist Consensus in Indiana, 1945–1958" (Ph.D. diss., University of Indiana, 1980), 53–54.

54. William B. Pickett, *Homer E. Capehart: A Senator's Life, 1897–1979* (Indianapolis: Indiana Historical Society, 1990), 163–64.

55. Poder, "The Senatorial Career," 108.

56. Irving Leibowitz, *My Indiana* (Englewood Cliffs, NJ: Prentice-Hall, 1964), 15.

57. Mary Brennan, *Wives, Mothers, and the Red Menace: Conservative Women and the Crusade against Communism* (Boulder: University Press of Colorado, 2008), 148.

58. Ibid.

59. Michelle Nickerson, *Mothers of Conservatism: Women and the Postwar Right* (Princeton, NJ: Princeton University Press, 2012), xxi.

60. Ibid.

61. Rebecca Klatch, *Women of the New Right* (Philadelphia: Temple University Press, 1987), 5.

62. Ibid., 11.

63. Kirsten Delegard, "'It Takes Women to Fight Women': Woman Suffrage and the Genesis of Female Conservatism in the United States," in *Women of the Right: Comparisons and Interplay across Borders*, ed. Kathleen M. Blee and Sandra McGee Deutsch (University Park: Pennsylvania State University Press, 2012), 211–25.

64. Brennan, *Wives, Mothers*, 152.

65. Ibid.

66. Elna C. Green, "From Antisuffragism to Anti-Communism: The Conservative Career of Ida M. Darden," *Journal of Southern History* 65, no. 2 (1999): 311.

67. Carleton, *Red Scare!*, 111–13; Patricia C. Walls, "Defending Their Liberties: Women's Organizations during the McCarthy Era" (Ph.D. diss., University of Maryland, 1994), 177.

68. George Norris Green, *The Establishment in Texas Politics: The Primitive Years, 1938–1957* (Westport, CT: Greenwood Press, 1979), 123.

69. Carleton, *Red Scare!*, 113.

70. Green, *Establishment*, 123; Carleton, *Red Scare!*, 112.

71. Green, *Establishment*, 123.

72. Carleton, *Red Scare!*, 124.

73. Ibid., 113.

74. Ibid., 116.

75. O'Leary cited in Green, *Establishment*, 125.

76. Carleton, *Red Scare!*, 113, 124.

77. John L. Niblack, "Asserts Minute Women Were Justified in Their Protests on ACLU Meeting," editorial, *Indianapolis News*, 16 December 1953.

78. June Melby Benowitz, *Days of Discontent: American Women and Right-Wing Politics, 1933–1945* (DeKalb: Northern Illinois University Press, 2002), 16; Catherine E. Rymph, *Republican Women: Feminism and Conservatism from Suffrage through the Rise of the New Right* (Chapel Hill: University of North Carolina Press, 2006), 62.

79. Ibid.

80. Benowitz, *Days of Discontent*, 16.

81. Ibid.

82. Rymph, *Republican Women*, 62.

83. Nickerson, *Mothers of Conservatism*, 16–17; Rymph, *Republican Women*, 62.

84. Nickerson, *Mothers of Conservatism*, 16.

85. Benowitz, *Days of Discontent*, 16–17.

86. Carleton, *Red Scare!*, 116.

87. Ibid., 141.

88. Ibid., 120–24.

89. Green, *Establishment*, 124.

90. Jim Jordan, "Legion Brands Civil Liberties Union 'Vicious Racket,'" *Indianapolis Times*, 22 November 1953.

91. "Denies Backing Legion in Dispute," *Indianapolis Times*, 22 November 1953.

92. Carleton, *Red Scare!*, 114.

93. Richard M. Clutter, "The Indiana American Legion, 1919–1960" (Ph.D. diss., University of Indiana, 1974), 105–6, 110, 120.

94. Ibid., 112–13.

95. Ibid., 272.

96. Erin Kempker, "Women at the Crossroads: Feminists, Conservatives, and Gender Politics in Indiana, 1950–1980" (Ph.D. diss., Purdue University, 2008), 25–29.

97. George E. Rundquist to W. Rowland Allen, 1949, folder 1, box 10, Rowland Allen Papers, Indiana Historical Society, Indianapolis (hereafter IHS).

98. "Incident in Indianapolis," transcript, 1953, p. 4, folder 6, box 10, Allen Papers.

99. Sorenson, "Anticommunist Consensus," 164.

100. "Incident in Indianapolis," transcript, 5–6.

101. "Indiana Rebuffs A.C.L.U.," *New York Times*, 18 November 1953; "Civil Liberties Unit to Meet in Church," *Indianapolis Star*, 19 November 1953.

102. "Incident in Indianapolis," transcript, 7.

103. Ibid., 8.

104. Jordan, "Legion Brands"; "Rival Camps Entrench for War of Words on Rights, Free Speech," *Indianapolis Star*, 21 November 1953.

105. "Rival Camps."

106. Walls, "Defending Their Liberties," 175.

107. Louis B. Greenberg to George Rundquist, Field Director ACLU, 1953, folder 4, box 10, Allen Papers.

108. "Incident in Indianapolis," transcript, 10.

109. Ibid. For more on the *See It Now* series, please see Thomas Rosteck, *"See It Now" Confronts McCarthyism: Television Documentary and the Politics of Representation* (Tuscaloosa: University of Alabama Press, 1994).

110. "Incident in Indianapolis," transcript, 6.

111. Sorenson, "Anticommunist Consensus," 189–93.

112. Tom Keating, "Birchers Got Start in City in 1958," *Indianapolis Star*, 7 September 1983.

113. Douglas E. Kneelands, "Birch Society, Age 10, Vows Red Rout," *New York Times*, 8 December 1968; Keating, "Birchers Got Start"; Jonathan M. Schoenwald, *A Time for Choosing: The Rise of Modern American Conservatism* (New York: Oxford University Press, 2001), 62.

114. Robert Welch, *The Blue Book of the John Birch Society* (Boston: Western Islands Publishing, 1961), 116–17.

115. Ibid., 119–21.

116. Ibid., 122.

117. "The John Birch Society," *Facts* 14, no. 5 (1961): 223, folder 12, box 11, Max Einstandig Papers, IHS.

118. Nickerson, *Mothers of Conservatism*, 138–40.

119. *Pro America Speaks* 9, no. 4 (May 1975), Southern California Unit, RH WL E559, Wilcox Collection, Kenneth Spencer Research Library, University of Kansas.

120. *Minute Women of the U.S.A., Inc.*, no. 1 (January 1954), folder 1-1, box 45-1, Hall-Hoag Papers, Hay Library, Brown University, Providence, RI.

121. Bernard Eismann and Donald Janson, *The Far Right* (New York: McGraw-Hill, 1963), 30.

122. "The John Birch Society," 221–28.

123. Robert Welch, *A Brief Introduction*, 1962, John Birch Society pamphlet, folder 16, box 12, Einstandig Papers.

124. Lisa McGirr, *Suburban Warriors: The Origins of the New American Right* (Princeton, NJ: Princeton University Press, 2001), 76.

125. "The John Birch Society," 223.

126. George Thayer, *The Farther Shores of Politics: The American Political Fringe Today* (New York: Simon and Schuster, 1967), 193.

127. Sara Diamond, *Roads to Dominion: Right-Wing Movements and Political Power in the United States* (New York: Guilford Press, 1995), 29; George H. Nash, *The Conservative Intellectual Movement in America since 1945* (New York: Basic Books, 1976).

128. Alan Brinkley, "The Problem of American Conservatism," *American Historical Review* 99, no. 2 (1994): 419.

129. Carleton, *Red Scare!*, 223.

130. Welch, *The Blue Book*, 77–78.

131. Nickerson, *Mothers of Conservatism*, 150.

132. Thayer, *The Farther Shores*, 179.

133. Nickerson, *Mothers of Conservatism*, 142, 147.

134. *Minute Women of the U.S.A., Inc.*, no. 19 (April 1957), RH WL D3490, Wilcox Collection, Kenneth Spencer Research Library (hereafter Spencer Library), University of Kansas, Lawrence (hereafter MW RH WL D3490 Collection).

135. Nickerson, *Mothers of Conservatism*, 142–48.

136. *Minute Women of the U.S.A., Inc.*, no. 8 (November 1955), MW RH WL D3490 Collection.

137. These "patriotic messages" were not limited to Indiana but were part of a national campaign. Thayer, *The Farther Shores*, 191.

138. Ibid.

139. "'Let Freedom Ring' Message," transcript of recorded message, 15 November 1965, folder 10, box 10, Einstandig Papers.

140. Robert Gordon to Regional Advisory Board Members, Lodge and Chapter ADL

Chairmen, Lodge and Chapter Presidents, Indianapolis ADL Committee Members, and Federation Directors, 8 September 1965, folder 12, box 11, Einstandig Papers; Marshall Schlossberg, speech to Indiana ADL Convention, South Bend, 16 April 1967, folder 13, box 127, Indiana Jewish Historical Society Collection, IHS.

141. "'Let Freedom Ring' Message," transcript of recorded message, 13 September 1965, folder 14, box 23, Allen Papers; "'Let Freedom Ring' Message, transcript of recorded message, 11 October 1965, folder 14, box 25, Allen Papers; "'Let Freedom Ring' Message," transcript of recorded message, 21 February 1966, folder 14, box 25, Allen Papers.

142. "'Let Freedom Ring' Message," transcript of recorded message, 24 March 1966, folder 14, box 25, Allen Papers.

143. This is not an exhaustive list, but it gives some insight into the nature and scope of the recordings. "'Let Freedom Ring' Message," transcript of recorded message, 14 March 1966, folder 14, box 25, Allen Papers.

144. Schlossberg, "Speech to the Indiana ADL Convention."

145. W. J. Griffith III, "Reds Instigate Riots Violence," *Indianapolis News*, 22 November 1967.

146. Nickerson, *Mothers of Conservatism*; Sorenson, "Anticommunist Consensus," 181.

147. Nancy Comisky, "Right Around the Corner," *Indianapolis Monthly* 4, no. 32 (2008): 52–58.

148. Kathryn Nikou, interview with the author, Indianapolis, 27 July 2011; Joan Gubbins, interview with the author, Cocoa Beach, FL, 23 June 2011.

149. Phyllis Schlafly founded the Eagle Forum in 1972 to counter feminism and the Equal Rights Amendment, along with other social issues. Frances Dodson Rhome to Coordinating Committee Members, 8 November 1977, folder 5, box 1, International Women's Year Records, IHS.

Chapter 2. Anticommunists and the World Government Conspiracy

1. *Minute Women of the U.S.A., Inc.*, no. 58 (March 1962), RH WL D3490, Wilcox Collection, Kenneth Spencer Research Library (hereafter Spencer Library), University of Kansas, Lawrence (hereafter RH WL D3490 Collection).

2. Kathryn S. Olmsted, *Real Enemies: Conspiracy Theories and American Democracy, World War I to 9/11* (New York: Oxford University Press, 2009), 3–5.

3. Ibid., 11.

4. Glen Jeansonne, *Women of the Far Right: The Mothers' Movement and World War II* (Chicago: University of Chicago Press, 1996), 6.

5. Kim E. Nielsen, *Un-American Womanhood: Antiradicalism, Antifeminism, and the First Red Scare* (Columbus: Ohio State University Press, 2001), 136.

6. Jeansonne, *Women of the Far Right*, 1.

7. Ibid., 143, 149.

8. Michelle Nickerson, *Mothers of Conservatism: Women and the Postwar Right* (Princeton, NJ: Princeton University Press, 2012), 28.

9. Ibid., 27–28, 30; Jeansonne, *Women of the Far Right*, 7, 178.

10. Nickerson, *Mothers of Conservatism*, 29.

11. D. J. Malloy, *The World of the John Birch Society: Conspiracy, Conservatism, and the Cold War* (Nashville, TN: Vanderbilt University Press, 2014), 182.

12. Lisa McGirr, *Suburban Warriors: The Origins of the New American Right* (Princeton, NJ: Princeton University Press, 2001), 178–79.

13. National Americanism Commission of the American Legion, "Preliminary Report on United World Federalists, Inc.," folder 6, box 121, Rosalind Kress Haley Collection, Eagle Forum Education Center Archives, St. Louis, Missouri (hereafter the Haley Collection).

14. National Americanism Commission of the American Legion, "World Federation or World Governments," report, folder 6, box 121, Haley Collection.

15. "When World Government Moves In," National Economic Council newsletter, no. 312 (June 1953), folder 6, box 121, Haley Collection.

16. *Minute Women of the U.S.A., Inc.*, no. 70 (September–October 1963), RH WL D3490 Collection.

17. "Assails UNESCO as 5th Column Aiding Soviets," *Chicago Daily Tribune*, 28 June 1953.

18. *Minute Women of the U.S.A., Inc.*, no. 11 (March 1956), RH WL D3490 Collection.

19. *Minute Women of the U.S.A., Inc.*, no. 38 (October 1959), RH WL D3490 Collection.

20. *Minute Women of the U.S.A., Inc.*, no. 54 (September–October 1961), RH WL D3490 Collection.

21. *Minute Women of the U.S.A., Inc.*, no. 2 (February 1955), RH WL D3490 Collection.

22. Rosemary Thomson, *The Price of LIBerty* (Carol Stream, IL: Creation House, 1978), 38.

23. Joan Gubbins, interview with the author, Cocoa Beach, FL, 23 June 2011.

24. Thomson, *The Price of LIBerty*, 38.

25. *Minute Women of the U.S.A., Inc.*, March 1968, RH WL E535, Wilcox Collection, Spencer Library (hereafter RH WL E636 Collection).

26. *Minute Women of the U.S.A., Inc.*, no. 54 (September–October 1961), RH WL D3490 Collection.

27. Rebecca Klatch, *Women of the New Right* (Philadelphia, PA: Temple University Press, 1987), 25–31.

28. *Pro America Speaks* 9, no. 4 (May 1975), Southern California Unit, RH WL E559, Wilcox Collection, Spencer Library (hereafter Pro America Collection).

29. Ibid.; Anthony C. Sutton, *Wall Street and the Bolshevik Revolution: The Remarkable True Story of the American Capitalists Who Financed the Russian Government* (repr., Clairview Books, 2012).

30. *Pro America Speaks* 8, no. 4 (March 1974), Pro America Collection.

31. Catherine E. Rymph, *Republican Women: Feminism and Conservatism from Suffrage through the Rise of the New Right* (Chapel Hill: University of North Carolina Press, 2006), 28.

32. Stephen D. O'Leary, *Arguing the Apocalypse: A Theory of Millennial Rhetoric* (New York: Oxford University Press, 1994); Ernest Lee Tuveson, *Redeemer Nation: The Idea of America's Millennial Role* (Chicago: University of Chicago Press, 1968).

33. Angela M. Lahr, *Millennial Dreams and Apocalyptic Nightmares: The Cold War Origins of Political Evangelicalism* (Oxford: Oxford University Press, 2007), 5–6.

34. J. Eric Oliver and Thomas J. Wood, "Conspiracy Theories and the Paranoid Style(s) of Mass Opinion," *American Journal of Political Science* 58, no. 4 (October 2014): 954.

35. Michael Barkun, *A Culture of Conspiracy: Apocalyptic Visions in Contemporary America* (Berkeley: University of California Press, 2003), 2.

36. Ibid., 10.

37. Jonathan R. Baer, "American Dispensationalism's Perpetually Imminent End Times," *Journal of Religion* 87, no. 2 (2007): 248–64; Lahr, *Millennial Dreams*, 5–6; William C. Martin, *With God on Our Side: The Rise of the Religious Right in America* (New York: Broadway Books, 1996), 7–9; Leo P. Ribuffo, *The Old Christian Right: The Protestant Far Right from the Great Depression to the Cold War* (Philadelphia, PA: Temple University Press, 1983), 83–85, 93–108; Mark S. Sweetnam, "Defining Dispensationalism: A Cultural Studies Perspective," *Journal of Religious History* 34, no. 2 (2010): 191–212; Daniel Wojcik, "Embracing Doomsday: Faith, Fatalism, and Apocalyptic Beliefs in the Nuclear Age," *Western Folklore* 55, no. 4 (Fall 1996): 297–331.

38. Lahr, *Millennial Dreams*, 1.

39. Ibid., 14.

40. Ibid., 35.

41. Barkun, *A Culture of Conspiracy*, 44.

42. *Minute Women of the U.S.A., Inc.*, no. 72 (January 1964), RH WL D3490 Collection.

43. *Minute Women of the U.S.A., Inc.*, August 1970, RH WL E535 Collection.

44. Barkun, *A Culture of Conspiracy*, 10, 15–28.

45. Ibid., 11.

46. Ibid.

47. Minute Women of the U.S.A., California branch newsletter, March 1955, box 1, folder 4, Phyllis Johnson Collection, Spencer Library.

48. Nickerson devotes a chapter to "Siberia, U.S.A." in *Mothers of Conservatism*, 103–35.

49. Quoted in ibid., 119.

50. Ibid., 113.

51. Ibid., 113–14.

52. Ibid., 114–15, 121–33.

53. Duane Tananbaum, *The Bricker Amendment Controversy: A Test of Eisenhower's Political Leadership* (Ithaca, NY: Cornell University Press, 1988), 41.

54. Ibid., 23.

55. Ibid., 42.

56. *Minute Women of the U.S.A., Inc.*, no. 2 (February 1954), Hall-Hoag Collection, John Hay Library (hereafter Hay Library), Brown University, Providence, Rhode Island (hereafter the HH Collection).

57. *Minute Women of the U.S.A., Inc.*, no. 1 (January 1954), HH Collection; *Minute Women of the U.S.A., Inc.*, no. 2 (February 1954), HH Collection.

58. Tannenbaum, *The Bricker Amendment Controversy*, 8.

59. *Minute Women of the U.S.A., Inc.*, no. 7 (December 1954), John Birch Society Collection, Hay Library (hereafter JBS Collection).

60. *Minute Women of the U.S.A., Inc.*, no. 1 (January 1954), HH Collection.

61. US Congress, *Journal of the House of Representatives of the United States*, 84th Cong., 2nd sess., January 3, 1956, 173.

62. Tananbaum, *The Bricker Amendment Controversy*.

63. *Minute Women of the U.S.A., Inc.*, no. 2 (February 1954), HH Collection.

64. *Minute Women of the U.S.A., Inc.*, no. 11 (March 1956), RH WL D3490 Collection.

65. Ibid.

66. *Minute Women of the U.S.A., Inc.*, no. 72 (January 1964), RH WL D3490 Collection.

67. "How to Fight the Reds," *Chicago Daily Tribune*, 18 May 1950.

68. "The Minute Women," *Chicago Daily Tribune*, 13 May 1950.

69. Cathal J. Nolan, "The Last Hurrah of Conservative Isolationism: Eisenhower, Congress, and the Bricker Amendment," *Presidential Studies Quarterly* 22, no. 2 (Spring 1992): 339.

70. Ibid.

71. Pro America had male members, and June Melby Benowitz argues that while it was open to men, it constituted a women's organization (*Days of Discontent: American Women and Right-Wing Politics, 1933–1945* [DeKalb: Northern Illinois University Press, 2002], 17).

72. *Minute Women of the U.S.A., Inc.*, no. 11 (March 1956), RH WL D3490 Collection.

73. *Minute Women of the U.S.A., Inc.*, no. 4 (April 1954), HH Collection.

74. *Minute Women of the U.S.A., Inc.*, no. 2 (February 1954), HH Collection.

75. Quoted in D. J. Mulloy, *The World of the John Birch Society: Conspiracy, Conservatism, and the Cold War* (Nashville, TN: Vanderbilt University, 2014), 183.

76. Robert Welch, Bi-MOM Record, November 1968, MOM folder, box 5, JBS Collection.

77. Ibid.

78. Ibid.

79. Ibid.

80. Benjamin R. Epstein and Arnold Forster, *The Radical Right: Report on the John Birch Society and Its Allies* (New York: Random House, 1967), 118–19.

81. McGirr also explains this connection, and she finds the earliest evidence for it in the society's magazine in 1962 (*Suburban Warriors*, 335). See also Robert S. Robins and Jerrold M. Post, *Political Paranoia: The Psychopolitics of Hatred* (New Haven, CT: Yale University Press, 1997), 190–94; Malloy, *The World of the John Birch Society*, 183.

82. David Brion Davis, *The Fear of Conspiracy: Images of Un-American Subversion from the Revolution to the Present* (Ithaca, NY: Cornell University Press, 1971), 327.

83. Quoted in Davis, *The Fear of Conspiracy*, 39.

84. Jedidiah Morse, "The Present Dangers and Consequent Duties of the Citizens," 1799, quoted in ibid., 45–48.

85. Ibid., 37.

86. Beyoncé's connection to the Illuminati is explored on numerous websites and YouTube videos: "Is Beyonce in the Illuminati," website, accessed 19 January 2017, http://www.beyonce-illuminati.com/; Chloe Kent, "Here's How Beyonce & the Illuminati Are Connected, Because the Two Go Way Back," *Bustle*, 7 February 2016, accessed 19 January 2017, https://www.bustle.com/articles/140194-heres-how-beyonce-the-illuminati-are-connected-because-the-two-go-way-back; Kenza Moller, "6 Signs Beyonce Is in the Illuminati, Regardless of What She Says in 'Formation,'" 16 February 2016, accessed 19 January 2017, https://www.romper.com/p/6-signs-beyonce-is-in-the-illuminati-regardless-of-what-she-says-in-formation-5745.

87. Welch, "More Stately Mansions," 1964, quoted in Davis, *The Fear of Conspiracy*, 328.

88. Ibid.

89. Ibid., 330, emphasis added.

90. Ibid., 329.

91. Martha F. Lee, "Nesta Webster: The Voice of Conspiracy," *Journal of Women's History* 17, no. 3 (2005): 92.

92. Donald I. Warren, *Radio Priest: Charles Coughlin, the Father of Hate Radio* (New York: Free Press, 1996), 188–98, 223.

93. Alan Brinkley, *Voices of Protest: Huey Long, Father Coughlin, and the Great Depression* (New York: Knopf, 1982), 83.

94. Epstein and Forster, *The Radical Right*, 110–14, 118–19; Mulloy, *The World of the John Birch Society*, 185; George Thayer, *The Farther Shores of Politics: The American Political Fringe Today* (New York: Simon and Schuster, 1967), 184–85.

95. Epstein and Forster, *The Radical Right*, 109.

96. Myron Feinsilber, "Birch Society Battles with Reds' Own Tactics," *Indianapolis News*, 16 October 1964.

97. Ibid.; "The John Birch Society," *Facts* 14, no. 5 (November–December 1961), published by the Anti-Defamation League, 226–27, folder 12, box 11, Max Einstandig Papers, Indiana Historical Society, Indianapolis (hereafter IHS).

98. Feinsilber, "Birch Society Battles."

99. Schuyler quoted in Oscar Renal Williams, *George S. Schuyler: Portrait of a Black Conservative* (Knoxville: University of Tennessee Press, 2007), 146–47.

100. Ibid., 147.

101. Veronica A. Wilson, "'To Tell All My People': Race, Representation, and John Birch Society Activist Julia Brown," in *Women of the Right: Comparisons and Interplay across Borders*, ed. Kathleen M. Blee and Sandra McGee Deutsch (University Park: Pennsylvania State University Press, 2012), 243.

102. Ibid., 248; speech on the John Birch Society, 1966, folder 10, box 10, Max Einstandig Papers, IHS.

103. Wilson, "'To Tell,'" 242.

104. Ibid., 250.

105. Ibid., 244.

106. Ibid., 243, 249.

107. Ibid., 252.

108. Ibid., 250.

109. Barkun, *A Culture of Conspiracy,* 9.

110. Ibid., 8.

111. Olmsted, *Real Enemies,* 11.

112. Barkun, *A Culture of Conspiracy,* 8–9.

113. Viren Swami et al., "Lunar Lies: The Impact of Informational Framing and Individual Differences in Shaping Conspiracist Beliefs about the Moon Landings," *Applied Cognitive Psychology* 27, no. 1 (2013): 78

114. Geoffrey Smith, "Isolationism, the Devil, and the Advent of the Second World War: Variations on a Theme," *International History Review* 4, no. 1 (February 1982): 57.

115. Sara Diamond, *Roads to Dominion: Right-Wing Movements and Political Power in the United States* (New York: Guilford Press, 1995), 58.

116. Oliver and Wood, "Conspiracy Theories," 954.

117. Ibid., 964.

118. Karen M. Sutton and Robbie M. Douglas, "The Hidden Impact of Conspiracy Theories: Perceived and Actual Influence of Theories Surrounding the Death of Princess Diana," *Journal of Social Psychology* 148, no. 2 (2008): 212.

119. Viren Swami, Tomas Chamorro-Premuzic, and Adrian Furnham, "Unanswered Questions: A Preliminary Investigation of Personality and Individual Difference Predictors of 9/11 Conspiracist Beliefs," *Applied Cognitive Psychology* 24, no. 6 (2010): 759.

120. Fran Mason, "A Poor People's Cognitive Mapping," in *Conspiracy Nation: The Politics of Paranoia in Postwar America* (New York: New York University Press, 2002), 40.

121. Oliver and Wood, "Conspiracy Theories," 961.

122. Nickerson, *Mothers of Conservatism,* 120.

123. *Minute Women of the U.S.A., Inc.*, no. 68 (May–June 1963), RH WL D3490 Collection.

124. Kathryn Nikou, interview with the author, Indianapolis, IN, 27 July 2011.

125. Gubbins interview.

126. Nickerson, *Mothers of Conservatism,* 121.

127. Theodore Sasson, "African American Conspiracy Theories and the Social Construction of Crime," *Sociological Inquiry* 65, no. 3/4 (November 1995): 281; William Paul Simmons and Sharon Parsons, "Beliefs in Conspiracy Theories among African Americans: A Comparison of Elites and Masses," *Social Science Quarterly* 86, no. 3 (September 2005): 596.

128. Mason, "A Poor People's Cognitive Mapping," 41.

129. Michael J. Wood, Karen M. Douglas, and Robbie M. Sutton, "Dead and Alive:

Beliefs in Contradictory Conspiracy Theories," *Social Psychological and Personality Science* 3, no. 6 (January 2012): 770.

130. Ibid., 767.

131. Ibid., 772.

132. Sasson, "African American Conspiracy Theories," 281.

133. *Minute Women of the U.S.A., Inc.*, no. 11 (March 1956), RH WL D3490 Collection.

134. Robert Welch, *The Blue Book of the John Birch Society* (Boston: Western Islands Publishing, 1961), 159.

135. Ibid.

136. Swami, Chamorro-Premuzic, and Furnham, "Unanswered Questions," 759; Wood, Douglas, and Sutton, "Dead and Alive," 772.

137. Diamond, *Roads to Dominion,* 55.

138. Swami, Chamorro-Premuzic, and Furnham, "Unanswered Questions," 759.

139. Sara Evans, *Tidal Wave: How Women Changed America at Century's End* (New York: Free Press, 2003), 53–55; Ruth Rosen, *The World Split Open: How the Modern Women's Movement Changed America* (New York: Viking, 2000), 66–70.

140. *Minute Women of the U.S.A., Inc.*, no. 58 (March 1962), RH WL D3490 Collection.

141. Ibid.

142. Ibid.

143. *Minute Women of the U.S.A., Inc.*, September 1970, RH WL E535 Collection.

144. Ibid.

145. Ibid.

146. "The Path to Regionalist World Government," Committee to Restore the Constitution, Inc., May 1977, folder 2, box 87, Haley Collection; "The Contrived Evolution of Regional Government," *Don Bell Reports*, 3 May 1974, folder 2, box 87, Haley Collection; "The 'Regional Governance' Conspiracy," Committee to Restore the Constitution, bulletin, July 1973, folder 1, box 87, Haley Collection; "Metro: Federal Rule by Bureaucrats," *Independent American*, 1976, folder 1, box 87, Haley Collection; "Beware! The United Nations Plans a One-World Government for You!," flyer, Network of Patriotic Letter Writers, folder 1, box 87, Haley Collection; *Say No to the New World Order*, KAI (Keep America Independent), pamphlet, folder 7, box 121, Haley Collection.

147. Barkun, *A Culture of Conspiracy,* 39–78.

148. Ibid., 39–40.

149. Mark Potok and Don Terry, "Margins to the Mainstream: Radical Right Conspiracy Theories Have Invaded American Politics," report for the Southern Poverty Law Center, 27 October 2015, accessed 26 February 2016, https://www.splcenter.org/fighting-hate/intelligence-report/2015/margins-mainstream.

150. Nickerson, *Mothers of Conservatism,* 140.

151. John Birch Society website, www.jbs.org, accessed 30 July 2015.

152. Theda Skocpol and Vanessa Williamson, *The Tea Party and the Remaking of Republican Conservatism* (New York: Oxford University Press, 2012), 33–34.

153. Potok and Terry, "Margins to the Mainstream."

154. Rick Biondi and Alex Newman, *World Federalism 101* (Create Space Independent Publishing Platform, 2014), 206.

155. Ibid., 206.

156. Ibid.

157. Ibid., 7.

158. Ibid., 206.

159. Christian Gomez, "A Review of 'World Federalism 101,'" *New American*, 28 February 2015, available online at http://www.thenewamerican.com/reviews/books/item/20182-a-review-of-world-federalism-101, accessed 26 February 2016.

160. Ibid.

161. *Minute Women of the U.S.A., Inc.*, February 1971, RH WL E535 Collection.

162. Robert Alan Goldberg, *Enemies Within: The Culture of Conspiracy in Modern America* (New Haven, CT: Yale University Press, 2001), 49, 64–65.

Chapter 3. The Battle over the ERA

1. Robert L. Jones Jr., speech to the Indiana House of Representatives, folder 13, box 1, Joline Ohmart Papers, Indiana Historical Society (hereafter IHS).

2. Rebecca E. Klatch, *Women of the New Right* (Philadelphia: Temple University Press, 1987), 206.

3. Michael Barkun, *A Culture of Conspiracy: Apocalyptic Visions in Contemporary America* (Berkeley: University of California Press, 2003), 9.

4. Kirsten Delegard, "'It Takes Women to Fight Women': Woman Suffrage and the Genesis of Female Conservatism in the United States," in *Women of the Right: Comparison and Interplay across Borders*, ed. Kathleen M. Blee and Sandra McGee Deutsch (University Park: Pennsylvania State University Press, 2012), 211–25.

5. Benita Roth, *Separate Roads to Feminism: Black, Chicana, and White Feminist Movements in America's Second Wave* (New York: Cambridge University Press, 2004), 3.

6. Alice Echols, *Daring to Be Bad: Radical Feminism in America, 1967–1975* (Minneapolis: University of Minnesota Press, 1989), 144–58.

7. Roth, *Separate Roads*, 216.

8. Delegard, "'It Takes Women,'" 212–13.

9. The House vote was 354 to 23 in favor, and in the Senate the vote was also overwhelmingly one-sided: 84 to 8. Mary Frances Berry, *Why ERA Failed: Politics, Women's Rights, and the Amending Process of the Constitution* (Bloomington: Indiana University Press, 1986), 63–64; Janet K. Boles, *The Politics of the Equal Rights Amendment: Conflict and the Decision Process* (New York: Longman, 1979); Mark R. Daniels and Robert E. Darcy, "As Time Goes By: The Arrested Diffusion of the Equal Rights Amendment," *Publius* 15, no. 4 (1985); Donald G. Mathews and Jane Sherron De Hart, *Sex, Gender, and the Politics of ERA: A State and the Nation* (New York: Oxford University Press, 1990); Jane J. Mansbridge, *Why We Lost the ERA* (Chicago: University of Chicago Press, 1986), 2.

10. Mansbridge, *Why We Lost*, 1.

11. Janet Allured, *The Second Wave in Louisiana, 1960–1985: Understanding Transnational Feminism in a Regional Context* (Athens: University of Georgia Press, forthcoming); Janet Allured, "Reflections on the Equal Rights Amendment and the South, 1972–1982," paper presented at the annual meeting of the Southern Historical Association, Mobile, AL, 2 November 2012; Melissa Estes Blair, *Revolutionizing Expectations: Women's Organizations, Feminism, and American Politics, 1965–1980* (Athens: University of Georgia Press, 2014); Judith Ezekiel, *Feminism in the Heartland* (Columbus: Ohio State University Press, 2002); Stephanie Gilmore, "The Dynamics of Second-Wave Feminist Activism in Memphis, 1971–1982: Rethinking the Liberal/Radical Divide," *NWSA Journal* 15, no. 1 (2003): 94–117; Gilmore, ed., *Feminist Coalitions: Historical Perspectives on Second-Wave Feminism in the United States* (Urbana: University of Illinois Press, 2008).

12. Gilmore, "The Dynamics," 95.

13. Estes Blair, *Revolutionizing Expectations*, 82–95.

14. Ezekiel, *Feminism in the Heartland*, 38.

15. Echols, *Daring to Be Bad*, 3–4, 6, 11.

16. Jo Freeman, *The Politics of Women's Liberation: A Case Study of an Emerging Social Movement and Its Relation to the Policy Process* (New York: McKay, 1975), 103.

17. Gilmore, "The Dynamics," 95; Ezekiel, *Feminism in the Heartland*, 29.

18. Ezekiel, *Feminism in the Heartland*, 39.

19. Chris Naragon, "A Local Revolution: The Actions of the Muncie-Delaware County, Indiana N.O.W. Chapter for Ratification of the ERA," report, May 1991, p. 2, Ball State University and Special Collections, Muncie, Indiana (hereafter BSU Collections); Betty Newcomb to NOW Member, 25 November 1972, National Organization for Women, Indiana Records box 1, folder 20, IHS (hereafter Indiana NOW Records).

20. Naragon, "A Local Revolution," 2–4; Erin Kempker, "Women at the Crossroads: Feminists, Conservatives, and Gender Politics in Indiana, 1950–1980" (Ph.D. diss., Purdue University, 2008), 117–19.

21. David J. Bodenhamer, Robert G. Barrows, and David Gordon Vanderstel, eds., *The Encyclopedia of Indianapolis* (Bloomington: Indiana University Press, 1994), 228; Betty Newcomb to Ann Scott, 28 February 1973, folder 5, box 2, Betty Newcomb Papers, BSU Collections.

22. Betty Newcomb to NOW Member, 27 July 1972, folder 16, box 1, Indiana NOW Records.

23. Betty Newcomb to Chapter President or Convener, 16 January 1973, folder 20, box 1, Indiana NOW Records, emphasis in original.

24. Janet Boles, "The Equal Rights Amendment as a Non-Zero-Sum Game," in *Rights of Passage: The Past and Future of the Era*, ed. Joan Hoff (Bloomington: Indiana University Press, 1986), 59.

25. Betty Newcomb to NOW Member, October 1972, folder 17, box 1, Indiana NOW Records.

26. Joline Moore Ohmart, "Outline for Speech," typed document, 12 May 1972, folder 11, box 2, Joline Ohmart Papers, IHS; Ruth Rosen, *The World Split Open: How the Modern Women's Movement Changed America* (New York: Viking, 2000), 89.

27. Indiana Women's Political Caucus meeting minutes, 12 October 1971, folder 1, box 2, Indiana Women's Political Caucus Records (hereafter IWPC Records), Indiana Historical Society, Indianapolis (hereafter IHS); Susan Svihlik and Frances Toler, eds., *W:M News* 3, no. 1 (January 1974), folder 26, box 1, IWPC Records; Virginia Dill McCarty, "From Petticoat Slavery to Equality: Women's Rights in Indiana Law," in *The History of Indiana Law*, ed. David J. Bodenhamer and Randall T. Shepard (Athens: Ohio University Press, 2006), 185.

28. McCarty, "From Petticoat Slavery," 185; *W:M News* 3, no. 1 (January 1974).

29. Rosen, *The World Split Open*, 89; IWPC meeting minutes, 12 October 1971.

30. IWPC meeting minutes, 12 October 1971.

31. Minutes of the Indiana ERA Ratification Committee, 21 November 1972, folder 38, box 1, Betty Newcomb Papers.

32. Betty Newcomb, "Proposal for ERA Ratification Strategy," typed document, 11 May 1972, folder 26, box 2, Betty Newcomb Papers.

33. Betty Newcomb to Ann Scott, 20 May 1972, folder 5, box 2, Betty Newcomb Papers.

34. Betty Newcomb to NOW Member, 27 July 1972; Newcomb to Ann Scott, 28 February 1973; McCarty, "From Petticoat Slavery," 185.

35. Audra Snyder Bailey, "HERA and the ERA," *W:M News* 3, no. 8 (August 1974): 4–5, folder 26, box 1, IWPC Records; Jan H. Blakslee, HERA Policy Committee minutes, 2 August 1973, HERA folder, box 24, Virginia Dill McCarty Papers (unsorted collection), IHS.

36. Audra Snyder Bailey, HERA State of the State report, 21 June 1975, folder 8, box 1, Hoosiers for the Equal Rights Amendment Collection (hereafter the HERA Collection), IHS.

37. This was true except for 1974, which might be understood as the Watergate effect. Linda Gail Seward, "The Equal Rights Amendment Campaign in Indiana: A Study of Ideas and Arguments" (Ph.D. diss., Purdue University, 1991), 87.

38. Ibid.

39. Catherine Rymph, *Republican Women: Feminism and Conservatism from Suffrage through the Rise of the New Right* (Chapel Hill: University of North Carolina Press, 2006), 219.

40. Michelle Nickerson, *Mothers of Conservatism: Women and the Postwar Right* (Princeton, NJ: Princeton University Press, 2012), xvii.

41. Freeman, *The Politics*, 236; Melissa Estes Blair, "Women's Organizations and Grassroots Politics: Denver, Durham, and Indianapolis 1960–1975" (Ph.D. diss., University of Virginia, 2008), 147.

42. Rymph, *Republican Women*, 202.

43. Donald Critchlow, *Phyllis Schlafly and Grassroots Conservatism: A Woman's Crusade* (Princeton, NJ: Princeton University Press, 2005), 211–14.

44. Erin M. Kempker, "Coalition and Control: Hoosier Feminists and the Equal Rights Amendment," *Frontiers: A Journal of Women Studies* 34, no. 2 (2013): 52–82.

45. Newcomb to Ann Scott, 20 May 1972.

46. Betty Newcomb to Kathy Rand, Midwest Regional Director, 1972, folder 16, box 1, Indiana NOW Records.

47. Betty Newcomb to Members of Indiana Coordinating Committee for Ratification of the ERA, Local LWV Presidents, and Local NOW Presidents and Conveners, folder 20, box 1, Indiana NOW Records.

48. Minutes of the Coordinating Committee for Passage of ERA in Indiana, 28 June 1972, folder 59, box 1, Betty Newcomb Papers.

49. Ibid.; Newcomb to NOW Member, 25 November 1972.

50. Newcomb to Chapter President or Convener, 16 January 1973.

51. Ibid.

52. Paula Coale, HERA Policy Council meeting minutes, 30 June 1974, folder 2, box 1, HERA Collection.

53. Policy Council meeting minutes, 20 January 1973, folder 6, box 2, IWPC Records.

54. Robert H. Bales, comments of Senator Sam J. Ervin on the Equal Rights Amendment, folder 18, box 4, Indiana NOW Records.

55. Beulah Coughenour, interview with the author, St. Petersburg, FL, 24 June 2011.

56. Joan Gubbins, interview with the author, Cocoa Beach, FL, 23 June 2011.

57. Coughenour noted that Phyllis Schlafly and her husband, Fred Schlafly, presented at the meeting, and together they explained the dangerous potential of the ERA (Coughenour interview).

58. Coughenour interview; Gubbins interview.

59. "Appointment of Two Members of the Intergovernmental Advisory Council on Education," 14 June 1982, Ronald Reagan Presidential Library, https://www.reaganlibrary.gov/sites/default/files/archives/speeches/1982/61482a.htm, accessed 27 January 2018.

60. Margaret Moore, "Women Win Offices in Election," *Indianapolis News*, 7 November 1968; Robbie Du Bois, "These 7 Give Assembly Woman's Touch," *Indianapolis Star*, 19 January 1969.

61. Eloise Scroggins, "Organizing on Their Own Terms: Women and the Equal Rights Amendment in Indiana" (M.A. thesis, University of Indiana, 2003), 94.

62. Gubbins interview.

63. Richard V. Pierard and James L. Wright, "No Hoosier Hospitality for Humanism: The Moral Majority in Indiana," in *New Christian Politics*, ed. David G. Bromley and Anson Shupe (Macon, GA: Mercer University Press, 1984), 205.

64. Joan M. Gubbins to Mary Lomont Till, 8 January 1973, folder 11, box 17, Indiana NOW Records; Joan M. Gubbins to Joline Ohmart, 27 February 1975, folder 3, box 1, Joline Ohmart Papers; Scroggins, "Organizing," 100.

65. Scroggins, "Organizing," 95.

66. Ibid.; Taylor University website, http://www.taylor.edu/about/mission.shtml, accessed 25 July 2007.

67. Coughenour also served as chairwoman for public works from 1978 through 2002. Indiana Waterworks website, http://www.indygov.org/egov/city/dww/governance/waterworks/member-2.htm, accessed 25 July 2007.

68. Coughenour interview.

69. In Illinois, another Heartland state where the ERA was hotly contested, the JBS provided support to anti-ERA efforts. See Berry, *Why ERA Failed,* 67.

70. Bonnie Britton, "Women Already Have Rights: Nancy Rider," *Indianapolis Star,* 14 October 1976.

71. Ruth Adams to Unratified States, 21 January 1977, 2, Indiana Folder, box 97, Records of ERAmerica, Manuscript Division, Library of Congress, Washington, DC (hereafter cited as ERAmerica Records).

72. While the organization did not appear to be very active in the state before the ERA, Coughenour remembered that in the ERA struggle Pro America represented the "more organized" group among conservative women. Gubbins noted that she joined Pro America in the early 1960s, and at that time it was led by Harvey. Coughenour interview; Gubbins interview; Margaret Moore, "ERA Issue Continues on Both Pro and Con Fronts," *Indianapolis News,* 15 August 1973.

73. "No Protest Expected at IWY Session," *Indianapolis Star,* 6 July 1977.

74. Jean H. Harvey, "'Pro America' Will Discuss S-1 Objections," *Indianapolis News,* 27 August 1973.

75. Debi Marquardt, "Four Week Newspaper Study: Coverage of 1973 Indiana Legislature and E.R.A.," report, November 1973, pp. 6–10, box 24, Virginia Dill McCarty Papers (unsorted collection).

76. David W. Brady and Kent L. Tedin, "Ladies in Pink: Religion and Political Ideology in the Anti-ERA Movement," *Social Science Quarterly* 56, no. 4 (1976): 568–69.

77. Lorena Martin, "ERA Red-Supported?," editorial, *Indianapolis News,* 18 January 1973.

78. Seward, "The Equal Rights Amendment," 166.

79. Scroggins, "Organizing," 94.

80. Ibid., 96.

81. Naragon, "A Local Revolution," 8; Scroggins, "Organizing," 94.

82. Scroggins, "Organizing," 88.

83. Seward, "The Equal Rights Amendment," 160.

84. Britton, "Women Already Have Rights."

85. Phyllis Schlafly, "What's Wrong with 'Equal Rights' for Women?," *Phyllis Schlafly Report* 5, no. 7 (February 1972), Eagle Forum, http://eagleforum.org/publications/psr/feb1972.html, accessed 27 January 2018.

86. Joan M. Gubbins to Joline Ohmart, 1975, folder 3, box 1, Joline Ohmart Papers.

87. Jones, speech.

88. Klatch, *Women of the New Right,* 139.

89. Nickerson, *Mothers of Conservatism,* 148, 150.

90. "Dangers of the Equal Rights Amendment," National Association of Pro America, Antis—Right Wing folder, box 22, ERAmerica Collection.

91. Alice Kessler Harris, *Out to Work: A History of Wage-Earning Women in the United States,* twentieth-anniversary ed. (New York: Oxford University Press, 2003), 301–19.

92. Ibid., 301.

93. Ibid.

94. Ibid., 318.

95. Linda K. Kerber, *No Constitutional Right to Be Ladies: Women and the Responsibilities of Citizenship* (New York: Hill and Wang, 1998), 309.

96. Quoted in Rosemary Thomson, *The Price of LIBerty* (Carol Stream, IL: Creation House, 1978), 16.

97. Klatch, *Women of the New Right*, 132.

98. Coughenour interview.

99. Seward, "The Equal Rights Amendment," 160.

100. Thomson, *The Price of LIBerty*, 17.

101. Coughenour interview.

102. Scroggins, "Organizing," 98.

103. Thomson, *The Price of LIBerty*, 12.

104. Ibid., 13, 17.

105. Ibid., 13.

106. Ibid., 44.

107. Klatch, *Women of the New Right*, 129.

108. Quoted in ibid., 50.

109. Ibid.

110. Ibid.

111. Coughenour interview.

112. Kathryn Nikou, interview with the author, Indianapolis, IN, 27 July 2011.

113. Critchlow, *Phyllis Schlafly and Grassroots Conservatism*, 221; Brady and Tedin, "Ladies in Pink," 570; Kent L. Tedin, "Religious Preference and Pro/Anti Activism on the Equal Rights Amendment Issue," *Pacific Sociological Review* 21, no. 1 (1978): 62.

114. Jerome L. Himmelstein, "The Social Basis of Antifeminism: Religious Networks and Culture," *Journal for the Scientific Study of Religion* 25, no. 1 (1986): 11.

115. Nikou interview.

116. Robbie Du Bois, "These 7 Give Assembly Woman's Touch," *Indianapolis Star*, 19 January 1969.

117. Ronnee Schreiber, *Righting Feminism: Conservative Women and American Politics* (Oxford: Oxford University Press, 2008), 50.

118. Ibid., 48.

119. Tedin, "Religious Preference," 62–63.

120. Ibid., 65.

121. Himmelstein, "The Social Basis," 13.

122. Ibid., 7.

123. Ibid., 12.

124. Scroggins, "Organizing," 98.

125. Klatch, *Women of the New Right*, 59–60.

126. Paul Kurtz, ed., *Humanist Manifestos I and II* (Amherst, NY: Prometheus Books, 1973).

127. Ibid., 8.

128. Ibid., 9.

129. Ibid., 13.

130. Ibid., 14.

131. Quoted in Klatch, *Women of the New Right,* 70.

132. "Can Indiana Rescind the Equal Rights Amendment?," typed document, Anti-ERA Materials (unsorted collection), IHS.

133. Joanne Reynolds to the Committees of Correspondence, Anti-ERA Materials (unsorted collection).

134. Thomson, *The Price of LIBerty,* 30–37.

135. Ibid., 35.

136. June C. Sterman, "Totalitarianism 'True Intent' of ERA," *Indianapolis News,* 26 February 1976.

137. Jan Buechler, "Naked Truth about ERA," editorial, *Indianapolis News,* 23 February 1979.

138. "Sen. Gubbins Scores ERA before Optimists," *Indianapolis News,* 4 March 1978.

139. Margaret Moore, "Anti-ERA Group Brings in Bread," *Indianapolis News,* 15 March 1973.

140. Klatch, *Women of the New Right,* 141.

141. Ibid.

142. Thomson, *The Price of LIBerty,* 15.

143. *Minute Women of the U.S.A., Inc.,* no. 68 (May–June 1963), 1, RH WL D3490, Wilcox Collection, Kenneth Spencer Research Library (hereafter Spencer Library), University of Kansas, Lawrence (hereafter RH WL D3490 Collection).

144. C. James Owen and York Wilbern, *Governing Metropolitan Indianapolis: The Politics of Unigov* (Berkeley: University of California Press), 80–84.

145. Pitschke was single, and she was in her early fifties in 1972. Social Security Death Index, Ancestry.com, accessed 29 May 2010.

146. Scroggins, "Organizing," 95.

147. "Attorney Evelyn Pitschke Replies to WISH-TV Editorial," 1 February 1973, folder 26, box 1, Indiana NOW Records; Shirley Wood, "Counseling on ERA 'Off-Key': A Letter-to-the-Editor of *Denver Post,*" newsletter article, *Muncie Delaware N.O.W. Newsletter,* March 1976, 7–8, Indiana NOW Records.

148. M. Catherine Barton to *The Jim Gerrard Show,* draft with handwritten notes, 15 December 1972, folder 21, box 1, Joline Ohmart Papers.

149. Virginia Dill McCarty to Suzanne Jones, 29 November 1973, folder 1, box 1, Indiana Women's Political Caucus Records, IHS; Scroggins, "Organizing," 89.

150. Moore, "ERA Issue Continues."

151. Evelyn Pitschke, "An Open Letter to the Members of the Congress of the United States of America," December 1977, 8, Anti-ERA Materials (unsorted collection); Pitschke, "The Effect of Section 2," *Phyllis Schlafly Report* 10, no. 4 (November 1976): 3–4, Anti-ERA Materials (unsorted collection); Pitschke, "Why Every Thinking

American Citizen Should Be against the So-Called Equal Rights Amendment," report, folder 18, box 1, Indiana Governor's Commission on the Status of Women in Indiana Records, IHS.

152. Seward, "The Equal Rights Amendment," 97.

153. Pitschke, "Why Every Thinking American."

154. Ibid.

155. Ibid.

156. Unknown author, "Pro America Resolutions," 1977, Anti-ERA Materials (unsorted collection).

157. Nola Meredith, "The Women's Lib Equal Rights Amendment," Anti—Misc Organizations folder, box 124, ERAmerica Collection.

158. "Where Does ProAmerica Stand in This Time of Danger?," Antis—Right-Wing folder, box 22, ERAmerica Collection.

159. Ibid.

160. Joan M. Gubbins, "Help! Someone Has Stolen My Child: A Report on Education in Indiana" essay available online at http://www.southern-style.com/someone%20has%20stolen%20my%20child.htm, accessed 16 August 2006.

161. "Sen. Gubbins Scores."

162. James H. Madison also points out that a 1971 survey found that Indiana ranked fortieth out of the fifty states in having an "effective response" to important issues of the day (*Hoosiers: A New History of Indiana* [Bloomington and Indianapolis: Indiana University Press and the Indiana Historical Society Press, 2014], 303).

163. Indicative of the state's commitment to low-budget bureaucracy and minimal intervention and activism, the Indiana legislature operated a full session in odd years only. Barbara Zimmer to Judy Head, 25 September 1973, folder 53, box 2, Betty Newcomb Papers.

164. Jo McCarty, "Report of Legislative Lobbyist," in "ERA Indiana Campaign Director Report," 1977, 5–8, folder 1, box 1, Jane S. Fribley Papers, IHS.

165. Lawrence Van Gelder, "After the Early Rush, the E.R.A. Is Now at a Standstill," *New York Times*, 1 April 1977, 34.

166. Berry, *Why ERA Failed*, 78.

167. The Democrats agreed to keep the ERA plank as part of their platform, but only after a heated and divisive debate (ibid., 67).

168. Critchlow, *Phyllis Schlafly and Grassroots Conservatism*, 137–62.

Chapter 4. Low-Key Feminism as a Strategy

1. Betty Newcomb to Members of Indiana Coordinating Committee for Ratification of the ERA, Local LWV Presidents, and Local NOW Presidents and Conveners, 1973, folder 20, box 1, Indiana National Organization for Women Records (hereafter Indiana NOW Records), Indiana Historical Society, Indianapolis (hereafter IHS).

2. Minutes for the IWPC Policy Council Meeting, 20 January 1973, folder 6, box 2, Indiana Women's Political Caucus Records (hereafter IWPC Records), IHS.

3. Virginia Dill McCarty, interview with Susan Brooks and Keith Carson, 4 October 2005, folders 6 and 7, box 1, Indianapolis American Inn of Court Oral Histories, IHS.

4. Betty Newcomb to Kathy Rand, 24 August 1972, folder 16, box 1, Indiana NOW Records.

5. Indiana Civil Rights Commission Public Inquiry on Problems of Discrimination Based on Sex, 14 November 1972, folder 17, box 1, Indiana NOW Records.

6. Mary Ann Wynkoop, *Dissent in the Heartland: The Sixties at Indiana University* (Bloomington: Indiana University Press, 2002), 137–41.

7. Ibid., 143.

8. Ibid., 148–52.

9. Ibid., 180.

10. Melissa Estes Blair, *Revolutionizing Expectations: Women's Organizations, Feminism, and the Transformation of American Politics, 1965–1980* (Athens: University of Georgia Press, 2014), 82–83.

11. Alice Echols, *Daring to Be Bad: Radical Feminism in America, 1967–1975* (Minneapolis: University of Minnesota Press, 1989), 4.

12. Mary Anne Butters, "Marchers Draw Support, Scorn," *Indianapolis Star*, 27 August 1971.

13. "The Ecology of Women: Indiana Women's Liberation First State Conference," 1972, folder 5, box 4, IWPC Records.

14. Estes Blair, *Revolutionizing Expectations*, 83.

15. "The Ecology of Women."

16. *Up Front*, no. 1 (4 September 1971), folder 5, box 6, Indiana NOW Records.

17. *IWL [Indianapolis Women's Liberation] Newsletter* 1, no. 8 (1971), folder 12, box 13, Indiana NOW Records; *IWL Newsletter* 2, no. 9 (1972), folder 3, box 4, Indiana NOW Records; Estes Blair, *Revolutionizing Expectations*, 83.

18. A handwritten list of contacts for IWL included 179 names, and not all had Indianapolis addresses. List of Members and Interested Women, folder 3, box 4, Indiana NOW Records; *IWL Newsletter* 1, no. 8 (April 1971), folder 12, box 13, Indiana NOW Records.

19. *IWL Newsletter* 1, no. 8 (April 1971).

20. Ibid.

21. Estes Blair, *Revolutionizing Expectations* 83–4; Norma Card to Kathy Rand, 2 July 1972, folder 17, box 1, Indiana NOW Records; Pat Mainardi, "The Politics of Housework," Redstockings, 1969, http://www.redstockings.org/index.php/june-1969-a-blast-of-redstockings-feminism, accessed 27 January 2018.

22. Estes Blair, *Revolutionizing Expectations*, 78.

23. Susan Svihlik and Frances Toler, eds., *W:M News* 3, no. 1 (January 1974), folder 26, box 1, IWPC Records; Audra Snyder Bailey, *Hold Fast to Dreams: The Sixty-Year Career of an Indiana Teacher* (Indianapolis: Guild Press of Indiana, 1996), 126.

24. Bailey, *Hold Fast to Dreams*, 126.

25. This seems to provide further evidence that rape acted, in Maria Bevacqua's words, as a "bridge issue," bringing together diverse women (radical, liberal, African

American, and, in this case, Republican). Bailey, *Hold Fast to Dreams*, 227; Estes Blair, *Revolutionizing Expectations,* 80; Maria Bevacqua, "Reconsidering Violence against Women: Coalition Politics in the Antirape Movement," in *Feminist Coalitions: Historical Perspectives on Second-Wave Feminism in the United States*, ed. Stephanie Gilmore (Urbana: University of Illinois Press, 2008), 166.

26. Indiana Governor's Commission on the Status of Women newsletter, 6 April 1973, folder 2, box 1, Governor's Commission on the Status of Women Collection (hereafter the GCSofW Collection), IHS.

27. Ibid.

28. Ibid.

29. Weekend Retreat at St. Mary-of-the-Woods College, "Win, Place, or Show," 21 February 1976, folder 10, box, 1, GCSofW Collection.

30. "The First Decade, 1976–1986," 5, folder 2001 FWWB, box 1, Fort Wayne Women's History Materials (unsorted collection, cited hereafter as FWWH Collection), IHS.

31. Previously, the bureau operated with revenue-sharing agreements; this was the first time it was included in the city budget. Sam Smith, "Woman's Bureau Center of Storm," *Fort Wayne News Sentinel,* 18 August 1975, newspaper clipping, box 3, FWWH Collection.

32. Miller quoted in Fort Wayne Women's Bureau Silver Anniversary, folder 2001 FWWB, box 1, FWWH Collection.

33. Smith, "Woman's Bureau."

34. Ibid.

35. Harriet Miller, "Eleven Month Progress & Status Report," Fort Wayne Women's Bureau, December 1975, box 2, FWWH Collection.

36. Mary Doherty, "Women and Politics," *Fort Wayne Free Press* 3, no. 6 (9–23 March 1972), box 3, FWWH Collection.

37. Betty Newcomb to Kathy Rand, 19 May 1972, folder 16, box 1, Indiana NOW Records.

38. Betty Newcomb to NOW Members, 25 November 1972, folder 20, box 1, Indiana NOW Records.

39. Butters, "Marchers Draw Support."

40. Linda Gail Seward, "The Equal Rights Amendment in Indiana: A Study of Ideas and Arguments" (Ph.D. diss., Purdue University, 1991), 108.

41. Ibid., 107.

42. Quoted in Estes Blair, *Revolutionizing Expectations,* 91.

43. *W:M News* was the name of the Indiana WPC newsletter. HERA publications made repeated reference to the ERA as "a matter of simple justice," using it as their slogan underneath an image of blind Justice. Audra Snyder Bailey, "Hera and the ERA," *W:M News* 3, no. 8 (1974): 4–5, folder 26, box 1, IWPC Records.

44. "Women Need Equality Too!!!," flyer, folder 15, box 2, Indiana NOW Records.

45. Virginia Dill McCarty to Betty Newcomb, 25 October 1972, folder 27, box 2,

Betty Newcomb Papers, Ball State University and Special Collections, Muncie, Indiana (hereafter BSU Collections).

46. The dearth of information prompted her to ask that the League of Women Voters, Indiana, forward any details or scuttlebutt they heard concerning the opposition. Newcomb to Local League Presidents, 13 November 1972, folder 5, box 2, Betty Newcomb Papers.

47. Policy Council meeting minutes, 20 January 1973, folder 6, box 2, IWPC Records.

48. Virginia Dill McCarty to Margaretta S. Tangerman, 27 December 1972, folder 6, box 3, IWPC Records.

49. Quoted in R. Douglass Hurt, "Midwestern Distinctiveness," in *The American Midwest: Essays on Regional History*, ed. Andrew R. L. Cayton and Susan E. Gray (Bloomington: Indiana University Press, 2007), 71.

50. James Madison, *The Indiana Way: A State History* (Bloomington: Indiana University Press, 1986), xiiv, 305.

51. Ricard M. Scammon, *America at the Polls: The Vote for President, 1920–1964* (Pittsburgh: University of Pittsburgh Press, 1965), 144, 146, 148; Gerhard Peters and John T. Woolley, "The American Presidency Project," http://www.presidency.ucsb.edu/elections.php, accessed January 3, 2017.

52. Judith Ezekiel, *Feminism in the Heartland* (Columbus: Ohio State University Press, 2002), 73.

53. A. Reed McFarlane to Betty Newcomb, Virginia D. McCarty, and Dorothy Fisher, 8 December 1972, folder 1, box 1, Betty Newcomb Papers.

54. Ibid.

55. Betty Newcomb to Ann Scott, 13 January 1973, folder 5, box 2, Betty Newcomb Papers.

56. Ibid.

57. Richard Pierce, *Polite Protest: The Political Economy of Race in Indianapolis, 1920–1970* (Bloomington: Indiana University Press, 2005), 1–2.

58. Ibid., 8, 124.

59. Ibid., 4.

60. Ibid., 125.

61. Vonda Metzger to Virginia Dill McCarty, 15 February 1972, folder 3, box 3, IWPC Records.

62. Ibid.

63. Metzger never states her age, but her letter implies that the WPC and McCarty do not understand the issues of the young women or offer help to young women wanting to combine political activism with the obligations of a new family. Virginia Dill McCarty to Vonda Metzger, 1 March 1972, folder 3, box 3, IWPC Records.

64. Ibid.

65. Betty Newcomb to Kathy Rand, no date, folder 16, box 1, Indiana NOW Records.

66. Quoted in Estes Blair, *Revolutionizing Expectations,* 86.

67. Quoted in Melissa Estes Blair, "Women's Organizations and Grassroots Politics:

Denver, Durham, and Indianapolis 1960–1975" (Ph.D. diss., University of Virginia, 2008), 193.

68. Estes Blair, *Revolutionizing Expectations*, 86–87.

69. The Indiana state legislature debated the ERA from 1973 to 1977. The House voted on the ERA three times (1973, 1975, 1977), and the Senate voted twice each in committee (1974, 1975) and on the floor (1973, 1977). Seward, "The Equal Rights Amendment," 84.

70. Virginia Dill McCarty and Betty Blumberg, facsimile for Council Members Information Only, 14 February 1975, folder 11, box 1, Hoosiers for the Equal Rights Amendment Collection (hereafter the HERA Collection), IHS; press release, 14 February 1975, folder 11, box 1, HERA Collection.

71. McCarty and Blumberg, facsimile.

72. Roberta Simons, Policy Council meeting minutes, 12 January 1975, folder 3, box 1, HERA Collection.

73. Lobbying was an important aspect of HERA's work, and it did ask volunteers to participate. However, Blumberg and McCarty trained volunteers and directed those efforts at the statehouse, while Policy Council representatives directed those efforts within congressional districts. Audra Snyder Bailey to Friend of HERA, 5 December 1974, folder 6, box 1, Audra Snyder Bailey Papers, IHS; Bailey, Deardourff and Eyre, Inc., report, 1975, folder 3, box 1, HERA Collection.

74. Dorothy E. Steinmeier to E. Laurie Scholl and Mandy Wertz, 9 July 1975, folder 4, box 1, HERA Collection.

75. Sue Errington, "State of the State" report, Great Lakes Regional Conference, Dayton, Ohio, 7–9 April 1978, folder 1, box 5, Indiana NOW Records.

76. Audra Snyder Bailey to HERA Members, 1 April 1975, folder 4, box 4, IWPC Records.

77. HERA did hold a rally for supporters in April 1975 called "The ERA Lives! Rally." It was a move that was highly debated, coming on the heels of the Valentine's Day defeat, and many questioned whether a rally would hurt or help the cause. Judith Head, "March 1, 1975, Rally Held by HERA," 14 March 1975, folder, 11, box 1, HERA Collection; HERA Policy and Organizational Councils meeting minutes, 15 November 1975, folder 3, box 1, HERA Collection.

78. Sydney Goddard, "ERA Demonstration at State House," 1976, folder 20, box 4, Indiana NOW Records.

79. Indiana NOW Elections Committee, ERA Strategy, 1977, folder 14, box 17, Indiana NOW Records.

80. Conference call between Elaine Latourell and Karen M. Williams, typed minutes, 25 July 1976, folder 13, box 2, Indiana NOW Records; Janet K. Boles, "Building Support for the ERA: A Case of 'Too Much, Too Late,'" *PS: Political Science* 15, no. 4 (Autumn 1982): 573.

81. Chris Naragon, "A Local Revolution: The Actions of the Muncie-Delaware County, Indiana N.O.W. Chapter for Ratification of the ERA," report, May 1991, 9, Stoeckel Special Collections, Ball State University, Muncie, Indiana.

82. Ibid., 9–10; "Overall Strategy for Senate," typed document, 1976, folder 12, box 17, Indiana NOW Records.

83. "Overall Strategy for Senate."

84. Naragon, "A Local Revolution," 9; ERA workshop agenda, 1976, folder 14, box 3, Indiana NOW Records; Indiana ERA Caravan schedule, handwritten document, folder 6, box 5, Indiana NOW Records.

85. Catherine E. Rymph, *Republican Women: Feminism and Conservatism from Suffrage through the Rise of the New Right* (Chapel Hill: University of North Carolina Press, 2006), 217–18.

86. Bailey, *Hold Fast*, 99, 83–114.

87. Audra Snyder Bailey to Senator, 9 April 1975, folder 4, box 1, HERA Collection.

88. Ibid.

89. Ibid.

90. Audra Snyder Bailey to the Executive Board, 29 March 1975, folder 10, box 1, HERA Collection.

91. Audra Snyder Bailey, confidential memo to HERA Democrats, 21 February 1975, folder 6, box 1, HERA Collection.

92. HERA Nominating Committee report, 21 May 1975, folder 7, box 1, HERA Collection; Laurie Scholl, "Press Release, RE: HERA Election," 21 June 1975, folder 10, box 1, HERA Collection.

93. Ruby Miller to Betty Newcomb, 5 November 1975, folder 1, box 2, Betty Newcomb Papers.

94. Diane Frederick, "Does GOP Oppose ERA?," *Indianapolis News*, 21 February 1979.

95. Audra Snyder Bailey to Members of the HERA Nominating Committee, 28 April 1975, folder 7, box 1, HERA Collection.

96. McCarty, interview with Brooks and Carson.

97. ERAmerica operated through 1982 and worked in several states during that time, primarily Georgia, Illinois, Missouri, the Carolinas, Oklahoma, and Florida, but only in Indiana was it successful. ERAmerica, report, November 1980, State Files Strategy Session folder, box 111, Records of ERAmerica, Manuscript Division, Library of Congress, Washington, DC (hereafter ERAmerica Collection); "The Equal Rights Amendment," report, November 1980, State Files Strategy Session folder, box 111, ERAmerica Collection; J. Klemesrud and T. Zabala, "New Team to Unify E.R.A. Campaign," *New York Times*, 8 March 1976, 43; "New Group Formed for Equal Rights," *New York Times*, 26 February 1976, 21.

98. Letter to contact person, Indiana folder, box 97, ERAmerica Collection.

99. Erin M. Kempker, "Coalition and Control: Hoosier Feminists and the Equal Rights Amendment," *Frontiers: A Journal of Women Studies* 34, no. 2 (2013): 52–82.

100. Beth Van Vorst Gray, "Equal Rights Amendment Ratification in Indiana Too Little . . . Too Late," blog post, 19 March 2010, http://broadripplesinthewater.blogspot.com/2010/03/equal-rights-amendment-ratification-in.html, last accessed 2 July 2012.

101. Jane Fribley to Ellen Kirby, 23 February 1980, folder 3, box 1, Jane S. Fribley Papers, IHS.

102. Ibid.

103. Indiana NOW Elections Committee, "ERA Strategy."

104. Ruth Adams to Unratified States, 21 January 1977, "Indiana" folder, box 97, ERAmerica Records.

105. Errington, "State of the State" report.

106. Frances Dodson Rhome to Coordinating Committee Members, 8 November 1977, folder 5, box 1, IWY Records.

107. Ibid.

108. Benita Roth, *Separate Roads to Feminism: Black, Chicana, and White Feminist Movements in America's Second Wave* (New York: Cambridge University Press, 2004), 107.

109. Virginia Dill McCarty to Jane McMichael, 14 August 1972, folder 5, box 3, IWPC Records.

110. Census figures from 1970 show that whites made up 92.8 percent of the state's population and African Americans 6.9 percent. Income level and age of caucus members covered the spectrum, though most (60 percent) put themselves in the middle categories with incomes between $5,000 ($29,321 today) and $20,000 ($117,282 today). Most significant is that over 19 percent of the caucus recorded incomes exceeding $30,000 ($175,923 today). Michael R. Haines, "Table Aa3397–3493: Indiana Population by Race, Sex, Age, Nativity, and Urban-Rural Residence: 1800–1990," in Historical Statistics of the United States Millennial Edition Online (online database), last accessed 20 April 2008.

111. Affirmative Action Program Supplement, 1972, folder 21, box 2, IWPC Records; U.S. Inflation Calculator, http://www.usinflationcalculator.com/, accessed 28 January 2018.

112. Emma G. Stafford, Policy Council meeting minutes, 21 October 1972, folder 5, box 2, IWPC Records.

113. Stafford, Policy Council meeting minutes, 21 October 1972.

114. Policy Council meeting minutes, 11 November 1972, folder 5, box 2, IWPC Records.

115. Though Republicans in the WPC did constitute a political minority, at roughly 30 percent of the 1972 membership, the response mocked the spirit of the affirmative action program. Affirmative Action Program Supplement; Virginia Dill McCarty, letter concerning IWPC membership, 18 September 1972, folder 9, box 4, IWPC Records

116. Winifred Breines, *The Trouble between Us: An Uneasy History of White and Black Women in the Feminist Movement* (Oxford: Oxford University Press, 2006), 10–11.

117. Hernandez quoted in Paula Giddings, *When and Where I Enter: The Impact of Black Women on Race and Sex in America* (New York: Quill William Morrow, 1984), 346.

118. Roth, *Separate Roads to Feminism,* 11, 194–95.

119. Breines, *The Trouble between Us,* 4.

120. Estes Blair, *Revolutionizing Expectations,* 83.

121. Doherty, "Women and Politics."

122. Harriet Miller to Mr. Prather, 11 May 1973, folder correspondence, box 2, FWWH Collection.

123. Harriet Miller to June Knight Shassere, 10 September 1973, folder correspondence, box 2, FFWB Collection.

124. Ibid.

125. Roth, *Separate Roads to Feminism,* 214–25.

126. Elizabeth Kaminski agrees that collective identity is important for drawing activists together but that it can also create conflict and fragmentation. See "Learning from Coalitions: Intersections and New Directions in Activism and Scholarship," in Gilmore, *Feminist Coalitions,* 288–89; Roth, *Separate Roads to Feminism,* 217–18.

127. Berenice Carroll, "Direct Action and Constitutional Rights: The Case of the ERA," in *Rights of Passage: The Past and Future of the Era,* ed. Joan Hoff (Bloomington: Indiana University Press, 1986), 65.

128. Ibid., 69.

129. Ezekiel, *Feminism in the Heartland,* 72.

130. Carroll, "Direct Action," 72.

131. Jo Freeman, *The Politics of Women's Liberation: A Case Study of an Emerging Social Movement and Its Relation to the Policy Process* (New York: McKay, 1975), 6.

132. Ibid., 236.

133. Kaminski, "Learning from Coalitions," 288–89.

134. Gayatri Chakravorty Spivak, *Outside in the Teaching Machine,* Routledge Classics (New York: Routledge, 2009), 3–4.

135. Ezekiel, *Feminism in the Heartland,* 29.

136. Toni Carabillo to David Abrams, 10 July 1977, Anti—Misc. Organizations folder, box 124, ERAmerica Collection.

137. Seward paraphrased Gubbins's explanation of the lobbyists as "belligerent and unattractive" based on an oral interview Seward conducted with Gubbins. Seward, "The Equal Rights Amendment," 107–8.

138. "Sen. Gubbins Scores ERA before Optimists," *Indianapolis News,* 3 March 1978.

139. Michael Barkun, *A Culture of Conspiracy: Apocalyptic Visions in Contemporary America* (Berkeley: University of California Press, 2003), 28.

140. Rebecca E. Klatch, *Women of the New Right* (Philadelphia: Temple University Press, 1987), 216.

141. Ronnee Schreiber, *Righting Feminism: Conservative Women and American Politics* (New York: Oxford University Press, 2008), 124–25.

142. Glen Jeansonne, *Women of the Far Right: The Mothers' Movement and World War II* (Chicago: University of Chicago Press, 1996), 189.

143. Barry Glassner, *The Culture of Fear: Why Americans Are Afraid of the Wrong Things* (New York: Basic Books, 1999).

144. Jane Fribley, "A Thanks and a Challenge," 1977, folder 9, box 1, Jane S. Fribley Papers.

Chapter 5. The International Women's Year as a Fulcrum

1. "Birch Society Celebrates Its 20th Birthday," *New York Times*, 11 December 1978, A14.

2. Judith P. Zinsser, "From Mexico to Copenhagen to Nairobi: The United Nations Decade for Women, 1975–1985," *Journal of World History* 13, no. 1 (Spring 2002): 139–40.

3. Martha Sonntag Bradley, *Pedestals and Podiums: Utah Women, Religious Authority, and Equal Rights* (Salt Lake City: Signature Books, 2005), 136.

4. William C. Martin, *With God on Our Side: The Rise of the Religious Right in America* (New York: Broadway Books, 1996), 131.

5. Mrs. James Lucas, executive secretary of the DAR, quoted in Mary C. Brennan, *Wives, Mothers, Red Menace: Conservative Women and the Crusade against Communism* (Boulder: University Press of Colorado, 2008), 71.

6. Sonntag Bradley, *Pedestals and Podiums*; Marjorie J. Spruill, "Gender and America's Right Turn," in *Rightward Bound: Making America Conservative in the 1970s*, ed. Bruce J. Schulman and Julian E. Zelizer (Cambridge, MA: Harvard University Press, 2008), 71; Neil J. Young, "'The ERA Is a Moral Issue': The Mormon Church, LDS Women, and the Defeat of the Equal Rights Amendment," *American Quarterly* 59, no. 3 (September 2007): 623–44.

7. Spruill, "Gender," 89.

8. "Report of the World Conference of the International Women's Year," Mexico City, 1975, United Nations report, http://www.un.org/womenwatch/daw/beijing/otherconferences/Mexico/Mexico%20conference%20report%20optimized.pdf, accessed 28 January 2018.

9. Zinsser argues that at the subsequent conferences in Copenhagen and Nairobi, delegates created a more radical agenda, so much so that the "Forward Looking Strategies" settled on in Nairobi confirm that women had become "central, not peripheral, to the realization of the broader goals for the United Nations" ("From Mexico," 144, 147–48).

10. Quoted in Sonntag Bradley, *Pedestals and Podiums*, 128–33.

11. National Commission on the Observance of International Women's Year, "*. . . To Form a More Perfect Union . . .*": *Justice for American Women* (Washington, DC: Superintendent of Documents, US Government Printing Office, 1976), 370–72.

12. Sonntag Bradley, *Pedestals and Podiums*, 135–36.

13. Ibid., 226.

14. Frances Dodson Rhome to Mrs. Russell Willis, 2 June 1977, folder 18, box 1, Governor's Commission on the Status of Women Collection (hereafter the GCSofW Collection), IHS.

15. Indiana State Meeting, Official Program Book, 1977, pp. 45–52, private collection of Dorothy Mennen, Lafayette, IN.

16. Ibid.

17. Donald Critchlow, *Phyllis Schlafly and Grassroots Conservatism: A Woman's Crusade*

(Princeton, NJ: Princeton University Press, 2005), 211, 214; Sonntag Bradley, *Pedestals and Podiums,* 116–23; Spruill, "Gender," 76–81.

18. Sonntag Bradley, *Pedestals and Podiums,* 237.

19. Mrs. David F. Starr and Mrs. Jan Hoffman, eds., *Indiana STOP ERA Hotline,* May 1977, folder 18, box 1, GCSofW Collection.

20. Ibid.

21. Ibid.

22. Spruill, "Gender," 81.

23. Rosemary Thomson, *The Price of LIBerty* (Carol Stream, IL: Creation House, 1978), 130.

24. Ibid., 129–30.

25. Kathryn Nikou, *Indiana STOP ERA Hotline,* July–August 1977, Anti-ERA Materials (unsorted collection), IHS; Frances Dodson Rhome to Coordinating Committee, 8 November 1977, folder 5, box 1, International Women's Year Records (hereafter IWY Records), IHS; "Section 7: Summary and Evaluation: Opposition," in *Hoosier Women Make History,* ed. Frances Dodson Rhome, vol. 2, 1977, p. 513, folder 8, box 2, IWY Records.

26. Beulah Coughenour, interview with the author, St. Petersburg, FL, 24 June 2011.

27. Citizens Review Committee, Submission of Seminar Instructors, "Section 5: Workshops," in Rhome, *Hoosier Women Make History.*

28. Kathryn Nikou, interview with the author, Indianapolis, IN, 27 July 2011.

29. Frances Dodson Rhome, "Final Report," in Rhome, *Hoosier Women Make History,* 490–512; Donna Snodgrass, "Indiana Delegation Heads for Houston," *Indianapolis Star,* 17 November 1977.

30. Rhome to Coordinating Committee, 8 November 1977.

31. Ibid.

32. *Indiana STOP ERA Hotline,* May 1977.

33. Julia Wrigley, in her investigation of right-wing women in the Boston antibusing movement, describes how women's activism often represents "protopolitics," activism that at least begins in political space unclaimed by men, parties, or institutions. At least part of the story of IWY is an explanation of how women can go from "protopolitics" to "pros at politics" in a short amount of time. See Julia Wrigley, "From Housewives to Activists: Women and the Division of Political Labor in the Boston Antibusing Movement," in *No Middle Ground: Women and Radical Protest,* ed. Kathleen Blee (New York: New York University Press, 1998), 252–53; Martin, *With God on Our Side,* 166.

34. Coughenour interview.

35. "No Protest Expected at IWY Session," *Indianapolis Star,* 6 July 1977.

36. Spruill, "Gender," 83.

37. Ibid.

38. National Association of Pro America, Indiana Chapter, "Last Call for State IWY Meeting," 13 July 1977, Anti-ERA Materials.

39. Erin M. Kempker, "Coalition and Control: Hoosier Feminists and the Equal Rights Amendment," *Frontiers: A Journal of Women Studies* 34, no. 2 (2013): 52–82.

40. Russell Lloyd to ERA Supporter, 1977, folder 1, box 1, Jane S. Fribley Papers, IHS.

41. Rhome to Coordinating Committee, 8 November.

42. Sharon L. Boothby to NOW Members and Friends, 29 June 1977, folder 10, box 1, IWY Records.

43. Sue Errington, "State of the State" report, Great Lakes Regional Conference, Dayton, Ohio, 7–9 April 1978, folder 1, box 5, Indiana NOW Records.

44. Ibid.

45. Sharon L. Boothby to NOW Members and Friends, 29 June 1977, folder 10, box 1, IWY Records.

46. Ibid.

47. Errington, "State of the State" report.

48. Official Program Book, 17–19.

49. Bonnie Britton and Donna Snodgrass, "Conservatives Prevail at State IWY," *Indianapolis Star*, 17 July 1977.

50. Native Americans accounted for less than 1 percent of the Indiana general population, which led state organizers to conclude that participants must have been confused about the meaning of the category. Michael R. Haines, "Table Aa3397–3493: Indiana Population by Race, Sex, Age, Nativity, and Urban-Rural Residence: 1800–1990," Historical Statistics of the United States, online database, accessed 6 April 2008; C. Mathew Snipp, "Table Ag331–391: Population of American Indians by Region and State, 1890–1990," Historical Statistics of the United States (online database), accessed 6 April 2008; Rhome to Coordinating Committee, 8 November.

51. Donna Bucove, ed., "Indiana State Meeting Report," 1977, pp. 81–114, folder 6, box 2, IWY Records.

52. Jane Fribley, "A Thanks and a Challenge," 1977, folder 9, box 1, Jane S. Fribley Papers.

53. Donna Snodgrass and Bonnie Britton, "IWY Delegates Issue Unresolved," *Indianapolis Star*, 18 July 1977; Rhome, "Final Report," 505.

54. "Preacher in a Public Area," cassette recording CT446: Perkins/Piper Interviews, 1977, IWY Records; Elizabeth Duff, "A Lady Senator Is Feminist Foe," *Philadelphia Inquirer*, 20 November 1977, box 1, Virginia Dill McCarty (unsorted collection), IHS.

55. Bucove, "Indiana State Meeting Report," 129.

56. "Section 7," 513.

57. Fribley, "A Thanks and a Challenge."

58. The other states were Alabama, Hawaii, Illinois, Mississippi, and Ohio. Sonntag Bradley, *Pedestals and Podiums*, 230–31.

59. Rhome, "Final Report," 491; Snodgrass and Britton, "IWY Delegates Issue Unresolved."

60. Daniel Manion to Molly Rucker, 22 July 1977, folder 15, box 7, IWPC Records.

For more information on Greg Dixon's leadership in the Moral Majority and Indiana politics, see Scott Matthew Brown, "Testing Absolute Church/State Separation: A Case Study of the Indianapolis Baptist Temple" (Ph.D. diss., University of Louisville, 2003); Richard V. Pierard and James L. Wright, "No Hoosier Hospitality for Humanism: The Moral Majority in Indiana," in *New Christian Politics*, ed. David G. Bromley and Anson Shupe (Macon, GA: Mercer University Press, 1984), 195–212.

61. Ruth Cartwright, "We Rose to a Point of Order," *Marion News Herald*, 22 July 1977.

62. Fribley, "A Thanks and a Challenge."

63. Sonntag Bradley, *Pedestals and Podiums*, 204–5.

64. Molly P. Rucker to Cathy Noe and US representative Andy Jacobs, 17 July 1986, folder 15, box 7, IWPC Records.

65. Rhome complained to convention center security about the disruptions and harassment and demanded that several men be ejected from the building. Convention center authorities, however, refused to evict them. "Section 7," 513; Britton and Snodgrass, "Conservatives Prevail."

66. Four resolutions, all relating to the status of the homemaker, made it to a vote in the business session, where they were voted down as a block. "Hoosier Judgment on Proposals," *Indianapolis Star*, 6 November 1977; P. J. Hayes, "Houston Session to Study Legislation," *Indianapolis Star*, 6 November 1977.

67. Britton and Snodgrass, "Conservatives Prevail."

68. The ten other states were Alabama, Hawaii, Kansas, Mississippi, Missouri, Montana, Nebraska, Ohio, Oklahoma, and Utah. Sonntag Bradley, *Pedestals and Podiums*, 237.

69. Britton and Snodgrass, "Conservatives Prevail."

70. Vice President Spiro Agnew (1969–73) was known for rhetorical flourish and alliteration.

71. Bonnie Britton, "IWY 'Citizens' Victory,' Review Leader Says," *Indianapolis Star*, 20 July 1977.

72. Cartwright, "We Rose."

73. R. Cartwright, "International Women's Year Meeting," *Marion News Herald*, 8 July 1977.

74. "Fact Sheet—International Women's Year," folder 18, box 1, GCSofW Collection.

75. National Association of Pro America, "Expose Objectives of National Women's Conference," Anti-ERA Materials.

76. *Indiana STOP ERA Hotline*, May 1977.

77. "Citizen's Review Committee Fact Sheet," folder 18, box 1, GCSofW Collection.

78. "Section 5," in Rhome, *Hoosier Women Make History*.

79. Spruill, "Gender," 80.

80. Donald Janson and Bernard Eismann, *The Far Right* (New York: McGraw-Hill, 1963), 53; Jonathan M. Schoenwald, *A Time for Choosing: The Rise of Modern American Conservatism* (Oxford: Oxford University Press, 2001), 4–13.

81. "Pro America Resolutions," 1977, Anti-ERA Materials.

82. Thomson, *The Price of LIBerty*, 17.

83. Ibid., 81.

84. Ibid., 128.

85. Ibid., 118.

86. CT:444 Bowman/Bates/Dolan Interviews, 1977, cassette recording, IWY Records.

87. Phillip J. Trounstine, "Effort to Expunge ERA Ok Is 'D-E-A-D,'" *Indianapolis Star*, 13 January 1978.

88. Toni Carabillo to David Abrams, 10 July 1977, Anti—Misc. Organizations folder, box 124, ERAmerica Collection.

89. Erin Kempker, "Women at the Crossroads: Feminists, Conservatives, and Gender Politics in Indiana, 1950–1980" (Ph.D. diss., Purdue University, 2008), 275–77; Archibald E. Roberts, *The Crisis of Federal Regionalism: A Solution* (Fort Collins, CO: Betsy Ross Press, 1976), 1.

90. George Norris Green, *The Establishment in Texas Politics: The Primitive Years, 1938–1957* (Westport, CT: Greenwood Press, 1979), 123; Kempker, "Women at the Crossroads," 14–60; *Minute Women of the U.S.A., Inc.*, no. 70 (September–October 1963), RH WL D3490, Wilcox Collection, Kenneth Spencer Research Library (hereafter Spencer Library), University of Kansas, Lawrence (hereafter RH WL D3490 Collection); *Minute Women of the U.S.A., Inc.*, March 1968, RH WL E535, Wilcox Collection, Spencer Library (cited hereafter as RH WL E535 Collection); *Minute Women of the U.S.A., Inc.*, March 1971, RH WL E535 Collection; *Minute Women of the U.S.A., Inc.*, Summer 1971, pt. 2, RH WL E535 Collection.

91. *Minute Women of the U.S.A., Inc.*, no. 70 (September–October 1963), RH WL D3490Collection.

92. Jo Hindman, quoted in *Minute Women of the U.S.A., Inc.*, March 1971, RH WL E535 Collection.

93. National Association of Pro America, Indiana Chapter, "Reject IWY Recommendations on International Interdependence," 1977, Anti-ERA Materials.

94. "Resolutions Passed by International Interdependence Workshop," 1977, folder 5, box 1, IWY Records.

95. Ibid.

96. Beverly Adams et al., "To Establish Justice," 269, online database.

97. Joan Gubbins et al., "To Establish Justice (Minority Report)," in *Women and Social Movements in the United States*, ed. Thomas Dublin and Kathryn Kish Sklar, 265, online database, accessed 9 May 2007.

98. Jerry Falwell and Tim LaHaye posited a "pre-tribulation tribulation" that would provide a window of time wherein through swift political action "Prophecy believers" might save the country from God's wrath. Angela M. Lahr, *Millennial Dreams and Apocalyptic Nightmares: The Cold War Origins of Political Evangelicalism* (Oxford: Oxford University Press, 2007), 15.

99. Ruth Y. Schiller to Indiana Women, 10 May 1977, folder 18, box 1, GCSofW Collection.

100. Evelyn Pitschke, "An Open Letter to the Members of the Congress of the United States of America," 8 December 1977, Anti-ERA Material.

101. Lillian Steele, "Open Letter to the People of Indiana," 1977, Anti-ERA Materials.

102. Lahr, *Millennial Dreams*, 12.

103. "Section 7," 513–14; Spruill, "Gender," 81.

104. Catholics accounted for the next largest group at 19 percent, while Jewish respondents accounted for 2 percent of the total. "Nonreligious" persons made up 6 percent of those surveyed. Rhome to Coordinating Committee, 8 November.

105. For more on the connections between anti-ERA activism and religious affiliation, see David W. Brady and Kent L. Tedin, "Ladies in Pink: Religion and Political Ideology in the Anti-ERA Movement," *Social Science Quarterly* 56, no. 4 (1976): 564–75; Jerome L. Himmelstein, "The Social Basis of Antifeminism: Religious Networks and Culture," *Journal for the Scientific Study of Religion* 25, no. 1 (1986): 1–15; Kent L. Tedin, "Religious Preference and Pro/Anti Activism on the Equal Rights Amendment Issue," *Pacific Sociological Review* 21, no. 1 (1978): 55–66.

106. Spruill, "Gender," 81–84; Thomson, *The Price of LIBerty*, 130.

107. Jane Fribley to Ellen Kirby, 23 February 1980, folder 3, box 1, Jane S. Fribley Papers.

108. Kempker, "Women at the Crossroads," 294–96; Pierard and Wright, "No Hoosier Hospitality," 196, 200.

109. Rucker to Noe and Jacobs.

110. Susan Marshall, "Rattle on the Right: Bridge Labor in Antifeminist Organizations," in Blee, *No Middle Ground*, 167–68.

111. Jan Kreuscher, "Minority Resolution Splits Hoosiers," *Indianapolis News*, 21 November 1977.

112. Ibid.

113. Jan Kreuscher, "IWY Conference Ignores Protest," *Indianapolis News*, 22 November 1977.

114. Rumors abounded among the Indiana delegation that these women, who reportedly wore shirts that said "Black terrorists," were also lesbians. The delegation insisted that Dishman's name be removed from the hotel registry to ensure that she would not be followed. Lillian Steele argues in the "Open Letter" that the Indiana delegation called upon the FBI to protect Dishman from an attack that a black lesbian threatened to carry out. It is unclear if they associated the threatening woman with the Weather Underground. Members of the Weather Underground were arrested by the FBI as they attempted to attend the national conference in Houston. R. Cartwright, "Lesbian Pornography Displayed at Indiana State Legislature," *Marion News Herald*, 10 February 1978; Lillian Steele, "Open Letter"; Pitschke, "An Open Letter"; Thomson, *The Price of LIBerty*, 149.

115. Thomson, *The Price of LIBerty*, 149.

116. Veronica A. Wilson, "'To Tell All My People': Race, Representation, and John Birch Society Activist Julia Brown," in *Women of the Right: Comparisons and Interplay*

across Borders, ed. Kathleen M. Blee and Sandra McGee Deutsch (University Park: Pennsylvania State University Press, 2012), 248.

117. Marshall, "Rattle on the Right," 174.

118. Gaye Steele, "Open Letter to the People of Indiana," 1977, Anti-ERA Material.

119. Estes Blair, *Revolutionizing Expectations*, 127–29.

120. Ibid., 127.

121. Robert Alan Goldberg, *Enemies Within: The Culture of Conspiracy in Modern America* (New Haven, CT: Yale University Press, 2001), 260.

122. Michael Barkun, *A Culture of Conspiracy: Apocalyptic Visions in Contemporary America*, Comparative Studies in Religion and Society (Berkeley: University of California Press, 2003), 189.

123. Theda Skocpol and Vanessa Williamson, *The Tea Party and the Remaking of Republican Conservatism* (Oxford: Oxford University Press, 2012), 200.

124. Goldberg, *Enemies Within*, 260.

125. Kathleen M. Fallon and Julie Moreau, "Righting Africa? Contextualizing Notions of Women's Right-Wing Activism in Sub-Saharan Africa," in Blee and Deutsch, *Women of the Right*, 69, 70.

126. Linda Steele, "Open Letter to the People of Indiana," Anti-ERA Materials.

127. Margaret Power, "Transnational Connections among Right-Wing Women: Brazil, Chile, and the United States," in Blee and Deutsch, *Women of the Right*, 21–35.

128. Jill A. Irvine, "Exporting the Culture Wars: Concerned Women for America in the Global Arena," in Blee and Deutsch, *Women of the Right*, 39.

129. Ibid., 48.

130. Susan Marshall argues that, contrary to the backlash notion, antifeminists organized contemporaneously with feminists and suffragists in the twentieth century. The antifeminist counterculture was "interactive not reactive" to the first-wave movement. Susan E. Marshall, *Splintered Sisterhood: Gender and Class in the Campaign against Woman Suffrage* (Madison: University of Wisconsin Press, 1997), 228, 235. See also Elna C. Green, *Southern Strategies: Southern Women and the Woman Suffrage Question* (Chapel Hill: University of North Carolina Press, 1997), xii.

131. Gaye Steele, "Open Letter."

132. Pitschke, "An Open Letter."

133. Phyllis Schlafly quoted in Rebecca Klatch, *Women of the New Right* (Philadelphia: Temple University Press, 1987), 124.

134. "Letter to Indiana Legislators," 1978, Anti-ERA Materials.

135. Rhome to Coordinating Committee, 8 November.

136. Virginia Dill McCarty and Donna L. Bucove to Workshop Coordinators, 19 July 1977, folder 3, box 1, IWY Records.

137. Barbara Zimmer, "Fiscal Officer's Comments on Financial Arrangements," 30 August 1977, folder 3, box 1, IWY Records.

138. This does not mean that feminist activism ended in the 1980s or that we are in a "postfeminist" era. Nancy Whittier, *Feminist Generations: The Persistence of the Radical Women's Movement* (Philadelphia: Temple University Press, 1995), 2–3.

139. "Appointment of Two Members of the Intergovernmental Advisory Council on Education," 14 June 1982, Ronald Reagan Presidential Library, https://www.reaganlibrary.gov/sites/default/files/archives/speeches/1982/61482a.htm, accessed 28 January 2018.

140. Virginia Dill McCarty, "From Petticoat Slavery to Equality: Women's Rights in Indiana Law," in *The History of Indiana Law*, ed. David J. Bodenhamer and Randall T. Shepard (Athens: Ohio University Press, 2006), 187; Sheila Suess Kennedy, "American Booksellers Association, et al. v. Hudnut," in *The Encyclopedia of Indianapolis*, ed. David J. Bodenhamer, Robert G. Barrows, and David Gordon Vanderstel (Bloomington: Indiana University Press, 1994), 253.

141. McCarty, "From Petticoat Slavery," 187.

142. Beulah Coughenour, interview with the author, St. Petersburg, FL, 24 June 2011.

143. Pat Robertson, *The New World Order* (Dallas: Word Publishing, 1991), 9.

144. Ibid., 8–9, emphasis mine.

145. Michael Lind, "Rev. Robertson's Grand International Conspiracy Theory," *New York Review of Books*, 2 February 1995, http://www.nybooks.com/articles/1995/02/02/rev-robertsons-grand-international-conspiracy-theo/, accessed 3 January 2017; Michael Lind, "Is Pat Robertson an Anti-Semite?," letter to the editor, *Commentary*, 1 January 1996, https://www.commentarymagazine.com/articles/is-pat-robertson-an-anti-semite/, 3 January 2017; Norman Podhortez, "In the Matter of Pat Robertson," *Commentary*, 1 August 1995, https://www.commentarymagazine.com/articles/in-the-matter-of-pat-robertson/, accessed 3 January 2017.

146. Ephraim Radner, "New World Order, Old World Anti-Semitism," *Christian Century* 112, no. 26 (13 September 1995): 844–50; Phillip H. Melling, *Fundamentalism in America: Millennialism, Identity and Militant Religion* (Edinburgh: Edinburgh University Press, 1999), 84.

147. Donald T. Critchlow and Nancy MacLean, *Debating the American Conservative Movement: 1945 to the Present* (Lanham, MD: Rowman & Littlefield, 2009), vii.

148. Quoted in Murray Friedman, *The Neoconservative Revolution: Jewish Intellectuals and the Shaping of Public Policy* (Cambridge: Cambridge University Press, 2005), 145.

Epilogue

1. "Ted Cruz Unloads on 'Pathological Liar' 'Bully' 'Serial Philanderer' Donald Trump," *LesGrossman News*, YouTube video, 3 May 2016, https://www.youtube.com/watch?v=E5NEfsfjf8s, accessed 7 January 2017.

2. Tim Alberta, "Why Cruz Is Going All-In on Indiana," *National Review*, 20 April 2016, http://www.nationalreview.com/article/434265/ted-cruz-bets-big-indiana-primary, accessed 7 January 2017.

3. Jonathan Merritt, "Can the Religious Right Give Ted Cruz the Win?," *Atlantic*, 22 December 2015, https://www.theatlantic.com/politics/archive/2015/12/can-the-religious-right-give-ted-cruz-the-win/421563/, accessed 20 January 2017.

4. "Donald Trump Opens Up about His Changes in Indiana," *Fox News*, YouTube Channel video, https://www.youtube.com/watch?v=d-ar39-E1Dk&app=desktop, accessed 7 January 2017; Jenna Johnson and Sean Sullivan, "Donald Trump Associates Ted Cruz's Father with JFK's Assassin," *Washington Post*, 3 May 2016, https://www.washingtonpost.com/news/post-politics/wp/2016/05/03/donald-trump-associates-ted-cruzs-father-with-jfks-assassin/?utm_term=.521bc6717b77, accessed 7 January 2017.

5. David Wright, Tal Kopan, and Julia Manchester, "Cruz Unloads with Epic Takedown of 'Pathological Liar,' 'Narcissist' Donald Trump," *CNN Politics*, 3 May 2016, http://www.cnn.com/2016/05/03/politics/donald-trump-rafael-cruz-indiana/index.html, accessed 7 January 2017.

6. Michael Finnegan, "Trump Ties Cruz's Father to JFK Assassination. His Source? The National Enquirer," *Los Angeles Times*, 3 May 2016, http://www.latimes.com/politics/la-na-trump-cruz-oswald-20160503-story.html, accessed 7 January 2017.

7. Eric Bradner, "5 Takeaways from the Indiana Primary," *CNN Politics*, 4 May 2016, http://www.cnn.com/2016/05/03/politics/primary-results-takeaways/, accessed 7 January 2017.

8. 270toWin, "Indiana," website, http://www.270towin.com/states/Indiana, accessed 20 January 2017.

9. Linda Qia, "Anatomy of a Talking Point: Donald Trump on the JFK Assassination," *PolitiFact*, 6 May 2016, http://www.politifact.com/truth-o-meter/article/2016/may/06/anatomy-talking-point-donald-trump-jfk-assassinati/, accessed 7 January 2017.

10. Alex Jones and Donald Trump video available through the *New York Times* website. Liam Stack, "He Calls Hillary Clinton a 'Demon.' Who Is Alex Jones?," *New York Times*, 13 October 2016, http://www.nytimes.com/2016/10/14/us/politics/alex-jones.html, accessed 5 January 2017; Edward Wong, "Trump Has Called Climate Change a Chinese Hoax. Beijing Says It Is Anything But," *New York Times*, 18 November 2016, http://www.nytimes.com/2016/11/19/world/asia/china-trump-climate-change.html?_r=0, accessed 6 January 2017; Darren Samuelsohn, "Fact: Trump Claimed Climate Change Is a Hoax Created by China," *Politico*, 26 September 2016, http://www.politico.com/blogs/2016-presidential-debate-fact-check/2016/09/fact-trump-claimed-climate-change-is-a-hoax-created-by-china-228711, accessed 6 January 2017; Michael Barbaro, "Donald Trump Clung to 'Birther' Lie for Years, and Still Isn't Apologetic," *New York Times*, 16 September 2016, http://www.nytimes.com/2016/09/17/us/politics/donald-trump-obama-birther.html, accessed 6 January 2017; Kyle Cheney, "No, Clinton Didn't Start the Birther Thing. This Guy Did," *Politico*, 16 September 2016, http://www.politico.com/story/2016/09/birther-movement-founder-trump-clinton-228304, accessed 6 January 2017.

11. Chris Megerian, "Donald Trump Has 'Got a Right' to Talk about Conspiracies, Republican Party Chairman Says," *Los Angeles Times*, 25 July 2016, http://www.latimes.com/nation/politics/trailguide/la-na-trailguide-updates-donald-trump-has-got-a-right-to-talk-1469401552-htmlstory.html, accessed 7 January 2017.

12. Ibid.

13. Ibid.

14. Jia Tolentino, "Trump and the Truth: The Sexual-Assault Allegations," *New Yorker*, 20 October 2016, http://www.newyorker.com/news/news-desk/trump-and-the-truth-the-sexual-assault-allegations, accessed 6 January 2017; Lisa Desjardins, "All the Assault Allegations against Donald Trump, Recapped," 14 October 2016 (updated 22 October 2016), http://www.pbs.org/newshour/rundown/assault-allegations-donald-trump-recapped/, accessed 6 January 2017.

15. Zeke Miller, "Donald Trump Has a Grand Unified Campaign Conspiracy Theory," *Time Magazine*, 13 October 2016, http://time.com/4530568/donald-trump-hillary-clinton-conspiracy/, accessed 5 January 2017.

16. Matt Shuham, "Trump Warns of Dark Conspiracy by Clinton, Media, and International Banks," Talking Points Memo Livewire, 13 October 2016, http://talkingpointsmemo.com/livewire/trump-conspiratorial-picture-florida, accessed 5 January 2017.

17. Ibid.

18. Ibid.

19. "Trump on Sexual Assault Allegations: 'I Am a Victim,'" *CNN Politics*, 15 October 2016, http://www.cnn.com/2016/10/14/politics/donald-trump-sexual-assault-allegations/, accessed 6 January 2017.

20. Amy Davidson, "Melania Trump, Conspiracy Theorist," *New Yorker*, 18 October 2016, http://www.newyorker.com/news/amy-davidson/melania-trump-conspiracy-theorist, accessed 5 January 2017.

21. Michelle Cottle, "Why White Women Continue to Back the GOP," *Atlantic*, 14 November 2016, http://www.theatlantic.com/politics/archive/2016/11/white-women-support-gop/507617/, accessed 20 January 2017.

22. Claire Cain Miller, "Why Women Did Not Unite to Vote against Donald Trump," *New York Times*, 12 November 2016, https://www.nytimes.com/2016/11/13/upshot/why-women-did-not-unite-to-vote-against-donald-trump.html?_r=0, accessed 20 January 2017.

23. Paul Starr, "Why Democrats Should Beware Sanders' Socialism," *Politico Magazine*, 22 February 2016, http://www.politico.com/magazine/story/2016/02/bernie-sanders-2016-socialism-213667, accessed 7 January 2017; Clare Foran, "Bernie Sanders Makes His Pitch for Socialism," *Atlantic Magazine*, 20 November 2015, http://www.theatlantic.com/politics/archive/2015/11/bernie-sanders-makes-his-pitch-for-socialism/416913/, accessed 6 January 2017; "The Bernie Manifesto: How Much of a Socialist Is Sanders?," *Economist*, 1 February 2016, http://www.economist.com/blogs/democracyinamerica/2016/02/bernie-manifesto, accessed 6 January 2017; Aaron Blake, "Here Are the Latest, Most Damaging Things in the DNC's Leaked Emails," *Washington Post*, 25 July 2016, https://www.washingtonpost.com/news/the-fix/wp/2016/07/24/here-are-the-latest-most-damaging-things-in-the-dncs-leaked-emails/?utm_term=.0c90d0d2405a, accessed 6 January 2017; Dana Houle, "No, the DNC Didn't Rig the Primary in Favor of Hillary," *New Republic*, 25 July 2016,

https://newrepublic.com/article/135472/no-dnc-didnt-rig-primary-favor-hillary, accessed 6 January 2017.

24. Cecilia Nowell, "At Women's Colleges, the Fight Goes On," blog entry, *Ms. Magazine,* 6 December 2016, http://msmagazine.com/blog/2016/12/06/womens-colleges-shattered-spirits-still-fighting-shatter-ceilings/, accessed 20 January 2017.

25. Mark Potok, "Donald Trump, Conspiracy Theory and the Radical Right," *Intelligence Report,* 27 October 2015, https://www.splcenter.org/fighting-hate/intelligence-report/2015/donald-trump-conspiracy-theory-and-radical-right, accessed 5 January 2017; "Fringe Racists, Conspiracy Theorists Make Bids for Office," *Intelligence Report,* 3 August 2016, https://www.splcenter.org/fighting-hate/intelligence-report/2016/fringe-racists-conspiracy-theorists-make-bids-office, accessed 5 January 2017.

26. Alex Jones promotes a host of conspiracy beliefs, including that the American government creates national crises like 9/11 to gain power. His show boasts of being broadcast on 160 radio stations, but, perhaps more importantly, it reaches millions on the internet. As of January 2017, his Facebook page has almost 1,400,000 likes and 1,285,000 followers, and he has over half a million followers on Twitter; his YouTube channel has over 1,890,000 subscribers. Eric Hananoki, "A Comprehensive Guide to Alex Jones: Conspiracy Theorist and Trump 'Valuable Asset,'" blog post, Media Matters for America, 1 December 2016, http://www.mediamatters.org/blog/2016/12/01/comprehensive-guide-alex-jones-conspiracy-theorist-and-trump-valuable-asset/214668, accessed 5 January 2017; Stack, "He Calls Hillary Clinton a 'Demon'"; "Alex Jones: 'It Is Surreal to Talk about Issues Here on Air and Then Word-for-Word Hear Trump Say It Two Days Later," 11 August 2016, video, Media Matters for America, https://mediamatters.org/video/2016/08/11/alex-jones-it-surreal-talk-about-issues-here-air-and-then-word-word-hear-trump-say-it-two-days-later/212339, accessed 5 January 2017.

27. "National Conspiracy Theories," poll results, Public Policy Polling, 2 April 2013, http://www.publicpolicypolling.com/pdf/2011/PPP_Release_National_Conspiracy Theories_040213.pdf, accessed 5 January 2017.

28. J. Eric Oliver and Thomas J. Wood, "Conspiracy Theories and the Paranoid Style(s) of Mass Opinion," *American Journal of Political Science* 58, no. 4 (October 2014): 963–64.

29. Quoted in Robert Alan Goldberg, *Enemies Within: The Culture of Conspiracy in Modern America* (New Haven, CT: Yale University Press, 2001), 238.

30. Michael Barkun, *A Culture of Conspiracy: Apocalyptic Visions in Contemporary America* (Berkeley: University of California Press, 2003), 260.

31. John Hayward, "Sarah Palin: President Trump Should Call for the Unshackling of the Political Bands Tying Us to the UN," interview with Raheem Kassam, 29 December 2016, http://www.breitbart.com/radio/2016/12/29/palin-trump-call-unshackling-political-bands-tying-us-u-n/, accessed 5 January 2017.

32. "Birch Society Celebrates Its 20th Birthday," *New York Times*, 11 December 1978, A14.

33. Rosemary Thomson quoted in Marjorie Julian Spruill, "Awake, Aware and Deeply Polarized: Mississippi Women and the International Women's Year Conferences of 1977," 40, paper presented at the annual meeting of the Cora Norman Lecture Series, Mississippi Humanities Council, Jackson, Mississippi, 2006.

34. Kathryn Olmsted, *Real Enemies: Conspiracy Theories and American Democracy, World War I to 9/11* (Oxford: Oxford University Press, 2009), 240.

Index

ERIN M. KEMPKER is an associate professor of history at the Mississippi University for Women.

WOMEN, GENDER, AND SEXUALITY IN AMERICAN HISTORY

Women Doctors in Gilded-Age Washington: Race, Gender, and Professionalization *Gloria Moldow*

Friends and Sisters: Letters between Lucy Stone and Antoinette Brown Blackwell, 1846–93 *Edited by Carol Lasser and Marlene Deahl Merrill*

Reform, Labor, and Feminism: Margaret Dreier Robins and the Women's Trade Union League *Elizabeth Anne Payne*

Private Matters: American Attitudes toward Childbearing and Infant Nurture in the Urban North, 1800–1860 *Sylvia D. Hoffert*

Civil Wars: Women and the Crisis of Southern Nationalism *George C. Rable*

I Came a Stranger: The Story of a Hull-House Girl *Hilda Satt Polacheck; edited by Dena J. Polacheck Epstein*

Labor's Flaming Youth: Telephone Operators and Worker Militancy, 1878–1923 *Stephen H. Norwood*

Winter Friends: Women Growing Old in the New Republic, 1785–1835 *Terri L. Premo*

Better Than Second Best: Love and Work in the Life of Helen Magill *Glenn C. Altschuler*

Dishing It Out: Waitresses and Their Unions in the Twentieth Century *Dorothy Sue Cobble*

Natural Allies: Women's Associations in American History *Anne Firor Scott*

Beyond the Typewriter: Gender, Class, and the Origins of Modern American Office Work, 1900–1930 *Sharon Hartman Strom*

The Challenge of Feminist Biography: Writing the Lives of Modern American Women *Edited by Sara Alpern, Joyce Antler, Elisabeth Israels Perry, and Ingrid Winther Scobie*

Working Women of Collar City: Gender, Class, and Community in Troy, New York, 1864–86 *Carole Turbin*

Radicals of the Worst Sort: Laboring Women in Lawrence, Massachusetts, 1860–1912 *Ardis Cameron*

Visible Women: New Essays on American Activism *Edited by Nancy A. Hewitt and Suzanne Lebsock*

Mother-Work: Women, Child Welfare, and the State, 1890–1930 *Molly Ladd-Taylor*

Babe: The Life and Legend of Babe Didrikson Zaharias *Susan E. Cayleff*

Writing Out My Heart: Selections from the Journal of Frances E. Willard, 1855–96 *Edited by Carolyn De Swarte Gifford*

U.S. Women in Struggle: A *Feminist Studies* Anthology *Edited by Claire Goldberg Moses and Heidi Hartmann*

In a Generous Spirit: A First-Person Biography of Myra Page *Christina Looper Baker*

Mining Cultures: Men, Women, and Leisure in Butte, 1914–41 *Mary Murphy*

Gendered Strife and Confusion: The Political Culture of Reconstruction *Laura F. Edwards*

The Female Economy: The Millinery and Dressmaking Trades, 1860–1930 *Wendy Gamber*

Mistresses and Slaves: Plantation Women in South Carolina, 1830–80 *Marli F. Weiner*

A Hard Fight for We: Women's Transition from Slavery to Freedom in South Carolina *Leslie A. Schwalm*

The Common Ground of Womanhood: Class, Gender, and Working Girls' Clubs, 1884–1928 *Priscilla Murolo*

Purifying America: Women, Cultural Reform, and Pro-Censorship Activism, 1873–1933 *Alison M. Parker*

Marching Together: Women of the Brotherhood of Sleeping Car Porters *Melinda Chateauvert*

Creating the New Woman: The Rise of Southern Women's Progressive Culture in Texas, 1893–1918 *Judith N. McArthur*

The Business of Charity: The Woman's Exchange Movement, 1832–1900 *Kathleen Waters Sander*

The Power and Passion of M. Carey Thomas *Helen Lefkowitz Horowitz*

For Freedom's Sake: The Life of Fannie Lou Hamer *Chana Kai Lee*

Becoming Citizens: The Emergence and Development of the California Women's Movement, 1880–1911 *Gayle Gullett*

Selected Letters of Lucretia Coffin Mott *Edited by Beverly Wilson Palmer with the assistance of Holly Byers Ochoa and Carol Faulkner*

Women and the Republican Party, 1854–1924 *Melanie Susan Gustafson*

Southern Discomfort: Women's Activism in Tampa, Florida, 1880s–1920s *Nancy A. Hewitt*

The Making of "Mammy Pleasant": A Black Entrepreneur in Nineteenth-Century San Francisco *Lynn M. Hudson*

Sex Radicals and the Quest for Women's Equality *Joanne E. Passet*

"We, Too, Are Americans": African American Women in Detroit and Richmond, 1940–54 *Megan Taylor Shockley*

The Road to Seneca Falls: Elizabeth Cady Stanton and the First Woman's Rights Convention *Judith Wellman*

Reinventing Marriage: The Love and Work of Alice Freeman Palmer and George Herbert Palmer *Lori Kenschaft*

Southern Single Blessedness: Unmarried Women in the Urban South, 1800–1865 *Christine Jacobson Carter*

Widows and Orphans First: The Family Economy and Social Welfare Policy, 1865–1939 *S. J. Kleinberg*

Habits of Compassion: Irish Catholic Nuns and the Origins of the Welfare System, 1830–1920 *Maureen Fitzgerald*

The Women's Joint Congressional Committee and the Politics of Maternalism, 1920–1930 *Jan Doolittle Wilson*

"Swing the Sickle for the Harvest Is Ripe": Gender and Slavery in Antebellum Georgia *Daina Ramey Berry*

Christian Sisterhood, Race Relations, and the YWCA, 1906–46 *Nancy Marie Robertson*

Reading, Writing, and Segregation: A Century of Black Women Teachers in Nashville *Sonya Ramsey*

Radical Sisters: Second-Wave Feminism and Black Liberation in Washington, D.C. *Anne M. Valk*

Feminist Coalitions: Historical Perspectives on Second-Wave Feminism in the United States *Edited by Stephanie Gilmore*

Breadwinners: Working Women and Economic Independence, 1865–1920 *Lara Vapnek*

Beauty Shop Politics: African American Women's Activism in the Beauty Industry *Tiffany M. Gill*

Demanding Child Care: Women's Activism and the Politics of Welfare, 1940–1971 *Natalie M. Fousekis*

Rape in Chicago: Race, Myth, and the Courts *Dawn Rae Flood*

Black Women and Politics in New York City *Julie A. Gallagher*

Cold War Progressives: Women's Interracial Organizing for Peace and Freedom *Jacqueline Castledine*

No Votes for Women: The New York State Anti-Suffrage Movement *Susan Goodier*

Anna Howard Shaw: The Work of Woman Suffrage *Trisha Franzen*

Nursing Civil Rights: Gender and Race in the Army Nurse Corps *Charissa J. Threat*

Reverend Addie Wyatt: Faith and the Fight for Labor, Gender, and Racial Equality *Marcia Walker-McWilliams*

Lucretia Mott Speaks: The Essential Speeches *Edited by Christopher Densmore, Carol Faulkner, Nancy Hewitt, and Beverly Wilson Palmer*

Lost in the USA: American Identity from the Promise Keepers to the Million Mom March *Deborah Gray White*

Women against Abortion: Inside the Largest Moral Reform Movement of the Twentieth Century *Karissa Haugeberg*

Colored No More: Reinventing Black Womanhood in Washington, D.C. *Treva B. Lindsey*

Beyond Respectability: The Intellectual Thought of Race Women *Brittney C. Cooper*

Leaders of Their Race: Educating Black and White Women in the New South *Sarah H. Case*

Glory in Their Spirit: How Four Black Women Took On the Army during World War II *Sandy Bolzenius*

Big Sister: Feminism, Conservatism, and Conspiracy in the Heartland *Erin M. Kempker*

The University of Illinois Press
is a founding member of the
Association of American University Presses.

University of Illinois Press
1325 South Oak Street
Champaign, IL 61820-6903
www.press.uillinois.edu